CONTENTS

CHAPTER 1

PROGRAMMING FUNDAMENTALS	1
Introduction	1
Subroutines: What They Arc and How to Use Them	2
Programming Style	4
Writing Your Programs	8
Make the IBM Work for You	10
About the Structure of the Book	13

CHAPTER 2

AN INPUT LINE EDITOR FOR THE IBM PC	15
Introduction	15
Line Editor Test Routines	20
Basic Line Editor Program	23
Displaying a Cursor	36
Processing a Key	37
Character-Accept and Display Routines	40
Processing Control Keys: Editing Routines	44
Error Processing	59
User Instructions	60
Complete Line Editor Program	61

CHAPTER 3

SCREEN TEXT EDITOR	75
Introduction	75
Part 1: Text Editor Program	77
Screen Editing Commands	84
Summary of Part 1	107
Part 2: Complete Text Editor Program	107
Command Display and Processor Routine	110
Enhancements	131
Editing Programs	131
User Instructions	132
Complete Screen Text Editor Program	136

CHAPTER 4

ANSWERING USERS' HELP REQUESTS	157
Introduction	157
Help Program	159
Pause Subroutine	164
Changing the Screen Intensity	165
Blinking Display	167
Error Processing	167
User Instructions	168
Complete Help Program	169

CHAPTER 5

A DATA ENTRY SCREEN PROCESSOR	173
Introduction	173
Creating a Data Entry Screen	176
Sample Variable-Exchange Routine	178
Data Entry Program	179
Changes to the Help Subroutine	182
Subroutine for Setting the Field Parameters	183
Displaying the Original Values	185
Editing Subroutine	186
Additional Option	189
Error Processing	190
User Instructions	190
Complete Data Entry Screen Program	192

BASIC SUBROUTINES
FOR THE IBM PC AND PCjr

BASIC SUBROUTINES FOR THE IBM PC AND PCjr

Alan G. Porter and Martin G. Rezmer

▲▼ Addison-Wesley Publishing Company, Inc.
Reading, Massachusetts • Menlo Park, California
Don Mills, Ontario • Wokingham, England • Amsterdam
Sydney • Singapore • Tokyo • Mexico City • Bogota
Santiago • San Juan

Library of Congress Cataloging in Publication Data
Porter, Alan G.
    BASIC subroutines for the IBM PC and PCjr.
    Includes index.
    1. IBM Personal Computer—Programming. 2. Basic
(Computer program language) 3. Subroutines (Computer
programs) I. Rezmer, Martin G. II. Title. III. Title:
B.A.S.I.C. subroutines for the IBM PC. IV. Title:
BASIC subroutines for the I.B.M. P.C.
QA76.8.I2594P67 1984   001.64'2   84–18455
ISBN 0–201–05662–3

BCDEFGHIJ-HA-898765

Second Printing, August 1985

For Shelley and Vicki
Thank you for your patience and support.

PREFACE

What do you do after reading the IBM BASIC manual? What can you do? How do you write a good program? How do you make programs professional looking and easier to use? This book is a first step toward these goals. After having read the IBM BASIC manual cover to cover several times, you may still find it difficult to perform certain functions with your IBM computer. Even though you are armed with an understanding of how INPUT, PRINT, and FOR–NEXT work, you may still have difficulty putting them together in a meaningful order. You know what you want the computer to do, but you are not a professional programmer, and so you do not know how to make the computer do it. In this book we present solutions to some of the most frequently encountered programming problems. We define what each problem is, show how to solve it, and give an exact solution (a program) in IBM BASIC. We also explain how you can modify the program for your own needs. The procedure here is to learn efficient programming techniques and good style by example—a very powerful teaching method.

This book is intended for use by people with widely varying skill levels—from the enthusiastic beginner with little programming experience to the advanced programmer. For the person learning to program we carefully explain how every program works and how we develop them. For the advanced programmer the programs provide ideas and building blocks that can be expanded and enhanced for use in individual programs.

The material is presented in modular fashion. That is, the materials from Chapter 2 (an input line editor) are expanded on in Chapter 3 to create a screen editor, and so on. The end result is a set of tools that can be used in every program you write. With these tools your programs will be more professional and easier to use, take less time to write, and be able to be modified easily when change becomes necessary.

CONTENTS

CHAPTER 6

A MENU SYSTEM	199
Introduction	199
Menu Program	202
Explanation of Program	205
Sample Menu Screen	207
User Instructions	209
Complete Menu Program	210

CHAPTER 7

REPORT GENERATION	213
Introduction	213
Simple Report Generator	216
Program Features	219
Printer Controls	227
Dot Commands	230
Standard Error Processing	236
How to Use This Program	236
User Instructions	237
Complete Report Generator Program	239

CHAPTER 8

PERSONAL CALENDAR: A SAMPLE PROGRAM	247
Introduction	247
Basic Calendar Program	249
User Instructions	264
Complete Personal Calendar Program	266

INDEX	271

PROGRAMMING FUNDAMENTALS

INTRODUCTION

This book is divided into the following subject areas.

• Line Editor	For easier entry of data.
• Screen Editor	A simple word processor for inputting programs and text.
• On-Line Help System	To answer questions as they occur.
• Data Entry System	When you need to enter more than one item of information.
• Menu System	To make getting somewhere easier.
• Report Generator	For putting it all down on paper.

• Sample Program   A personal calendar to show how this can all work together for you.

Subroutines are provided that show how to input data into the computer, how to store and work with these data, and then how to output the data to the screen or printer.

The final chapter provides a stand-alone program that summarizes all of these techniques into a personal calendar program.

In this chapter we discuss subroutines, programming style and technique, and efficient methods for writing and testing your own programs. We also present the common structure used in the following chapters in order to prepare you for getting the most out of this book.

SUBROUTINES: WHAT THEY ARE AND HOW TO USE THEM

Simply stated, a *subroutine* is a program that is used over and over again in one program or in many programs. A subroutine can be as small as two lines or as large as several thousand lines. In general, however, subroutines are kept small so that they will be understandable and manageable. Ideally, a subroutine will only perform one function, such as allowing alphanumeric input from the keyboard. By performing only one function, it will always behave as expected, and you will not be surprised by an unusual response. If a subroutine is to perform several functions, it can be made by combining several single-function subroutines.

A subroutine is distinguished from a "regular" program by two BASIC statements: GOSUB and RETURN. A GOSUB is used by the "calling" program (the main or originating program) to access the subroutine, and a RETURN is used by the subroutine, upon completing its task, to return to the calling program. Except for these two statements, a subroutine is a regular BASIC program.

GOSUB–RETURN   When the program encounters GOSUB, it unconditionally branches to the referenced line number. Upon encountering a RETURN, the program branches back to the statement immediately following the most recently executed GOSUB.

EXAMPLE

```
5000    GOSUB 6000
5100    PRINT X%*3
5200    END
6000    INPUT X%
6100    RETURN
RUN
?100
300
```

In this GOSUB example, when line 5000 is encountered, the program execution sequence jumps to line 6000 and asks for the input of X%. The number 100 is input from the keyboard and execution resumes at line 5100 and the result of X%*3 is printed on the screen (300).

The reason for the existence of a subroutine is fairly straightforward: to make the computer do as much of your work as possible. If you have a function in your program that is required several times, you have the option of retyping the function in several places or typing it in once, adding RETURN as the last line, and using a GOSUB when you want to use it. Why should you do all the work when the computer will gladly do it at the mere typing of the command GOSUB? Subroutines serve one additional purpose; they make the programs consistent. If the same subroutine is used throughout your programs, then this function will be performed exactly the same way each time. You will not have to remember the exact details of how it works everytime you wish to use it in the program.

Let's use a common example. How do we start our car? A modern automobile simply requires us to get in and turn the key. The manufacturers have created a "subroutine" (actually, a group of subroutines nested together) to perform the required tasks for us when we turn the key. The action of turning the key starts the subroutine chain that does the following tasks.

- Determines if the choke is needed,
- Turns on the fuel pump,

- Runs the electrical system checkout,
- Engages the starter.

And we are done. We get the same results every time—unless the system has broken down on us!

The following chapters will present a series of subroutines that you can use in your own programs. These subroutines present only one of many possible ways to solve each problem and can be modified for your own requirements.

PROGRAMMING STYLE

We like to consider computer programming as an art form. As with all art forms the creator has a "style." This style can determine whether the creation is a work of beauty or something else. Some of us were not born with enormous amounts of style; we have to study others and copy where we can. Style also evolves with time; most of us get better as we gain experience. We rarely, however, go back to an older creation and improve or update its style. It is therefore important to do as good a job as possible the first time through.

The subroutines in this volume reflect our style. Some people will like it and others will not, but that is art. In the following subsections we summarize some of the elements of our programming style. The elements of style that are most important are those that lead to an increase in understanding and improve the readability of the program. We try to adhere to them as much as possible, but, being human, we do slip from time to time. We hope that by studying our style, you will be able to add those characteristics that you like to your own style.

Meaningful Variable Names

It will come as no surprise to you that not all variable names are meaningful. Even a variable name that is meaningful to you may be totally confusing to another person reading your program. We are fortunate that IBM BASIC allows variable names of up to 40 significant characters. Thus it is our convention to use as long a name as necessary to give a clear definition of the variable being addressed.

It is important to remember that for programs in BASIC, variables are used by the entire program (which is why they are commonly called global variables). Any variable can be assigned a value at any point in a program, and that value can be used at any other place in the program. This procedure is how information is passed to and from subroutines. Before calling a subroutine, we assign values to the variables used by that subroutine. After the subroutine has completed its task, those same variables are still available for use by the rest of the program, even though some of the values may have changed in the subroutine. Therefore, the more meaningful a variable name is, the less likely it is to be misused and changed incorrectly in a program.

Line Numbers and Subroutines

We use lots of subroutines in our programs. Since we must use line numbers and not labels (names) to address subroutines, a consistent procedure must be used to keep them all straight in our mind. We do not renumber the subroutines. Once a subroutine is created and assigned a starting line number, we keep that line number intact. It may look nice to have an entire program evenly numbered, but even numbering is not worthwhile if the subroutines keep moving around. Therefore, we only renumber the main program sections if we must; we do not renumber the subroutine sections.

Our choice of line numbers for the subroutines is not totally random. There is a plan.

First, we want you to be able to add these routines to existing programs, and since most people tend to start numbering programs at 10, we elected to use larger-value line numbers. This way our routines will not conflict with yours and neither will they require renumbering.

Second, by carefully selecting line numbers, we can make a program run as quickly as possible. When BASIC looks for a line number (as in GOSUB 10000 or GOTO 11000), it first checks to see if the current line number is larger or smaller than the one being searched for. If the current line number is smaller, it begins the search for the desired line at the current line. If the current line number is larger, it begins the search with the first line number in memory.

For example, consider the following program.

```
100
  .
  .
  .
1000   PRINT "HELLO"
1100   GOSUB 2000
1200   GOTO 1000
2000   PRINT "RANDY"
2100   RETURN
```

When BASIC executes line 1100

```
GOSUB 2000
```

it begins the search for line 2000 at line 1200. But when it executes line 1200

```
GOTO 1000
```

it must begin searching at the first line in memory, which is line 100.

If this program were a large one, a lot of time would be wasted going from line 100 to line 1000, simply because there are a lot of line numbers to check. Getting to line 2000, however, will be faster because there are fewer line numbers to check. Therefore, because of this characteristic of BASIC, we have tried to place subroutines at a line larger than the line calling the GOSUB or GOTO. Obviously this is not always possible, but it is an easy constraint to live with.

Finally, these programs were not developed overnight; nor were they carefully arranged to look perfect. They evolved, and features have been added and deleted along the way. Therefore, since we do not continuously rearrange the line numbers, occasionally two seemingly related subroutines can be separated by large line number differences. This does not degrade the performance of the programs; it only goes to show that we are normal programmers and cannot and do not think of everything in perfect order.

Remark Statements, or What's This?

Most programmers fail to use enough remark (REM) statements in their programs.

REM   REM statements are nonexecuting line statements. They are used in programs to provide notes and reminders to the original program author and to others who may subsequently need to go back into the program and figure out its purpose or method.

IBM BASIC also allows us to use a single quotation mark, " ' ", in place of REM. It is a nice shortcut, which we use to make the programs less cluttered and more readable.

EXAMPLE

```
1090   REM
1095   REM
1100   REM
1105   X = 11.005      ' THIS IS A FIXED VALUE
1110   Y = 5.026       ' THIS IS A FIXED VALUE
1115   '
1120   '
1125   '
```

In this example lines 1090–1100 and 1115–1125 are used to isolate what is found between them. This makes reading the program easier and calls attention to lines 1105 and 1110. The remarks after lines 1105 and 1110 indicate what the values are, where they came from, or what they are used for. Use any description desired to remind yourself what these lines are for.

When the original author of a REMless program is gone, who will support and modify the work? Usually, no one; the REMless program will be thrown out, and a new one will be written from scratch by another programmer. Therefore, it is good practice to use remark statements as much as possible to help both yourself and subsequent users of a program.

In the programs in this book we have used remark lines to separate major sections of the program and to explain, in detail, how the program works and what it does. We use remarks wherever possible in the body of a routine to help clarify the processes it is going through. Even groups of blank REM lines add to the clarity of a program by separating the text.

Since program branches, such as GOTO and GOSUB, use line numbers, we use a remark with each one to clarify where the program is going. We also often branch to a REM line that contains the meaning of the routine.

Regardless of who you are or what your position is, the debugging of a program is tedious. But the more remarks you have in a program, the sooner you can fix it and get on to another program.

Multiple Statements on a Line

Most versions of the BASIC language allow you to put several program statements on the same line, usually separated by a colon. IBM also allows this procedure. In general, this technique is a poor one, and we do not use it or recommend it, but it does enhance the execution speed of completed programs by eliminating the need to process extra line numbers. As far as we are concerned, only remark statements should be tagged onto a line. Please feel free to add on Remark statements as often as you like. Certain commands such as IF–THEN statements frequently require multiple commands on the same line, and they are acceptable there. If the line is very long, however, it should probably be made into a subroutine and a GOSUB used.

WRITING YOUR PROGRAMS

As you write your own programs, you will develop your own personal programming style, which may be very different from ours as we have described it so far. However, all of your programs should incorporate two important features: They should be user friendly, and they should be tested.

User-Friendly Programs

A user-friendly program is also a programmer-friendly program. A program is considered to be user friendly if it is understandable, predictable, and easy to use. If the program meets these requirements, then the user will be friendly to the programmer. If the program does not meet these requirements, then the user will be very unfriendly to the programmer. Therefore the easier it is to use your program, the happier everyone will be.

The Lazy Programmer

We think of ourselves as being lazy programmers but in a positive sense. We strive to make our programs easy for us to work with and to write, but we never do anything for ourselves that makes more work for the user of our programs. We create programs to be useful and helpful to others. The programs will usually be used hundreds of times but only written once. Therefore, although we do not try to maximize our work, we do not take a shortcut if it will penalize us later or penalize the user forever.

The Idiot-Proof Program

We do not write idiot-proof programs! We write user-friendly programs. Our users are not idiots; they are people trying to get a job done, and we are supposed to help them. We recognize the fact that our users do not usually have the same skills that we have, but then we may not be able to do their jobs either. Idiot-proof programs tend to be inflexible and demeaning. They show everyone that the programmer thinks the user is inferior and incompetent. This is wrong.

A program should be flexible and adjust automatically to the skills of the user. It should be simple and easy to use, yet it should not hinder an experienced person who is using the program for the hundredth time that day. It should have an on-line help system to answer the questions for the novice or casual user or for the expert who simply forgot something. The program should reflect respect for the user, not contempt. Plainly and simply, we are here to help the user.

Testing Your Programs

All programs should be thoroughly tested before they are given to users. Testing is time-consuming; and the larger a program is, the more variables and conditions there are to test. You should remember that a running program is the most essential element of a program that is user friendly, and the only way to verify that a program works is to test it. We readily admit that we have delivered programs that users subsequently found errors in (there may even be undiscovered errors in this book). Unless you spend years testing, you may never find all the errors in your programs, but you must try to be as thorough as possible. If you test a program in steps, as it is being developed, many problems can be discovered and corrected before they become serious. It is also beneficial to have another person test your work as you progress. A second opinion can be very valuable.

Another minor point: Programs do not have bugs; they have errors which are made by humans. Rarely does the computer make a mistake, and our users should not dislike a computer because we made a mistake. We should try to find and correct errors as quickly as possible, even the little ones. A tiny sliver in your foot can become very painful and annoying if left in too long.

We do not want to belabor the point or imply that we are setting down some sort of gospel, but we do believe that your attitude is as important as your raw programming skills.

MAKE THE IBM WORK FOR YOU

The whole purpose in writing a program is to have the computer do some of your work. When you design the program, think about the problems that may arise and how the computer can automatically solve them as they are encountered. This idea leads us to the building-block concept.

The building blocks we are providing in this book are intended to make the IBM work for both the programmer and the user. The programmer benefits by being able to use ready-made pieces over and over again, and the user benefits by having a consistent and professional program to work with.

IBM BASIC

The result of IBM and Microsoft working closely together in the development of the PC system is a very powerful version of BASIC. They have also provided us with some very valuable development tools. One of these tools is the line editor in IBM BASIC, which allows almost painless editing. In this book we have used the same key definitions as defined by IBM. You will find this to be convenient; it is an excellent example of user friendliness (making a new program operate like an old one). IBM also has provided us with many other handy features such as the ability to merge two programs together to make one larger program and a renumber command to make your programs aesthetically pleasing.

We suggest that you review the BASIC Program Editor Section of the BASIC manual and practice the editing commands. Also review the Merge and Renumber commands. You will need to use the Merge command for this book, but Renumber is not necessary.

The IBM BASIC Compiler

The BASIC that comes with your computer is an interpretive language. This means that as the program is executed, every line is deciphered (interpreted) every time it is encountered. Although this provides an excellent development environment, it slows the program execution down. A compiler is a program that converts your program into a machine language equivalent, thereby speeding up the program by eliminating the redundant reinterpretation of every line. The disadvantage of using a compiler is that it takes a long time to compile a program every time a debug change is made, thus slowing the development process.

IBM sells a BASIC compiler. In general it will make a program run ten to twenty times faster than the interpreter. It is not perfectly compatible with the interpretive version, but the differences—extensions and improvements to commands—are minor. We think the compiler is a good investment and does more to improve the speed of execution of a program than anything else.

The compiler has the further advantage of allowing you to distribute unalterable programs. In other words, the compiled program cannot be changed (accidentally or otherwise) by your users. Hence, the users cannot introduce errors into the program.

Helpful Hints

The following suggestions and hints are offered for your convenience. Their use in your programs will improve the efficiency of your programming and your programs.

- Hint 1. Do not use multiple statements per line. Multiple statements on a line make the program much more difficult to read and debug.

- Hint 2. Wait until the program has been completely debugged and tested before deleting the remark statements from your programs to make them run faster. After all, the remark statements are there to help you find things, an important aid in debugging. If future adaptations to the program are likely, you should save a printout of your program with its Remark statements.

- Hint 3. Use integers instead of real numbers and arrays whenever possible. This conserves memory space and allows the program to run faster.

- Hint 4. Always use variables instead of constants. Your programs will run faster.

- Hint 5. Place the most frequently used variables at the top of your program to speed up program execution. IBM BASIC is an interpretive language. This means that it deciphers each line every time it is executed. Variable names are added to the internal list of names as they are encountered, and every variable is found every time by seeking through the name list starting at the first name. Names at the front of the list, therefore, are found quicker than names at the end.

- Hint 6. Frequently referenced line numbers should be located as early in the program as possible to speed up program execution.

We cannot overemphasize these hints. They are the small things that make a big difference in program performance.

ABOUT THE STRUCTURE OF THE BOOK

The real learning experience in this book lies in studying our examples. Although individual cases may vary, probably the easiest way to read this book is to go through the text of each chapter lightly to get a feel for what is to be done. Then study the programs carefully to learn how each was created.

Diagraming the flow of the program can be very helpful. Read the text again in more detail, and then type in the program, verifying your progress at each test point. As each example is completed you should have a good feeling for what we have presented. Please enjoy yourself, and remember to back up your diskettes as you go.

The following chapters are divided into sections: design, user features, and programmer features. In using these section topics, we are trying to show you how to structure your thinking to help you create programs more efficiently. Here are the points we are trying to make:

Design	Define the basic program function.
User features	Define specific user functions and the special conditions to be met.
Programmer features	Define specific features needed to meet the design criteria.

As each new BASIC command is encountered in the text, we will provide a brief explanation and example. These examples are given to refresh your memory only, and we suggest that you review your IBM BASIC manual for more detailed definitions.

The format of the program listings in the chapters that follow need not be precisely duplicated in the computer. We have taken artistic license in the placement of the remark statements (through the use of our word processor) to make the listings easier to read.

Many of the chapters build on one another. For instance, the program presented in Chapter 2, the line editor, gets combined with the additional material in Chapter 3 to yield the screen editor. The following list describes which chapters are added together to yield the new one.

Chapter 2	Stand-alone
Chapter 3	Chapters 2 + 3
Chapter 4	Stand-alone
Chapter 5	Chapters 2 + 4 + 5
Chapter 6	Chapters 2 + 4 + 6
Chapter 7	Stand-alone
Chapter 8	Chapters 2 + 4 + 5 + 6 + 7 + 8

For Chapters 2 and 3 the programs are entered by using the IBM's built-in editing capability. Once you have a finished product from Chapter 3, you can use the resulting screen editor to enter and edit the programs in the remaining chapters—a real timesaving tool.

Each chapter also includes a sample user manual. The user manual is something that most people forget because it comes at the end of a long, trying project. It is, however, the users' first and most lasting impression of your work, and some skill should be developed in writing the manual.

AN INPUT LINE EDITOR FOR THE IBM PC

INTRODUCTION

One feature is common to almost every program: The program asks a question and the user types in an answer. In a BASIC program you normally get the user's answer by using an INPUT statement.

INPUT The INPUT statement requests an input from the user at the keyboard, and the program will not proceed until the input is made.

EXAMPLE

```
5000    INPUT AGE%
5100    PRINT AGE%*2
```

```
RUN
? 34
68
OK
```

In this example line 5000 causes the user to be prompted on the screen (by a question mark) to supply a number for the variable AGE% (34). Once the number is typed in at the keyboard, line 5100 is executed and the result is printed on the screen (68).

The INPUT statement accepts all user input. The programmer must test every entry for a valid response (i.e., a number in the proper range, or a name with only alphabetical characters), and the user re-enters the information if the program detects an error. This process is repeated for every INPUT statement.

Why not have the IBM do some of the programmer's work and at the same time give the user some additional editing capabilities? This task can be done with a line editor. A *line editor* is a subroutine that accepts data entered on the keyboard and processes any special editing characters entered. These characters perform such functions as inserting a space or deleting a character. The line editor is also used to control the exact characters the user is allowed to enter. For example, you could restrict the user to entering numbers only, with no other characters allowed, or you could ask for a simple yes or no response. Of course, many more functions are available with a line editor.

The line editor program is one of the largest routines in this book. It is presented first because it is used as a building block for most of the routines in the following chapters. We have attempted to present this routine in an understandable manner, but don't be too concerned if you must reread a couple of sections before understanding it.

The development of the line editor program will progress through a discussion of the major components needed, the methods for displaying the cursor, processing input keystrokes, editing routines, and finally a set of user instructions. The sections that follow immediately will review the thought process we want you to go through each time you consider a programming problem.

In this chapter, as in all the following chapters, you will encounter program modules that are to be entered into your computer, tested, and debugged. These modules will result in complete working programs, one for each chapter of the book.

Design

Before writing a computer program, you must define what problem is to be solved and exactly what you want the program to do—a task we call *design*. The problem we wish to begin solving in this chapter is an unfriendly user interface to the computer. INPUT does not display the default or existing value; therefore the user cannot edit an existing value, and the program has no control over what the user enters. The solution to these problems is a line editor.

As general characteristics the line editor should display the original text, if any, and allow the user to edit it. Periods should be used to show the user the maximum number of characters that can be entered. For example, to enter a field (a piece of information the user is entering or editing) 10 characters long, we could have the following displays:

```
. . . . . . . . . .
Hello.....
110.27....
```

Our line editor includes these features. The editor should also allow the user to edit and correct mistakes in the text. We want the computer to do some error checking for us, and so the line editor should be able to selectively control the type of data entered. It should be able to force numeric entries, or a yes or no response, or to accept any text. Also, since one of the most useful features of a program is an on-line help capability, the line editor should be able to notify the program of a user's help request. All these features are incorporated in our line editor program.

The specific features of the line editor can be divided into those directed toward the user and those directed toward the programmer. We will address the user features first.

User Features

IBM BASIC has program-editing capability. We have implemented the IBM commands as well as additional features in our editor. For convenience, we have also used the same command keys in our editor as the IBM uses. So we implement these editing functions:

- Move cursor left one position.
- Move cursor right one position.
- Skip to the previous word.
- Skip to the next word.
- Skip to end of line.
- Skip to front of line.
- Insert a character and slide the text to the right.
- Delete the current character and move the remaining text to the left.
- Delete text from the current character to the end of the line.
- Delete next word.
- TAB.
- Restore original text.
- Restore deleted text.
- HELP key.

The line editor will show one period per allowed character on the screen with the programmer selecting the maximum allowable number of characters per field when setting up the screen. This is handy in cases like ZIP code fields, where only 5 spaces are required, or where one space is needed for a middle initial.

As mentioned, an important part of any program is the on-line help system. The line editor supports the help system by allowing the user to request help by pressing the F1 key. (The help system will be presented in detail in Chapter 4.)

Programmer Features

The programmer's features relate to how the programmer interfaces to the line editor. This interface should be as simple as possible, because we do not want it to add more work in creation than it saves in entry. Thus for the basic editor we require five pieces of information:

1. Screen row number where the input is to take place,
2. Screen column number where the input is to take place,
3. A "mask" to define the type of information to be entered,
4. The maximum length of the field,
5. The original text to be edited, if any.

The programmer uses a special symbol, which we call a *mask*, to tell the subroutine what keys may be pressed by the user. As examples of masks we use, an "a" will allow any key to be pressed and accepted, and a "#" will only allow numbers, the negative sign, and the decimal point to be pressed and accepted. This is done by having the program check every key pressed and verifying that it is valid for the current mask.

The line editor accepts six types of input data: help request, number, yes/no, capital or uppercase letters, and any text. The yes/no field only accepts the letters *Y* or *N*, and the any-text field accepts any printable ASCII character. A number field may contain the following symbols:

    - . 0 1 2 3 4 5 6 7 8 9

A Word of Advice

Before you start to enter the first lines of the program given in the next section, we have two suggestions.

First, it is important to type in the program with all of the remark statements intact. The remarks will help you in the debugging of the program, and they are also used as entry points for most of the GOSUBs.

Second, use of IBM's built-in editing capability can save many hours of time and frustration in the entry of the line editor program presented in this chapter and the screen editor program in Chapter 3. If you are not already familiar with these commands, we suggest you review them in your BASIC reference manual.

LINE EDITOR TEST ROUTINE

What follows is the first program module, which you are to enter. The programs (one for each chapter) are broken down into modules for several reasons. First, it is easier to understand and enter small modules; and second, it is far easier to test and debug small pieces of a program.

This first module is a test program for the line editor modules that follow. It allows you to define a field at any location on the screen and then use the line editor to input and edit.

The line editor test routine program is as follows:

```
100   ' CHAPTER 2 - LINE EDITOR TEST ROUTINE
110   ' ASKS FOR INITIAL CONDITIONS THEN IT USES THE LINE EDITOR.
120   ON ERROR GOTO 60000          ' STANDARD ERROR PROCESSING ROUTINE
130   KEY OFF                      ' TURN THE FUNCTION KEYS OFF
140   CLS
150   PRINT "Chapter 2 - LINE EDITOR TEST ROUTINE"
160   INPUT "Enter MASK ";MASK$
170   INPUT "Enter FIELD LENGTH ",MAXSIZE%
180   INPUT "Enter TEXT ";ENTRY$
190   INPUT "Enter ROW  ";ROW%
200   INPUT "Enter COL  ";COL%
210   CLS
220   GOSUB 50000                  ' THE LINE EDITOR
230   LOCATE 20,1
240   PRINT
250   IF HELP% = 1 THEN PRINT "HELP REQUESTED"
260   PRINT
```

```
270    PRINT ">";ENTRY%;"<"
280    LOCATE 23,1
290    INPUT "Press ENTER TO CONTINUE OR ENTER END TO EXIT.";A$
300    IF A$ < > "" THEN END
310    GOTO 150
320    '
330    '
340    '
```

KEY   The KEY statement allows the programmer to assign his or her own functions to any or all of the ten special function keys at the left side of the IBM keyboard. KEY ON shows the function key assignments on the 25th line of the display screen, and KEY OFF erases the 25th line, freeing it for other use without changing the function key assignments.

CLS   The CLS statement clears the display screen and returns the cursor to the home position (upper left-hand corner of screen).

PRINT   The PRINT command causes a line feed (increments one line) when encountered without option parameters. With options, the values of the list following the PRINT command are evaluated and printed.

LOCATE   This statement is used to position the cursor at the desired screen location.

IF–THEN   The IF statement is followed by an expression that is evaluated, and if found to be true the THEN or GOTO clause is executed. The THEN can be followed either by additional statements or a line number assignment, while the GOTO is always followed by a line number assignment.

ON ERROR GOTO   This statement allows "error trapping." That is, if the program detects an error—disk drive not ready or bad line number, for example—the program execution can be directed to an error-handling subroutine (written by the programmer) that, it is hoped, will produce an intelligible error message for the user. Line 220 indicates a subroutine starting at line 5000. For this, and any later references to lines not in the specific subroutine being discussed, you can check the lines indicated by refering to the end of this chapter where the entire line editor program is printed.

TEST POINT

Test points, encountered here for the first time, will appear regularly from now on to enable you to test each program module before adding the next module. We will point out the most pertinent conditions to test for, which will simplify your debugging to small modules.

Perform the following steps after the line editor test program has been entered:

1. Save the program on your diskette.
2. Type RUN (CR) where (CR), carriage return, means press the EN-TER key.

The program should clear the screen and ask you to ENTER MASK. Enter the desired mask and press ENTER. Then you will be asked for the field length, the text to fill the mask, and also for the row and column location for display on the screen. After you press ENTER, the process should repeat itself. When you wish to stop going through this loop, type END (CR) on the PRESS ENTER TO CONTIN-UE OR ENTER END TO EXIT line.

It is always a good idea to provide your users with a consistent and straightforward way to exit your programs. For example, in the line editor test program you are allowed to enter the word END as a response. Terrible problems can occur if your users get in the habit of using control break or reset to exit programs. For example, if users press control break when working with diskette files, there may be some information in the diskette buffer area that has not been saved on the disk. It will be saved only if the file is closed properly. There-fore, resetting may cause a loss of data if the diskette has not been updated completely.

FIG. 2.1   Overview of line editor program

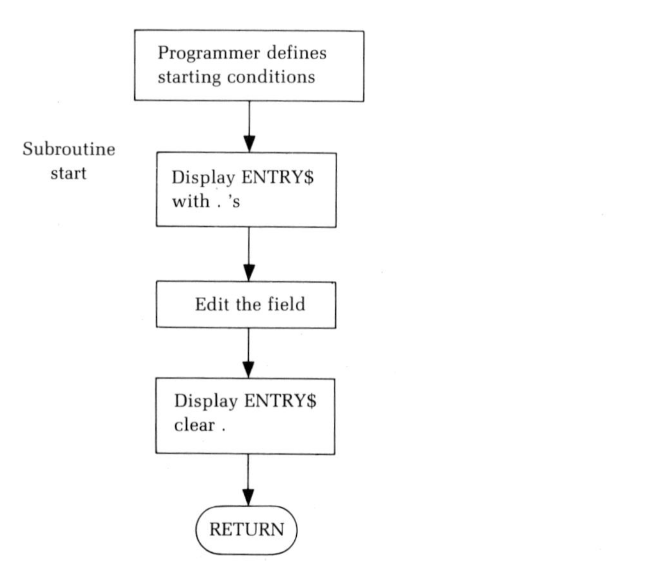

BASIC LINE EDITOR PROGRAM

A flowchart for the basic line editor process is shown in Figure 2.1. This flowchart gives a general overview of the program to be developed. Basically, the flowchart says that the programmer defines the characteristics of the field to be entered and the current contents of the field. The line editor first displays the field with periods, and then it allows the user to enter and/or edit the field. Finally, the field will be redisplayed and the periods erased.

The basic line editor program is as follows:

```
50000      ' BASIC LINE EDITOR (SET TO LINE NUMBER 50000)
50005      '
50010      '
50015      ' THIS IS A BASIC LINE EDITOR
50020      '
50025      ' THE PROGRAMMER CALLS IT USING THE FOLLOWING VARIABLES
50030      '
50035      ' ROW%          = SCREEN LINE NUMBER
50040      ' COL%          = SCREEN COLUMN NUMBER
50045      ' ENTRY$        = TEXT TO BE EDITED
50050      ' MASK$         = DATA TYPE TO BE ACCEPTED
50055      ' WHERE:
50060      ' a = ALPHANUMERIC UPPER AND LOWER CASE
50065      ' A = ALPHANUMERIC FORCE UPPER CASE
50070      ' # = NUMBER FIELD ONLY
50075      ' Y = YES/NO FIELD
50080      ' MAXSIZE%   = MAXIMUM FIELD LENGTH
50085      '
50090      PLACE% = 1                  ' SET THE STARTING POSITION
50095      '
50100      FILL$ = "."                 ' DISPLAY DOTS
50105      HELP% = 0                   ' CLEAR THE HELP FLAG
50110      FRONT% = 1                  ' FIRST CHARACTER DISPLAYED
50115      CTRL% = 0                   ' CLEAR THE EXIT FLAG
50120      GOSUB 52660                 ' DISPLAY ENTRY$
50125      GOSUB 50160                 ' EDIT THE STRING
50130      FILL$ = " "                 ' CLEAR THE SCREEN
50135      '
50140      RETURN                      ' GO BACK TO CALLER
50145      '
50150      ' *********************
50155      '
```

The explanations for various parts of this program and its GOSUBs are given in the following subsections.

Explanation of Variables

The basic line editor program consists mostly of remark statements. It is always good practice, at the beginning of a program or a subroutine, to use remarks statements to define who wrote it, when it was last changed, what it does, and the purpose of the major variables used. Several of these remarks are shown in lines 50000–50085.

The % symbol in the names means that these variables are integer variables. An *integer* is a whole number between −32,767 and +32,767. Throughout this book we will use integers whenever possible. We do so for several reasons. First, most programmers do not use integer variables; therefore by using integer variables, we can avoid variable name conflicts within your programs. For example, A, A%, and A$ are all treated as individual and unique variables, even though they have similar names. Second, integer variables require less memory space than floating-point (decimal-point numbers) variables, and we want the subroutines to be as compact as possible.

The variables ROW% and COL% (lines 50035 and 50040) are used to position the text on the screen. ROW% is a number between 1 and 24. COL% is a number between 1 and 79. HELP% will be set equal to 1 if the user requests help; otherwise, it will be set equal to 0.

ENTRY$ (line 50045) contains the text to be edited. If there is no text to be edited, then ENTRY$ is cleared by the line

```
ENTRY$ =""
```

MASK$ (line 50050) is used to define the type of the field to be edited. MAXSIZE% (line 50080) defines the maximum number of characters allowed.

```
MASK$ = "a"
MAXSIZE% = 10
```

means "accept any character up to a maximum length of ten characters." A # is used for numeric fields; a Y for yes/no fields and an A for uppercase letters. Figure 2.2 contains several examples of how these various parameters are used. As always, help is available to the user anytime, no matter what the type definition.

Notice that we have not restricted the variable names to only two characters, but we have tried to use meaningful names—not just names meaningful today as we design the program, but names still meaningful twelve months from now when we return to make further enhancements.

FIG. 2.2.   Field parameter examples

MASK$	MAXSIZE%	DESCRIPTION
a	20	Accept any 20 characters.
a	8	Accept any 8 characters.
A	20	Accept any characters and capitalize all letters.
#	6	Accept a 6-digit number.
#	10	Accept a 10-digit number.
Y		Allow only Y or N entry.

FILL$ (line 50100) is the character used to illustrate the field's maximum length. For example, if FILL$ equals a "." and the field is to be six characters long, then the line editor will display

. . . . . .

six dots, to show the field's maximum length.

TEST POINT

At this point the program is not yet functional, but it is a good idea to test what is entered to make sure it at least returns you to the beginning of the program. Execute the program and it should stop at line 50120.

Explanation of the Display Subroutine

The display subroutine, called by line 50120 GOSUB 52660, is flowcharted in Figure 2.3. This routine displays the text in the current

FIG. 2.3 Display subroutine

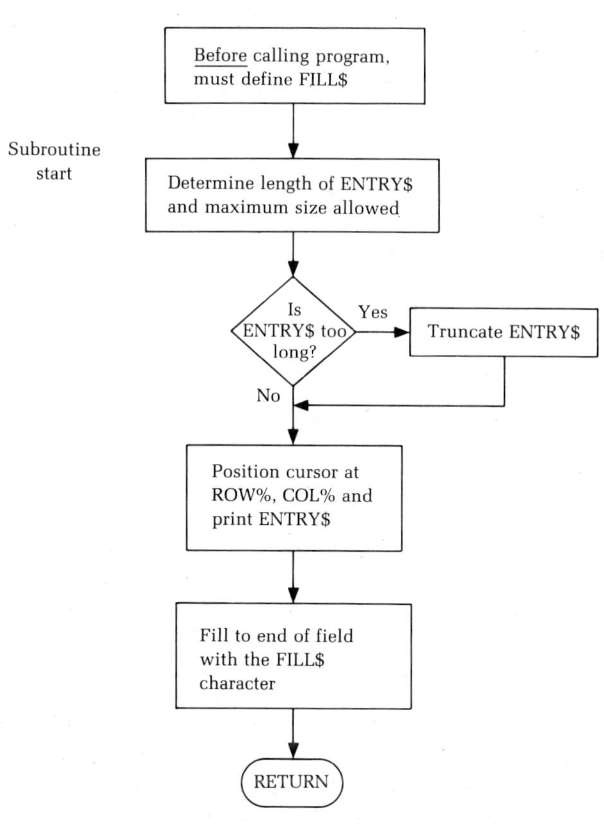

ENTRY$ at the requested screen position and the requested length of the field, using the FILL$ character. If there is no text to display, then it will simply show one dot for each character allowed.

FILL$ must be set before this subroutine is called. Figure 2.1 shows that the first time this subroutine is used it displays a period; the last time it is used, a blank or space character is used as FILL$. The space will remove the periods and clean up the screen display. You can use any printable ASCII or graphics character for FILL$.

The display program corresponding to the flowchart in Figure 2.3 is as follows.

```
52630     ' ENTRY POINT FOR EDIT ROUTINES
52635     '
52640     FRONT% = 1                          ' MAKE SURE CURSOR IS AT
                                                 FRONT
52645     IF PLACE% > 79 - COL% THEN
              PLACE% = 79 - COL%              ' IN CASE OFF SCREEN
52650     '
52655     '
52660     ' DISPLAY TEST$
52665     ' FILL$ IS THE FILL CHARACTER
52670     ' TXTSIZE% IS THE LENGTH OF ENTRY$
52675     ' MAXSIZE% IS THE MAXIMUM ALLOWED LENGTH
52680     '
52685     '
52690     TXTSIZE% = LEN (ENTRY$)             ' HOW LONG IS THE
                                                 CURRENT FIELD?
52695     '
52700     ' IS ENTRY$ TOO LONG?
52705     '
52710     IF TXTSIZE% > MAXSIZE% THEN ENTRY$ =
              LEFT$ (ENTRY$,MAXSIZE%):TXTSIZE% = MAXSIZE%
52715     '
52720     ' POSITION THE CURSOR
52725     '
52730     LOCATE ROW%,COL%                    ' ROW POSITION
52735     '
52740     ' PRINT THE TEXT
52745     '
52750     IF MAXSIZE% > 79 - COL% THEN X = (79 - COL%) ELSE X =
              MAXSIZE%
52755     PRINT MID$(ENTRY$,FRONT%,X);        ' NO LINE FEED
52760     '
52765     ' PRINT THE FILL CHARACTER
52770     '
52775     IF (TXTSIZE% - FRONT%) >
              X THEN RETURN                   ' NO FILL$ TO PRINT
52780     FOR XX = (TXTSIZE% - FRONT%) TO (X - 2)
52785         PRINT FILL$;
52790     NEXT XX
52795     RETURN                              ' ALL DONE
52800     '
52805     ' ********************
52810     '
```

You may be wondering why this subroutine's line numbers are not consecutive with the previous routine. The display subroutine is used quite frequently by the line editor. Since the line editor is to become part of a larger program we do not want BASIC to search the entire program every time we need to display something. For this reason, we put the display routine after all the other line editor subroutines so that BASIC can find it quickly.

The display subroutine starts by using the LEN (LENgth) command (line 52690) to determine the length of ENTRY$.

LEN The LEN command returns the number of characters contained in the referenced string as an integer value between 0 and 255.

EXAMPLE

```
5000   A$="HAPPY DAYS"
5100   PRINT A$;LEN(A$)
RUN
HAPPY DAYS 10
```

As the example shows, the number of characters and spaces in A$, HAPPY DAYS, is equal to 10.

Next, a test is made in the display program (line 52710) to see if ENTRY$ is larger than MAXSIZE%. This test can fail only the first time the line editor is called, because the editor will not allow the user to enter too many characters. If ENTRY$ is too long then the editor will truncate the extra characters.

LEFT$ The LEFT$(A$,N) command returns the character string starting at the left end of A$ for N characters.

EXAMPLE

```
5000   A$="HAPPY DAYS"
5100   PRINT LEFT$(A$,4)
RUN
HAPP
```

In this example of LEFT$, we take the characters in A$ starting at the left-most position and count to the right four positions for the result, HAPP.

Our line editor allows the user to enter more characters than will fit on one line of the screen. The display routine will only show the characters that fit between the beginning screen column position and column 79 (lines 52750 and 52755). For example, if COL% = 40 and MAXSIZE% = 100, the display routine shows the 39 characters that will fit between column 40 and 79.

Why do we stop at column 79 and not 80? After a character is printed in the 80th column, BASIC automatically advances the cursor to the next line; when on the 24th screen line, BASIC will scroll the screen up. This is not a very desirable characteristic in a line editor, and rather than checking the screen row numbers and treating the 24th line as a special case, we simply do not use the screen's 80th column.

MID$(A$,N,X)   The MID$ command returns the character string starting at N in the string A$ for X characters. If X is not present, then the program continues until the end of the string is reached.

EXAMPLE

```
5000   A$ = "HAPPY DAYS"
5100    PRINT MID$(A$,7,3)
RUN
DAY
```

In this example of MID$, we count 7 characters into A$ and extract the next 3 characters encountered. This results in DAY being extracted from A$.

After ENTRY$ fits into the alloted space, the cursor is positioned and ENTRY$ is printed (line 52755). Finally, a FOR–NEXT loop (lines 52780 through 52790) is used to fill the remainder of the field with the FILL$ character.

FOR–NEXT The FOR–NEXT looping command executes the statements after the FOR statement until the NEXT statement is encountered. Then the counting variable is incremented, and the process is repeated until the counting variable reaches the maximum value desired. Once the maximum value is reached, the program execution proceeds to the statement following the NEXT. A STEP statement can also be used in a FOR–NEXT loop to increment the loop in values other than 1 (the default value).

EXAMPLE

```
5000    FOR I=1 TO 5
5100      PRINT I
5200    NEXT
RUN
1
2
3
4
5
```

In this FOR–NEXT loop we simply count up from 1 to 5 by ones.

EXAMPLE

```
5000    FOR I=1 TO 20 STEP 5
5100      PRINT I
5200    NEXT
RUN
1
6
11
16
```

This FOR–NEXT loop counts up in intervals of 5.

EXAMPLE

```
5000    FOR I=10 TO 1 STEP −1
5100      PRINT I
```

```
5200   NEXT
RUN
10
9
8
7
6
5
4
3
2
1
```

This example shows how to count down by using a negative step.

At this point in the display subroutine, we have positioned EN-TRY$ on the screen and shown the field's maximum length.

The variables X and XX are "garbage" variables. That is, they have only immediate meaning and may be changed by any routine. They are used to count loops and to hold values temporarily. Remember that garbage variables may be used by a subroutine that you call. Always use a unique name if you want to make sure that your variable remains unchanged by any branches to subroutines.

TEST POINT

The display program is the first subroutine that really does something; it displays any preexisting text and periods to indicate the number of allowable characters. Now it is time to test it.

How do you select a series of tests to perform? Experienced programmers test both the midpoints and extremes of a program. Programs tend to be stable in the midranges of their operation but can fail at the extremes of their operations. The best way to illustrate what is meant by this statement is to look at what tests should be performed on this subroutine.

Take a moment now and think about what tests you might perform. Although this routine is simple, there are a number of extremes that need to be tested. First, identify the important variables used in this subroutine. They are as follows.

`ENTRY$`	Text field
`MASK$`	Field type
`MAXSIZE%`	Field length
`ROW%`	Screen row number
`COL%`	Screen column number

Next, identify the extreme values for each of the following variables.

VARIABLE	TEXT EXTREME
`ENTRY$`	Length = 0 (i.e., null or blank field) Length = MAXSIZE% Length > MAXSIZE%
`MAXSIZE%`	Length = 1 Length = screen width Length = 255
`ROW%`	Line 1 Line 24 or 25
`COL%`	First column = 1 Last column = 80

Since this subroutine is to be controlled by the programmer, certain extremes that will cause an error condition have been intentionally ignored. These errors occur if ROW% or COL% point to locations off the screen, as when one or both are equal to 0, or when ROW% > 25 or COL% > screen width. Also, if MASK$ is a blank string, an error will occur. If you find yourself being forgetful, then you can add simple tests before line 50100 in the basic line editor program to verify that ROW%, COL%, MAXSIZE%, and MASK$ have valid values. The meaning of *extremes* should become apparent to you as you read through the above list. As you test your own programs in the future try to observe where your errors occur. In many cases you will discover that you have exceeded some limit or extreme.

Make sure that the routine works properly for all ENTRY$ text fields. Test it with no text, too much text, and the maximum acceptable amount of text. Also, be sure to test those combinations of extremes that appear to be extremely extreme cases—for example, ROW% = 24 or 25, MAXSIZE% = screen width, and ENTRY\$ > MAXSIZE%.

Lines 24 and 25 are both extremes on the IBM. Normally you cannot use line 25 and line 24 is considered the last screen line, but it is possible (using the KEY OFF command) to use line 25. So both lines become extremes.

FIG. 2.4   Subroutine for editing the field

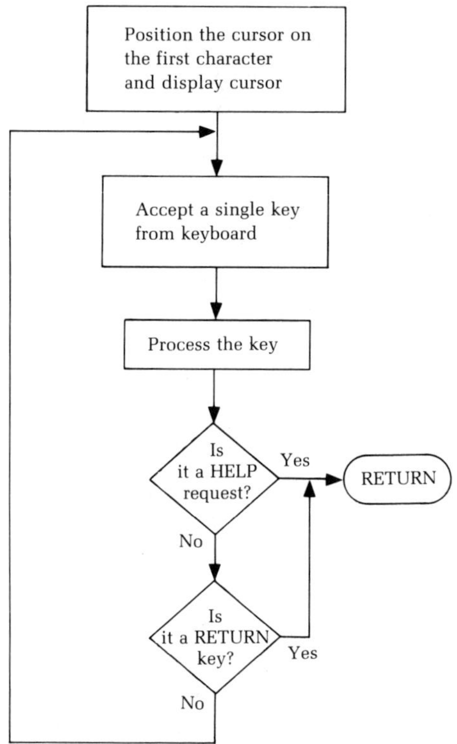

Explanation of the Edit Subroutine

The flowchart shown in Figure 2.4 describes the process for editing the field. This subroutine is called by line 50125, GOSUB 50160, in the basic line editor program. The flowchart details the following sequence of events: Position and display a cursor over the first character in the field. Next, accept a single character from the keyboard, process it, and then get another one. When ENTER is pressed, or if a help request is made, then return to the calling program.

Here is the program that edits the field.

```
50160      ' EDIT THE ENTRY$ FIELD
50165      IF LEN(MASK$)>1 THEN MASK$=
               LEFT$(MASK$,1)                    ' USE ONLY ONE LETTER
50170      ORG.ENTRY$ = ENTRY$                   ' KEEP ORIGINAL IN CASE
                                                     THEY CHANGE MIND
50175      TXTSIZE% = LEN(ENTRY$)                ' NEEDED FOR SPECIAL
                                                     ROUTINES
50180      LOCATE ROW%,1                         ' POSITION CURSOR
50185      GOSUB 52500                           ' PRINT THE CHARACTER
50190      '
50195      ' ACCEPT A KEY FROM THE KEYBOARD
50200      '
50205      A.KEY$ = INKEY$
50210      IF LEN(A.KEY$) =
               0 THEN GOTO 50205                 ' LOOP UNTIL ENTRY MADE
50215      '
50220      ' IF HERE THEN A KEY PUSHED
50225      '
50230      IF LEN(A.KEY$) = 1
               THEN A.KEY% =
               ASC(A.KEY$) ELSE A.KEY% =
               ASC(RIGHT$(A.KEY$,1)) +
               300                               ' CONVERT KEY TO A NUMBER
50235      '
50240      ' PROCESS THE KEY
50245      '
50250      GOSUB 50285                           ' KEY% PROCESSOR
50255      ' EXIT IF HELP REQUESTED OR SPECIAL KEY ENTERED
50260      IF HELP% <> 0 OR CTRL% <>
               0 THEN GOSUB 52630 : RETURN       ' REDISPLAY AND EXIT
```

```
50265     GOTO 50205                                    ' GET THE NEXT KEY
50270     '
50275     ' ****************************
50280     '
```

INKEY\$ (line 50205) accepts characters from the keyboard. INKEY\$ returns a string either 0, 1, or 2 characters long depending on the key pressed.

If no key is pressed, INKEY\$ returns a string of length 0. When an alphanumeric or control key is pressed, INKEY\$ returns a string of length 1 with the ASCII value of the key. A length of 2 indicates that a special IBM function or number pad key has been pressed. Every special key is assigned an ASCII character code according to APPENDIX G of the IBM BASIC manual. The ASCII character code values are presented in Figure 2.5.

DISPLAYING A CURSOR

In the field-editing program (line 50185, GOSUB 52500), the current character is displayed blinking and in high intensity. When there is no character to display, then an underline is used.

The following program will display a blinking high-intensity character.

```
52500     ' DISPLAY THE CHARACTER IN HIGH INTENSITY
              (SET TO LINE NUMBER 52500)
52505     ' THIS GIVES THE ILLUSION OF CURSOR MOVEMENT
52510     '
52515     LOCATE ROW%,(COL% + PLACE% -
              FRONT%)                       ' POSITION CURSOR
52520     COLOR 31,0                        ' HIGH INTENSITY
                                                BLINKING
52525     XX$ = MID$(ENTRY$,PLACE%,1)       ' MOVE FOR THE NEXT IF
52530     IF XX$ = "" OR XX$ =
              " " THEN XX$ = "_"            ' SHOW UNDERLINE FOR SPACE
52535     PRINT XX$;                        ' PRINT THE INVERSE
52540     COLOR 7,0                         ' RESTORE TO NORMAL
                                                VIDEO
```

```
52545      LOCATE ROW%,(COL% + PLACE% -
              FRONT%)                          ' REPOSITION THE CURSOR
52550      RETURN
52555      '
52560      ' ********************
52565      '
```

PLACE% is used to keep track of the current cursor position; however, PLACE% could have been set by the calling program. For example, if we wanted to begin editing at the end of a field instead of at the beginning, we would set PLACE% equal to the length of the field instead of 1.

The COLOR command is used to set the colors of the background, foreground, and the border of the screen. You may use these options if your system is equipped with a color monitor and an interface card; otherwise, you will be limited to turning blinking characters on and off.

After the cursor is positioned over the current character, the COLOR 31,0 command turns the blinking high-intensity mode on (line 52520), and then the character is printed. Line 52540 returns the screen to low intensity, and then the cursor is repositioned over the character (line 52545).

TEST POINT

Running the program will cause the text field to be displayed and the cursor to be positioned over the first character. If there is a character in the first position, it will be shown blinking and in high intensity; otherwise, an underline will be shown. After the text and the cursor are displayed, the program will be waiting for a key to be entered. Since we have not entered this yet, enter control break to exit.

PROCESSING A KEY

The program polls the keyboard for a character on line 50205. Line 50210 determines whether or not a key has been pressed. If the length of A.KEY$ is greater than 0, then a key has been pressed. If the length

FIG. 2.5   ASCII character codes

Hex. No.	Binary No.	0	1	2	3	4	5	6	7	8	9	A	B	C	D	E	F
		0000	0001	0010	0011	0100	0101	0110	0111	1000	1001	1010	1011	1100	1101	1110	1111
0	0000	0	16	SP 32	Ø 48	@ 64	P 80	` 96	p 112	128	144	SP 160	Ø 176	@ 192	P 208	` 224	p 240
1	0001	1	DC1 17	! 33	1 49	A 65	Q 81	a 97	q 113	129	DC1 145	! 161	1 177	A 193	Q 209	a 225	q 241
2	0010	2	DC2 18	" 34	2 50	B 66	R 82	b 98	r 114	130	DC2 146	" 162	2 178	B 194	R 210	b 226	r 242
3	0011	3	DC3 19	# 35	3 51	C 67	S 83	c 99	s 115	131	DC3 147	# 163	3 179	C 195	S 211	c 227	s 243
4	0100	4	DC4 20	$ 36	4 52	D 68	T 84	d 100	t 116	132	DC4 148	$ 164	4 180	D 196	T 212	d 228	t 244
5	0101	5	21	% 37	5 53	E 69	U 85	e 101	u 117	133	149	% 165	5 181	E 197	U 213	e 229	u 245
6	0110	6	22	& 38	6 54	F 70	V 86	f 102	v 118	134	150	& 166	6 182	F 198	V 214	f 230	v 246
7	0111	BEL 7	23	´ 39	7 55	G 71	W 87	g 103	w 119	BEL 135	151	´ 167	7 183	G 199	W 215	g 231	w 247
8	1000	BS 8	CAN 24	(40	8 56	H 72	X 88	h 104	x 120	BS 136	CAN 152	(168	8 184	H 200	X 216	h 232	x 248
9	1001	HT 9	25	) 41	9 57	I 73	Y 89	i 105	y 121	HT 137	153	) 169	9 185	I 201	Y 217	i 233	y 249
A	1010	LF 10	26	* 42	: 58	J 74	Z 90	j 106	z 122	LF 138	154	* 170	: 186	J 202	Z 218	j 234	z 250
B	1011	VT 11	ESC 27	+ 43	; 59	K 75	[91	k 107	{ 123	VT 139	ESC 155	+ 171	; 187	K 203	[219	k 235	{ 251
C	1100	FF 12	28	, 44	< 60	L 76	\ 92	l 108	| 124	FF 140	156	, 172	< 188	L 204	\ 220	l 236	| 252
D	1101	CR 13	29	- 45	= 61	M 77	] 93	m 109	} 125	CR 141	157	- 173	= 189	M 205	] 221	m 237	} 253
E	1110	SO 14	30	. 46	> 62	N 78	^ 94	n 110	~ 126	SO 142	158	. 174	> 190	N 206	^ 222	n 238	~ 254
F	1111	SI 15	31	/ 47	? 63	O 79	_ 95	o 111	DEL 127	SI 143	159	/ 175	? 191	O 207	_ 223	o 239	DEL 255

of A.KEY\$ is 0, then no keys have been pressed, and so the program branches back to line 50205 to poll the keyboard again. The program stays on these two program lines until a key is pressed.

Once a key is pressed, line 50230 determines what its length is and assigns a value to A.KEY%. If a regular ASCII key has been pressed, then the length is 1 and the ASCII value of the key is stored in A.KEY%. When the length is 2, a special function key has been entered. The values assigned these keys conflict with the normal ASCII characters. IBM expects you to distinguish the keys by knowing the length of A.KEY\$. In our program we have found it easier to work with the keys if we convert them to numbers instead of keeping them as strings. Therefore, to help us tell the keys apart we will add 300 to the ASCII value of A.KEY\$ when its length is 2.

ASC format y=ASC(X\$)   This function allows the program to extract the ASCII value of the first character of the string X\$.

Subroutine GOSUB 50285 (line 50250 of the field-editing program) is used to display or process the key pressed by the user. A key can be either control plus another key, a numeric keypad key, a function key, or a regular text key.

Program function keys and the numeric keypad keys are used for editing text and moving the cursor. If you refer to the keyboard section of the *IBM Guide to Operations,* you will see that we use the keys the same way as described by IBM.

The program that tests the key is:

```
50285   ' TEST FOR CONTROL KEY
50290   '
50295   IF A.KEY% <= 31 OR A.KEY% >
            126 THEN GOSUB 51000: RETURN     ' PROCESS AND RETURN
50300   '
50305   ' MUST BE AN ALPHANUMERIC
50310   '
50315   ' TEST THE MASK TO DETERMINE DATA TYPE
50320   '
50325   IF MASK$ = "a" THEN
            GOSUB 50900 : RETURN             ' ACCEPT ANYTHING
50330   IF MASK$ = "A" THEN
            GOSUB 50480 : RETURN             ' FORCE UPPER CASE
```

```
50335    IF MASK$ = "#" THEN GOSUB 50380: RETURN
50340    IF MASK$ = "Y" THEN GOSUB 50430: RETURN
50345    '
50350    ' BAD MASK CHARACTER
50355    '
50360    RETURN
50365    '
50370    ' ****************************
50375    '
```

If the user presses a control or special key, a branch is made to the control-character subroutine, GOSUB 51000 (line 50295). If any other key is pressed, the program checks and branches to the appropriate character-checking subroutine.

As examples, MASK$ = "a," then a branch is made to subroutine 50900, the universal-character-accept routine. If MASK$ = "#", then a branch to subroutine 50380 verifies that a number has been entered.

When a valid character is entered, it is added to ENTRY$ and displayed; otherwise, it is ignored. The MASK$ checks occur on lines 50325–50340.

In our version of the editor, only five data types are allowed. You can add other branches to this routine if more data types are desired. For example, you may wish to have a data type for positive integers.

Processing the Input Keys

After a key is pressed, the program must determine whether it is a special key (character) or an alphanumeric key and if it is a valid character. This process is flowcharted in Figure 2.6.

CHARACTER-ACCEPT AND DISPLAY ROUTINES

When a valid alphanumeric character is entered, it is added to EN-TRY$ and displayed on the screen. Then the cursor is moved right one position.

There are several checks performed in the character-accept routine. First, if the insert mode is on (INSERT% = 1), a space is inserted

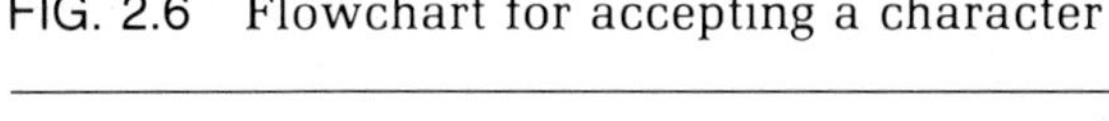

FIG. 2.6   Flowchart for accepting a character

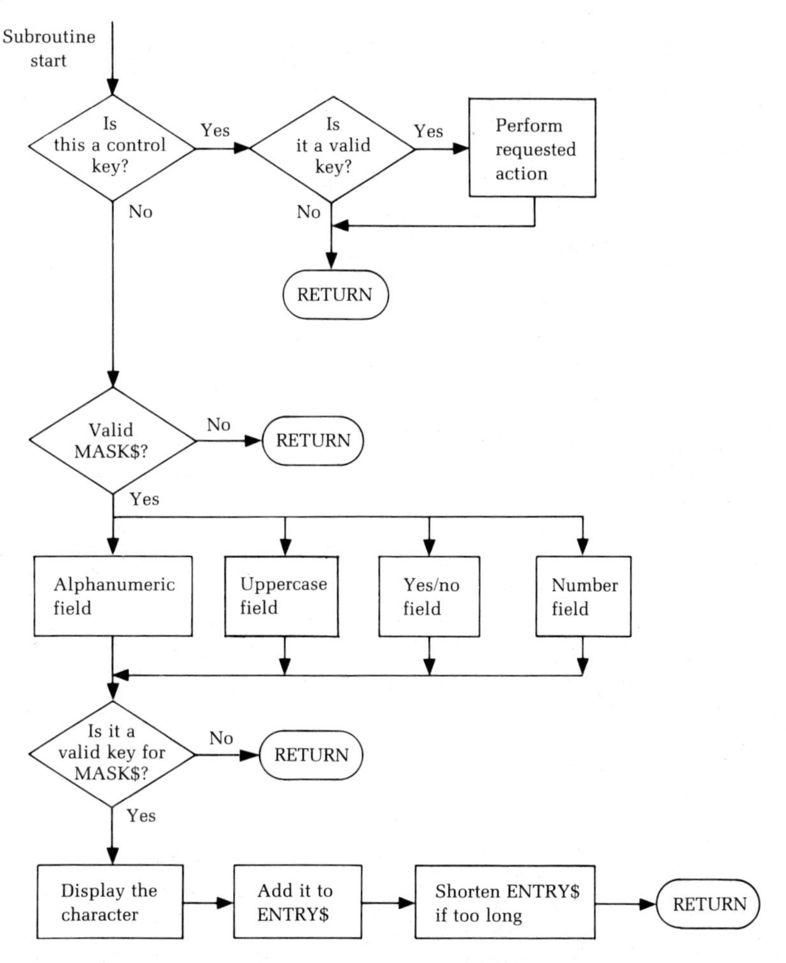

into ENTRY\$ before the character is added. Second, checks are made to determine how to add the character; there are different ways to add the character depending on where the character is to be added to ENTRY\$. Finally, if the new field is too long, it is truncated to MAXSIZE% length.

The program to check for and accept an alphanumeric character is:

```
50900      ' PRINT A.KEY% AND ADD TO ENTRY$ (SET TO LINE NUMBER 50900)
50905      '
50910      IF INSERT% = 1 THEN GOSUB 51405     ' INSERT A SPACE FIRST
50915      ' ADD TO END OF ENTRY
50920      IF PLACE% > LEN(ENTRY$) THEN ENTRY$ =
               ENTRY$ + A.KEY$ : GOTO 50935
50925      ' ADD TO MIDDLE OF STRING
50930      MID$(ENTRY$,PLACE%,1) = A.KEY$
50935      TXTSIZE% = LEN (ENTRY$)
50940      ' IF TOO BIG TRUNCATE IT
50945      IF TXTSIZE% > MAXSIZE% THEN ENTRY$ =
               LEFT$ (ENTRY$,MAXSIZE%)
50950      '
50955      ' NEED TO MOVE RIGHT ONE PLACE
50960      '
50965      GOSUB 51520                          ' RIGHT ARROW
50970      RETURN
50975      '
50980      ' **************************
50985      '
```

The programs that test for yes/no and number fields are listed next.

```
50380      ' ACCEPT A NUMBER
50385      '
50390      ' TEST TO SEE IF IT IS A VALID NUMERIC TYPE OF CHARACTER
50395      '
50400      IF (A.KEY% < 45) OR (A.KEY% >
               57) THEN RETURN                  ' BAD KEY
50405      IF A.KEY% = 47 THEN RETURN            ' BAD KEY ALSO
50410      GOSUB 50900                           ' GOOD KEY SO
                                                     ACCEPT IT
50415      RETURN
50420      ' *************************************
50425      '

50430      ' TEST FOR YES OR NO
```

```
50435     IF (A.KEY% = 121) OR (A.KEY% =
             110) THEN A.KEY% = A.KEY% -
             32 : A.KEY$ = CHR$(A.KEY%)        ' UPPERCASE CONVERT
50440     IF (A.KEY% <> 89) AND (A.KEY% <>
             78) THEN RETURN                   ' CAPITAL Y OR N
50445     ENTRY$ = A.KEY$                      ' RETURN ONE LETTER
                                                   ONLY
50450     LOCATE ROW%,COL%                     ' PRINT FULL WORD
50455     IF A.KEY% = 78 THEN PRINT "NO "; ELSE
             PRINT "YES";
50460     GOSUB 52500                          ' POSITION AND
                                                   DISPLAY BRIGHT
50465     RETURN
50470     ' *****************************************
50475     '
```

For each data type, if A.KEY% is in the correct range, then the
key-accept routine at line 50900 is called to add the key to ENTRY$. If
a bad key is entered, then the routine RETURNs and the key is effectively ignored.

It is not uncommon to want the user to enter all uppercase, or
capital, letters. Rather than forcing the user to use the shift or caps-
lock key, we will simply test each character entered and convert any
lowercase letters to uppercase. This is a good example of a user-
friendly feature. The user will never be inconvenienced by having to
retype a field to change the case. The user may not even notice that
you have taken a little extra care or that the program has done a little
more work, but it is these simple things that improve the ease of use
and quality of a program.

The uppercase character routine is:

```
50480     ' FORCE UPPERCASE ENTRY
50485     '
50490     IF A.KEY% >= 97 AND A.KEY% <=
             122 THEN A.KEY% = A.KEY% -
             32 : A.KEY$ = CHR$(A.KEY$)        ' IF LOWERCASE CONVERT TO
                                                   UPPERCASE
50495     GOSUB 50900                          ' ACCEPT IT NOW
50500     RETURN
50505     '
50510     '
50515     '
```

PROCESSING CONTROL KEYS: EDITING ROUTINES

The line editor uses the function and special keys to move the cursor and edit the text. These characters are summarized in Figure 2.7. We have tried to duplicate BASIC's use of the keys. Therefore, if you are familiar with the BASIC editor, you already know how to use this editor. If you have a word processor that uses the keys differently, then redefine the keys to be compatible with the word processor for convenience.

The right and left arrows are used quite cleverly to move the cursor right and left. The arrow keys will not erase the characters as they pass over them. Control-left arrow is used to skip to the previous word. The DEL (delete) key deletes a character and compresses the field. Pressing the INS (insert) key turns the insert mode on and allows characters to be added into the middle of the field. The insert mode is kept on until any special character (including INS) is entered. The END key is used to jump to the end of the line. Control-right arrow is used to skip to the next word, and control END will delete everything from the cursor to the end of the field. The TAB key will skip right to the next TAB stop. The shift TAB causes the cursor to jump to the beginning of the field. The ESC (escape) key will restore the original field after it has been incorrectly changed. The next word can be deleted using the F2 key. Any text deleted using the control END key can be restored using shift F2.

FIG. 2.7   Editing Controls

Right arrow	Move right one character.
Control-right arrow	Move right one word.
Left arrow	Move left one character.
Control-left arrow	Move left one word.
END	Move to end of line.
Control END	Erase to end of line.
TAB	Move right one TAB stop.

Shift TAB	Move to front of line.
F2	Erase next word.
Shift F2	Restore delete buffer.
ESC	Restore original text.
INS	Toggle insert mode.
DEL/backspace	Erase current character.
Shift F1	Help.
Enter	Done, go to next field.

Subroutine 51000 in the program that follows uses conditional IF statements to branch to these editing routines. To add new editing features, you would simply add more conditionals and insert the code in the space before line 51280.

The following subroutine processes the control keys. The individual editing routines for the various control characters are described in the following subsections.

```
51000    ' PROCESS A CONTROL KEY (SET TO LINE NUMBER 51000)
51005    '
51010    ' EXIT KEYS SUCH AS RETURN SET CTRL%
51015    '
51020    '
51025    ' VALUE           DESCRIPTION          ACTION
51030    '   9             TAB                  TAB RIGHT
51035    '  13             ENTER                ALL DONE EXIT
51040    '  27             ESC                  RESTORE ORIGINAL TEXT
51045    ' 315             SHIFT TAB             JUMP TO FRONT OF LINE
51050    ' 359             F1                   EXIT MODE KEY
51055    ' 384             SHIFT F1             HELP
51060    ' 360             F2                   DELETE NEXT WORD
51065    ' 385             SHIFT F2             RESTORE DELETE BUFFER
51070    ' 375             LEFT ARROW           JUMP LEFT ONE CHARACTER
51075    ' 377             RIGHT ARROW          JUMP RIGHT ONE CHARACTER
51080    ' 379             END                  JUMP TO END OF LINE
51085    ' 380             DOWN ARROW           JUMP DOWN ONE LINE
                                                    (used in chapter 3)
```

```
51090    ' 382          INS               TOGGLE INSERT MODE
51095    ' 383 OR 8     DEL OR BACKSPACE  DELETE CURRENT CHARACTER
51100    ' 415          CTRL LEFT ARROW   JUMP LEFT ONE WORD
51105    ' 416          CTRL RIGHT ARROW  JUMP RIGHT ONE WORD
51110    ' 417          CTRL END          DELETE TO END OF LINE
51115    '
51120    CTRL% = 0                        ' CLEAR EXIT FLAG
51125    IF A.KEY% = 382 THEN GOSUB
            51370: RETURN                 ' INSERT
51130    INSERT% = 0                      ' TURN INSERT OFF
51135    '
51140    '
51145    IF A.KEY% = 9 THEN
            GOSUB 51960 : RETURN          ' TAB
51150    IF A.KEY% = 13 THEN CTRL% =
            1 : RETURN                    ' ENTER
51155    IF A.KEY% = 27 THEN GOSUB
            52075 : RETURN                '  ESC RESTORE ORIGINAL
                                             ENTRY$
51160    '
51165    '
51170    IF A.KEY% = 315 THEN GOSUB
            51855 : RETURN                ' FRONT OF LINE
51175    IF A.KEY% = 384 THEN HELP% =
            1 : RETURN                    ' SHIFT F1 HELP REQUEST
51180    '
51185    IF A.KEY% = 359 THEN CTRL% =
            27 : RETURN                   ' F1 EXIT MODE
51190    IF A.KEY% = 360 THEN GOSUB
            51910 : RETURN                ' DELETE NEXT WORD
51195    '
51200    '
51205    '
51210    IF A.KEY% = 375 THEN GOSUB
            51470 : RETURN                ' LEFT ARROW
51215    IF A.KEY% = 377 THEN GOSUB
            51520 : RETURN                ' RIGHT ARROW
51220    IF A.KEY% = 379 THEN GOSUB
            51800 : RETURN                ' END
51225    IF A.KEY% = 383 OR A.KEY% =
            8 THEN GOSUB 51300 : RETURN   ' DELETE CHARACTER
51230    IF A.KEY% = 385 THEN GOSUB
            52020 : RETURN                ' RESTORE DELETE BUFFER
51235    '
51240    '
```

```
51245      '
51250      '
51255      IF A.KEY% = 415 THEN GOSUB
              51660 : RETURN                    ' CTRL RIGHT ARROW
51260      IF A.KEY% = 416 THEN GOSUB
              51575 : RETURN                    ' CTRL LEFT ARROW
51265      IF A.KEY% = 417 THEN GOSUB
              51740 : RETURN                    ' CTRL END
51270      '
51275      '
51280      RETURN
51285      '
51290      ' * * * * * * * * * * * * * * * * * * * * * * * * * * * *
51295      '
```

Displaying a Character

After a valid key has been pressed, the following subroutine will display the character on the screen. If a character has been removed and the field shortened, then the FILL$ character will be displayed at the end of the field.

The program for displaying characters is as follows.

```
52570      ' POSITION AND DISPLAY NORMAL
52575      '
52580      LOCATE ROW%,(COL% + PLACE% − FRONT%)
52585      XX$ = MID$ (ENTRY$,PLACE%,1)          ' PRINT ONE LETTER
52590      IF XX$ = "" THEN XX$ = FILL$          ' IF NULL THEN
                                                   MAKE IT A SPACE
52595      PRINT XX$;
52600      '
52605      LOCATE ROW%,(COL% + PLACE% − FRONT%)  ' REPOSITION THE
                                                   CURSOR
52610      RETURN
52615      '
52620      ' * * * * * * * * * * * * * * * * * * * * * * * * * *
52625      '
```

TEST POINT

The display subroutine is tested in conjunction with the character-accept and display routine. RUN the program and press any key. This key's character should be displayed on the screen in a NORMAL video, and the cursor should move one position to the right.

Moving the Cursor Right and Left

The right and left arrow subroutines, which are presented below, are very simple. First, the program redisplays the current cursor position in low intensity. Next, it increments or decrements PLACE%, and then it displays the new cursor position in high intensity. Notice in the program that follows that both routines test the size of PLACE% and that it is changed only if it meets the boundary condition.

```
51470   ' LEFT ARROW
51475   '
51480   GOSUB 52570                         ' DISPLAY NORMAL
51485   IF PLACE% > 1 THEN PLACE% =
            PLACE% - 1                      ' MOVE LEFT ONE
51490   IF PLACE% < FRONT% THEN FRONT% =
            PLACE% : GOSUB 52660            ' REDISPLAY LINE
51495   GOSUB 52500                         ' DISPLAY INVERSE
51500   RETURN
51505   '
51510   ' *********************************
51515   '

51520   ' RIGHT ARROW
51525   '
51530   IF MID$ (ENTRY$,PLACE%,1) = ""
            THEN RETURN
51535   GOSUB 52570                         ' DISPLAY AS NORMAL
51540   IF PLACE% < MAXSIZE% THEN
            PLACE% = PLACE% + 1
51545   IF (PLACE% + COL% - FRONT%) > 78 THEN FRONT% =
            PLACE% - 78 + COL% :
            GOSUB 52660                      ' REDISPLAY
51550   GOSUB 52500                          ' DISPLAY AS INVERSE
51555   RETURN
51560   '
51565   ' ****************************
51565   '
51570   '
```

TEST POINT

Enter some text and then press the left arrow. The cursor should move left one position each time you press the key. Press the left arrow key until you return to the beginning of the field. Continue pressing the left arrow to make sure the routine works properly with the cursor in the first character position. Repeat the test using the right arrow.

Jump to the Next Word

Skipping to the next word on the line moves the cursor to the first character of the word to the right of the current cursor position. To do this operation, the program looks at each character to the right of the cursor and stops at the first one after the next space or group of spaces. If the cursor is positioned over a word, then it must move right to the first space and then over any spaces to the first nonspace.

The following routine allows the user to skip to the next word.

```
51575   ' SKIP TO NEXT WORD
51580   '
51585   '
51590   IF PLACE% = > TXTSIZE%
            THEN RETURN                ' ALREADY AT END
51595   GOSUB 52570                    ' REMOVE CURSOR
51600   PLACE% = PLACE% + 1            ' LOOK FOR FIRST SPACE
51605   IF PLACE% = TXTSIZE% THEN GOTO 51630
51610   IF MID$ (ENTRY$,PLACE%,1) <>
            " " THEN GOTO 51600     ' IS IT A SPACE?
51615   PLACE% = PLACE% + 1            ' MOVE RIGHT ONE
51620   IF PLACE% + TXTSIZE% THEN GOTO 51630
51625   IF MID$ (ENTRY$,PLACE%,1) =
            " " THEN GOTO 51615     ' SKIP OVER SPACES
51630   IF (PLACE% + COL% - FRONT%) > 78 THEN FRONT%
            = PLACE% - 78 + COL% :
            GOSUB 52660                ' REDISPLAY LINE
51635   GOSUB 52500                    ' DISPLAY CURSOR
51640   RETURN
51645   '
51650   ' ******************************
51655   '
```

TEST POINT

Enter the sentence

```
"THIS IS A TEST"
```

Now use the left arrow to move to the beginning of the field. Enter a control-right arrow, and the cursor should jump to the front of the next word. Repeat this exercise with several sentences and vary the number of spaces between words.

Jump to the Previous Word

To skip to the previous word, we first want to force the cursor to move over any spaces, in case we are at the front of a word, and then to position the cursor at the character immediately to the right of the next space. The following program performs the skip to the previous word.

```
51660   ' SKIP TO PREVIOUS WORD
51665   '
51670   IF PLACE% = 1 THEN RETURN          ' AT THE FRONT ALREADY
51675   GOSUB 52570                        ' REMOVE CURSOR
51680   PLACE% = PLACE% - 1                ' LOOK FOR SPACE
51685   IF PLACE% = 1 THEN
            GOTO 51715                     ' FORCE MOVE AT LEAST ONE SPACE
51690   IF MID$ (ENTRY$,PLACE%,1) =
            " " THEN GOTO 51680            ' SKIP OVER GROUP OF SPACES
51695   PLACE% = PLACE% - 1
51700   IF PLACE% = 1 THEN GOTO 51715
51705   IF MID$ (ENTRY$,PLACE%,1) <>
            " " THEN GOTO 51695            ' IS IT A SPACE?
51710   PLACE% = PLACE% + 1                ' POSITION OVER FIRST
                                              LETTER
51715   IF PLACE% < FRONT% THEN
            FRONT% = PLACE% : GOSUB
            52660                          ' REDISPLAY LINE
51720   GOSUB 52500                        ' DISPLAY THE CURSOR
51725   RETURN
51730   '
51735   ' ***************************
```

TEST POINT

Enter the sentence

```
"PREVIOUS WORD TEST."
```

Then enter a control-left arrow, and the cursor should move left one word. Repeat the tests you did for jumping to the next word.

Jump to the End of the Line

We skip to the end of the line by testing the length of the field and placing the cursor there. The following program gives the routine.

```
51800    ' SKIP TO END OF LINE
51805    '
51810    GOSUB 52570                      ' MOVE THE CURSOR
51815    PLACE% = LEN (ENTRY$) + 1
51820    IF PLACE% > MAXSIZE% THEN
            PLACE% = MAXSIZE%             ' DO NOT GO PAST END
51825    IF (PLACE% + COL%) > 79 THEN
            FRONT% = PLACE% - 78 +
            COL% : GOSUB 52660            ' REDISPLAY THE LINE
51830    GOSUB 52500                      ' SHOW THE CURSOR
51835    RETURN
51840    '
51845    ' ****************************
51850    '
```

TEST POINT

Enter some text, move the cursor left, and press the END key. The cursor should jump to the end of the line.

Deleting a Character

The delete subroutine uses MID$ and LEFT$ commands to compress the field, and then it displays the new text and the cursor. In the delete program that follows, you will note that there are several conditional tests. These tests check for special circumstances at the boundaries of the subroutine. Many routines require special handling at the minimum or maximum points of the routine. In this case the special handling is needed when the cursor is at the very beginning or end of the field.

As you develop programs, you should carefully design and test the boundaries or extremes of the routine, because most errors will occur at the boundaries and not in the middle range of a routine. You will not always be able to think of every possible error condition, but you can think of the majority of the limits of a routine so that they can be tested.

The delete subroutine is as follows.

```
51300   ' DELETE AND PACK
51305   '
51310   TXTSIZE% = LEN (ENTRY$)
51315   IF TXTSIZE% = 0 THEN RETURN    ' NOTHING TO DELETE
51320   IF TXTSIZE% = 1 THEN ENTRY$
            = " ":PLACE% = 1: GOTO
            51340                       ' DELETE WHOLE LINE
51325   IF PLACE% = 1 THEN ENTRY$ = MID$ (ENTRY$,2):
            GOTO 51340
51330   IF PLACE% > = TXTSIZE% THEN ENTRY$ = LEFT$
            (ENTRY$,TXTSIZE% - 1):PLACE% = PLACE% - 1:
            GOTO 51340
51335   ENTRY$ = LEFT$ (ENTRY$,(PLACE% - 1)) + MID$
            (ENTRY$,PLACE% + 1)
51340   GOSUB 52660                     ' PRINT NEW STRING
51345   GOSUB 52500                     ' PRINT INVERSE
51350   RETURN
51355   '
51360   ' ****************************
51365   '
```

TEST POINT

At this point you should be able to enter text and move the cursor back and forth. To test the delete routine, enter some text and then delete a character at the following positions.

1. Cursor on the first character,
2. Cursor in middle of text,
3. Cursor on last character,
4. Cursor at the end of the line past end of text.

Inserting Characters

Characters are inserted by an insert-mode toggle. In other words, we turn, or toggle, the insert mode on or off. The INS key is used to turn the mode on, and this or any other special key can turn the insert mode off.

Once the insert mode is turned on, any regular characters typed will be inserted into the field, with any characters to the right of the cursor being shifted to the right one place for each character inserted. Any characters at the very end of the field will spill off into that never-never land of lost characters.

The actual insertion is done by first inserting a space into the field and printing the line. Next, the desired character is written over this space. Finally, the cursor is moved right one place. The LEFT$ command is essential in this routine.

Any characters pushed off the end of the field because of the insertion are lost. A variation you could implement is to allow insertion only until the field is full and then stop. If users did not want the characters at the end, they would have to move the cursor there and erase them.

The program for inserting characters is as follows.

```
51370    ' TOGGLE THE INSERT MODE
51375    '
51380    IF INSERT% = 1 THEN INSERT% = 0: RETURN     ' TURN IT OFF
51385    INSERT% = 1                                 ' TURN IT ON
51390    RETURN
51395    ' ***********************************
51400    '
51405    ' INSERT A CHARACTER
51410    '
51415    '
```

```
51420     ' IS IT THE FIRST CHARACTER?
51425     IF PLACE% = 1 THEN ENTRY$ = " " + ENTRY$: GOTO 51440
51430     ' INSERT IN THE MIDDLE
51435     ENTRY$ = LEFT$ (ENTRY$,PLACE% - 1) + " " +
              MID$ (ENTRY$,PLACE%)
51440     GOSUB 52660                                   ' PRINT THE FIELD
51445     GOSUB 52570                                   ' REPOSITION CURSOR
51450     RETURN
51455     '
51460     ' ********************************
51465     '
```

TEST POINT

Begin by entering some text on the line and moving the cursor into the middle of the text. Now press INS followed by some other letters. As each letter is entered, the text should split, with the right side sliding right one place for each new letter entered. The cursor should step right one place. Press another special key—left arrow, for example—and make sure that the insert mode is turned off. Next, toggle the insert mode back on and verify that a second INS also turns inserting off. Finally, move the cursor to the beginning and the end of the text and check that the insert mode works there.

Erase to the End of the Line

This erase feature is very handy. You will frequently decide to change everything to the right of the cursor, and the erase routine allows you to do so in one keystroke. Erasing to the end of the line only requires a LEFT$ command and then a redisplay of the field. As an added convenience and as a precaution against accidental erasure, we will save all the deleted text in a variable called PRESERVE$. The shift F2 key is used to restore the deleted text.

The subroutine to erase to the end of the line is as follows.

```
51740     ' ERASE TO END OF LINE
51745     '
51750     ' PRESERVE DELETED PIECE BEFORE DESTRUCTION
```

```
51755    IF PLACE% = 1 THEN PRESERVE$ = ENTRY$ :
            ENTRY$ = "": GOTO 51770              ' ERASE WHOLE LINE
51760    PRESERVE$ = MID$(ENTRY$,PLACE%)        ' SAVE THE END
51765    ENTRY$ = LEFT$ (ENTRY$,PLACE% - 1)
51770    GOSUB 52660                            ' PRINT THE FIELD
51775    GOSUB 52500                            ' DISPLAY THE CURSOR
51780    RETURN
51785    '
51790    ' *******************************
51795    '
```

To restore the delete buffer:

```
52020    ' RESTORE DELETE BUFFER
52025    '
52030    ' INSERT IF LINE NOT BLANK OTHERWISE EQUATE TO PRESERVE$
52035    IF LEN(ENTRY$) = 0 THEN ENTRY$ =
            PRESERVE$ : GOTO 52045              ' NOTHING THERE
52040    IF PLACE% = 1 THEN ENTRY$ =
            PRESERVE$ + ENTRY$ ELSE ENTRY$ =
            LEFT$(ENTRY$,PLACE%-1) +
            PRESERVE$ + MID$(ENTRY$,PLACE%)
52045    GOSUB 52660                            ' REDISPLAY LINE
52050    GOSUB 52500                            ' SHOW CURSOR
52055    RETURN
52060    '
52065    '
52070    '
```

TEST POINT

Enter some text and move the cursor left. Now enter control END, and
everything to the right of the cursor should disappear. Next, restore
the text using shift F2. Test this routine at the beginning, the middle,
and the end of the line. You should notice that the restore key can insert PRESERVE$ into the middle of the field. This is useful for moving
text.

Restoring the Original Field

Frequently, after several changes have been made on a line, you will
discover that you entered the wrong information and you have to
erase all the changes and restore the line to its original state. This lit-

tle user-friendly subroutine does this for you when you press the ESC (escape) key. With the following subroutine, we are simply preparing ourselves to be helpful to the user.

```
52075     ' RESTORE ORIGINAL ENTRY$
52080     '
52085     ENTRY$ = ORG.ENTRY$
52090     GOSUB 51855                           ' REDISPLAY AND JUMP TO
                                                    FRONT OF TEXT
52095     RETURN
52100     '
52105     '
52110     '
```

Tab Stops

Tabs are set eight spaces apart.

Tab stops are a convenient feature to include in the line editor. Their use in program development provides increased readability. In a letter they facilitate indenting text. Every eighth character, the TAB key will move the cursor right to the next tab stop. If there is text on the line, it will skip over the text. However, if the cursor moves past the end of the text on the line, spaces are added to the line.

The TAB routine is as follows.

```
51960     ' TAB KEY
51965     '
51970     GOSUB 52570                           ' REMOVE CURSOR
51975     PLACE% = (INT(PLACE%/8) + 1) * 8      ' SLIDE THE CURSOR RIGHT
51980     IF PLACE% > MAXSIZE% THEN
              PLACE% + MAXSIZE%                  ' CAN'T GO PAST END OF LINE
51985     IF (PLACE% + COL% - FRONT%) >
              79 THEN FRONT% = PLACE% -
              79 + COL%                          ' ADJUST FOR WINDOW
51990     IF PLACE% > LEN(ENTRY$) THEN
              ENTRY$ = ENTRY$ + SPACE$
              (PLACE% - LEN(ENTRY$))             ' ADD SPACES TO END
51995     GOSUB 52660                           ' REDISPLAY THE LINE
52000     GOSUB 52500                           ' SHOW CURSOR
```

```
52005    RETURN
52010     '
52015     '
```

TEST POINT

At this point you will do two tests. First, enter some text and return the cursor to the beginning of the line. Next, press TAB and the cursor should move over to the eighth column. Since the line contains text, no blanks will be inserted. Next, move the cursor to the front of the line and delete all of the text by using the delete-to-end-of-line command. Now press TAB and eight spaces should be inserted and the cursor positioned on column 8.

The F1 Key

Pressing the F1 key will cause the CTRL% flag to be set and the line editor to return to the calling program. This feature is used extensively later in the book.

Jump to the Front of the Line

When the shift TAB is pressed, the cursor is positioned at the front of the line. On a long line this is easier than pressing the left arrow key or the control-left arrow key several times.

This routine simply resets the pointers, FRONT% and PLACE%, and then redisplays the line and the cursor. It is necessary to redisplay the line just in case you are editing a line that is too long and does not fit in the available viewing area.

Here is the subroutine that jumps to the front of the line.

```
51850     '
51855     'SKIP TO FRONT OF THE LINE
51860     '
51865    GOSUB 52570              'REMOVE THE CURSOR
51870    PLACE% = 1               ' RESET THE POINTERS
51875    FRONT% = 1
51880    GOSUB 52660              ' REDISPLAY THE LINE
```

```
51885   GOSUB 52500                        ' DISPLAY THE CURSOR
51890   RETURN
51895   '
51900   '
51905   '
```

TEST POINT

Enter some text, press the Shift and TAB keys simultaneously, and the cursor should jump to the beginning of the line. Continue editing the text on the line and again press both keys to verify that the subroutine is correct.

Deleting a Word

Frequently you will want to delete an entire word, not just one character. The following routine will delete from the cursor to the end of the current word. It does this by searching for the first space to the right of the cursor.

Here is the subroutine that deletes a word.

```
51910   ' DELETE NEXT WORD AND REDISPLAY
51915   '
51920   IF PLACE% > LEN(ENTRY$) OR
            LEN(ENTRY$) = 0 THEN
            RETURN                          ' DONE YET?
51925   IF MID$(ENTRY$,PLACE%,1) <>
            " " THEN GOSUB 51300 :
            GOTO 51920                      ' DELETE ONE CHARACTER AT
                                            '   A TIME
51930   IF PLACE% > LEN(ENTRY$) OR
            LEN(ENTRY$) = 0 THEN
            RETURN                          ' ERROR TEST
51935   IF MID$(ENTRY$,PLACE%,1) =
            " " THEN GOSUB 51300            ' REMOVE TRAILING SPACES
51940   RETURN
51945   '
51950   '
51955   '
```

TEST POINT

Enter the sentence "This is a test," move the cursor to the first character of any word, and press F2. The word should disappear and the line should compress.

Test this at the beginning, the middle, and the end of a line. Do it until the entire line is erased, and then try it again.

ERROR PROCESSING

There are two types of error processing used throughout this book. The first type is correctable or controllable user errors. In other words, these are errors we can easily anticipate and then write programs to correct. For example, shifting lowercase letters to uppercase letters is a case in which we have prepared ourselves for an error and have not penalized the user. The second error type is a BASIC or system error. This type of error occurs when the computer cannot interpret a command. Two examples are when diskettes are not in the drive and when the incorrect files are on the diskette. We handle regularly expected operation errors throughout the entire program. For system errors a special subroutine is used. This same routine is used in the following chapters. We call this routine, which follows, the Standard Error-Processing Routine.

```
60000   ' STANDARD ERROR PROCESSING ROUTINE
60005   '
60010   X = ERR                         'ERROR NUMBER
60015   Y = ERL                         ' LINE NUMBER OF ERROR
60020   RESUME 60025
60025   KEY OFF                         ' TURN OFF SO WE CAN USE 25TH LINE
60030   LOCATE 25,1                     ' POSITION CURSOR ON 25TH LINE
60035   PRINT "Error ";X;"
            ON LINE ";Y
60040   BEEP                            ' RING THE BELL
60045   END                             ' THAT'S ALL FOLKS
60050   '
60055   '
60060   '
```

TEST POINT

The quickest way to test this routine is to enter the routine and save the program and then to delete line 50000 and run the program. After you enter the field-description data, the screen should clear and an error number will be printed for line 220 and the program will stop. This is a missing line number error since we were trying to branch to 50000, which we just deleted.

ERR AND ERL   These are both variables used in error processing. ERR contains the error code for the last error, and ERL contains the line number where the error was detected.

RESUME   This is the command used to continue program execution after an error-recovery procedure has been performed.

BEEP   This command beeps the speaker.

USER INSTRUCTIONS

Whenever it is appropriate, we will include a sample set of instructions that can be included in your operator's manual. We naturally are assuming that every program that you write includes an operator's manual. Portions of the operator's manual can be extracted and used as help files.

The line editor program allows you to enter and edit text. You can move the cursor left and right, insert and delete characters anywhere on the line, and request help from the computer.

The line editor will check every character that you enter and verify that it is acceptable. For example, if the program is requesting a number, then it will allow you to enter only numbers, not letters. When it wants a yes or no response, it will only allow you to enter a Y or an N.

Periods (.) are displayed to illustrate the maximum length of the field to be entered. In certain instances it will be possible to enter text that will exceed the space shown. When this happens the text shown in the window will slide left until you reach the end of the line, at which time the cursor will stop moving.

Whenever you have any doubts about how you should respond to an input, you can request help by pressing shift F1. If help is available, then a message will be displayed for you. After you have read the message, press ENTER and the program will continue.

The following list summarizes the editing commands available.

Right arrow	Move right one character.
Control-right arrow	Move right one word.
Left arrow	Move left one character.
Control-left arrow	Move left one word.
END	Move to end of line.
Control END	Erase to end of line.
TAB	Move right one TAB stop.
Shift TAB	Move to front of line.
F2	Erase next word.
Shift F2	Restore delete buffer.
ESC	Restore original text.
INS	Toggle insert mode.
DEL/backspace	Erase current character.
Shift F1	Help.
Enter	Done, go to next field.

When you are in the insert mode, you will keep inserting letters until you enter any arrow key.

COMPLETE LINE EDITOR PROGRAM

The complete program listing for the line editor follows. It may look like a formidable program, but if the remark statements were removed, the program would be about 160 lines long. Considering what this routine does, that length is not excessive.

```
100        ' CHAPTER 2 - LINE EDITOR TEST ROUTINE
110        ' ASKS FOR INITIAL CONDITIONS THEN IT
              USES THE LINE EDITOR
120        ON ERROR GOTO 60000                          ' STANDARD ERROR
                                                            PROCESSING ROUTINE
130        KEY OFF                                      ' TURN THE FUNCTION
                                                            KEYS OFF
140        CLS
150        PRINT "CHAPTER 2 - LINE EDITOR TEST
              ROUTINE"
160        INPUT "ENTER MASK ";MASK$
170        INPUT "ENTER FIELD LENGTH ",MAXSIZE%
180        INPUT "ENTER TEXT ";ENTRY$
190        INPUT "ENTER ROW ";ROW%
200        INPUT "ENTER COL ";COL%
210        CLS
220        GOSUB 50000                                  ' THE LINE EDITOR
230        LOCATE 20,1
240        PRINT
250        IF HELP% = 1 THEN PRINT "HELP
              REQUESTED"
260        PRINT
270        PRINT ">";ENTRY$;"<"
280        LOCATE 23,1
290        INPUT "PRESS ENTER TO CONTINUE OR ENTER
              END TO EXIT.";A$
300        IF A$ < > "" THEN END
310        GOTO 150
320        '
330        '
340        '

50000      ' BASIC LINE EDITOR (SET TO LINE NUMBER 50000)
50005      '
50010      '
50015      ' THIS IS A BASIC LINE EDITOR
50020      '
50025      ' THE PROGRAMMER CALLS IT USING THE
              FOLLOWING VARIABLES
50030      '
50035      ' ROW%     = SCREEN LINE NUMBER
50040      ' COL%     = SCREEN COLUMN NUMBER
50045      ' ENTRY$   = TEXT TO BE EDITED
50050      ' MASK$    = DATA TYPE TO BE ACCEPTED
50055      ' WHERE:
```

```
50060    ' a = ALPHANUMERIC UPPER AND LOWERCASE
50065    ' A = ALPHANUMERIC FORCE UPPERCASE
50070    ' # = NUMBER FIELD ONLY
50075    ' Y = YES/NO FIELD
50080    ' MAXSIZE% = MAXIMUM FIELD LENGTH
50085    '
50090    PLACE% = 1                          ' SET THE STARTING
                                                 POSITION
50095    '
50100    FILL$ = "."                         ' DISPLAY DOTS
50105    HELP% = 0                           ' CLEAR THE HELP FLAG
50110    FRONT% = 1                          ' FIRST CHARACTER
                                                 DISPLAYED
50115    CTRL% = 0                           ' CLEAR THE EXIT FLAG
50120    GOSUB 52660                         ' DISPLAY ENTRY$
50125    GOSUB 50160                         ' EDIT THE STRING
50130    FILL$ = " "                         ' CLEAR THE SCREEN
50135    '
50140    RETURN                              ' GO BACK TO CALLER
50145    '
50150    ' *********************
50155    '
50160    ' EDIT THE ENTRY$ FIELD
50165    IF LEN(MASK$)>1 THEN MASK$=
             LEFT$(MASK$,1)                   'USE ONLY ONE LETTER
50170    ORG.ENTRY$ = ENTRY$                 ' KEEP ORIGINAL IN
                                                 CASE THEY CHANGE
                                                 MIND
50175    TXTSIZE% = LEN(ENTRY$)              ' NEEDED FOR SPECIAL
                                                 ROUTINES
50180    LOCATE ROW%,1                       ' POSITION CURSOR
50185    GOSUB 52500                         ' PRINT THE CHARACTER
50190    '
50195    ' ACCEPT A KEY FROM THE KEYBOARD
50200    '
50205    A.KEY$ = INKEY$
50210    IF LEN(A.KEY$) = 0 THEN GOTO 50205  ' LOOP UNTIL ENTRY
                                                 MADE
50215    '
50220    ' IF HERE THEN A KEY PUSHED
50225    '
50230    IF LEN(A.KEY$) = 1 THEN A.KEY% =
             ASC(A.KEY$) ELSE A.KEY% =
             ASC(RIGHT$(A.KEY$,1)) + 300      ' CONVERT KEY TO A
                                                 NUMBER
```

```
50235    '
50240    ' PROCESS THE KEY
50245    '
50250    GOSUB 50285                                   ' KEY% PROCESSOR
50255    ' EXIT IF HELP REQUESTED OR SPECIAL KEY
             ENTERED
50260    IF HELP% <> 0 OR CTRL% <> 0 THEN GOSUB
             52630 : RETURN                            ' REDISPLAY AND EXIT
50265    GOTO 50205                                    ' GET THE NEXT KEY
50270    '
50275    ' ***************************
50280    '
50285    ' TEST FOR CONTROL KEY
50290    '
50295    IF A.KEY% <= 31 OR A.KEY% > 126 THEN
             GOSUB 51000: RETURN                        ' PROCESS AND RETURN
50300    '
50305    ' MUST BE AN ALPHANUMERIC
50310    '
50315    ' TEST THE MASK TO DETERMINE DATA TYPE
50320    '
50325      IF MASK$ = "a" THEN GOSUB 50900 :
             RETURN                                     ' ACCEPT ANYTHING
50330    IF MASK$ = "A" THEN GOSUB 50480 : RETURN      ' FORCE UPPERCASE
50335    IF MASK$ = "#" THEN GOSUB 50380: RETURN
50340    IF MASK$ = "Y" THEN GOSUB 50430: RETURN
50345    '
50350    ' BAD MASK CHARACTER
50355    '
50360    RETURN
50365    '
50370    ' ***************************
50375    '
50380    ' ACCEPT A NUMBER
50385    '
50390    ' TEST TO SEE IF IT IS A VALID NUMERIC
             TYPE OF CHARACTER
50395    '
50400    IF (A.KEY% < 45) or (A.KEY%) > 57) THEN
             RETURN                                     ' BAD KEY
50405    IF A.KEY% = 47 THEN RETURN                    ' BAD KEY ALSO
50410    GOSUB 50900                                   ' GOOD KEY SO ACCEPT IT
50415    RETURN
50420    ' ******************************************
```

```
50425      '
50430      ' TEST FOR YES OR NO
50435      IF (A.KEY% = 121) OR (A.KEY% = 110) THEN
               A.KEY% = A.KEY% - 32 : A.KEY$ =
               CHR$(A.KEY%)                          ' UPPER CASE CONVERT
50440      IF (A.KEY% <> 89) AND (A.KEY% <> 78)
               THEN RETURN                           ' CAPITAL Y OR N
50445      ENTRY$ = A.KEY$                           ' RETURN ONE LETTER
                                                         ONLY
50450      LOCATE ROW%,COL%                          ' PRINT FULL WORD
50455      IF A.KEY% = 78 THEN PRINT "NO "; ELSE
               PRINT "YES";
50460      GOSUB 52500                               ' POSITION AND DISPLAY
                                                         BRIGHT
50465      RETURN
50470      ' *****************************************
50475      '
50480      ' FORCE UPPER CASE ENTRY
50485      '
50490      IF A.KEY% >= 97 AND A.KEY% <= 122         ' IF LOWERCASE
               THEN A.KEY% = A.KEY% - 32 : A.KEY$ =      CONVERT TO
               CHR$(A.KEY%)                              UPPERCASE
50495      GOSUB 50900                               ' ACCEPT IT NOW
50500      RETURN
50505      '
50510      '
50515      '
50900      ' PRINT A.KEY% AND ADD TO ENTRY$ (SET TO
               LINE NUMBER 50900)
50905      '
50910      IF INSERT% = 1 THEN GOSUB 51405           ' INSERT A SPACE FIRST
50915      ' ADD TO END OF ENTRY
50920      IF PLACE% > LEN(ENTRY$) THEN ENTRY$ =
               ENTRY$ + A.KEY$ : GOTO 50935
50925      ' ADD TO MIDDLE OF STRING
50930      MID$(ENTRY$,PLACE%,1) = A.KEY$
50935      TXTSIZE% = LEN (ENTRY$)
50940      ' IF TOO BIG TRUNCATE IT
50945      IF TXTSIZE% > MAXSIZE% THEN ENTRY$ =
               LEFT$ (ENTRY$,MAXSIZE%)
50950      '
50955      ' NEED TO MOVE RIGHT ONE PLACE
50960      '
50965      GOSUB 51520                               ' RIGHT ARROW
```

```
50970     RETURN
50975     '
50980     ' ***************************
50985     '
51000     ' PROCESS A CONTROL KEY (SET TO LINE
              NUMBER 51000)
51005     '
51010     ' EXIT KEYS SUCH AS RETURN SET CTRL%
51015     '
51020     '
51025     ' VALUE           DESCRIPTION              ACTION
51030     '   9             TAB                      TAB RIGHT
51035     '  13             ENTER                    ALL DONE EXIT
51040     '  27             ESC                      RESTORE ORIGINAL TEXT
51045     ' 315             SHIFT TAB                JUMP TO FRONT OF LINE
51050     ' 359             F1                       EXIT MODE KEY
51055     ' 384             SHIFT F1                 HELP
51060     ' 360             F2                       DELETE NEXT WORD
51065     ' 385             SHIFT F2                 RESTORE DELETE BUFFER
51070     ' 375             LEFT ARROW               JUMP LEFT ONE CHARACTER
51075     ' 377             RIGHT ARROW              JUMP RIGHT ONE CHARACTER
51080     ' 379             END                      JUMP TO END OF LINE
51085     ' 380             DOWN ARROW               JUMP DOWN ONE LINE (USED
                                                        IN CHAPTER 3)
51090     ' 382             INS                      TOGGLE INSERT MODE
51095     ' 383 or 8        DEL OR BACKSPACE         DELETE CURRENT CHARACTER
51100     ' 415             CTRL LEFT ARROW          JUMP LEFT ONE WORD
51105     ' 416             CTRL RIGHT ARROW         JUMP RIGHT ONE WORD
51110     ' 417             CTRL END                 DELETE TO END OF LINE
51115     '
51120     CTRL% = 0                              ' CLEAR EXIT FLAG
51125     IF A.KEY% = 382 THEN GOSUB 51370:
              RETURN                             ' INSERT
51130     INSERT% = 0                            ' TURN INSERT OFF
51135     '
51140     '
51145     IF A.KEY% = 9 THEN GOSUB 51960 : RETURN    ' TAB
51150     IF A.KEY% = 13 THEN CTRL% = 1 : RETURN     ENTER
51155     IF A.KEY% = 27 THEN GOSUB 52075 : RETURN   ' ESC RESTORE ORIGINAL
                                                        ENTRY$
51160     '
51165     '
51170     IF A.KEY% = 315 THEN GOSUB 51855 :
              RETURN                                  ' FRONT OF LINE
```

```
51175    IF A.KEY% = 384 THEN HELP% = 1 : RETURN      ' SHIFT F1 HELP
                                                            REQUEST
51180    '
51185    IF A.KEY% = 359 THEN CTRL% = 27 : RETURN     ' F1 EXIT MODE
51190    IF A.KEY% = 360 THEN GOSUB 51910 :
             RETURN                                   ' DELETE NEXT WORD
51195    '
51200    '
51205    '
51210    IF A.KEY% = 375 THEN GOSUB 51470 :
             RETURN                                   ' LEFT ARROW
51215    IF A.KEY% = 377 THEN GOSUB 51520 :
             RETURN                                   ' RIGHT ARROW
51220    IF A.KEY% = 379 THEN GOSUB 51800 :
             RETURN                                   ' END
51225    IF A.KEY% = 383 OR A.KEY% = 8 THEN GOSUB
             51300 : RETURN                           ' DELETE CHARACTER
51230    IF A.KEY% = 385 THEN GOSUB 52020 :
             RETURN                                   ' RESTORE DELETE
                                                            BUFFER
51235    '
51240    '
51245    '
51250    '
51255    IF A.KEY% = 415 THEN GOSUB 51660 :
             RETURN                                   ' CTRL LEFT ARROW
51260    IF A.KEY% = 416 THEN GOSUB 51575 :
             RETURN                                   ' CTRL RIGHT ARROW
51265    IF A.KEY% = 417 THEN GOSUB 51740 :
             RETURN                                   ' CTRL END
51270    '
51275    '
51280    RETURN
51285    '
51290    ' ******************************
51295    '
51300    ' DELETE AND PACK
51305    '
51310    TXTSIZE% = LEN (ENTRY$)
51315    IF TXTSIZE% = 0 THEN RETURN                  ' NOTHING TO DELETE
51320    IF TXTSIZE% = 1 THEN ENTRY$ = "":PLACE%
             = 1: GOTO 51340                          ' DELETE WHOLE LINE
51325    IF PLACE% = 1 THEN ENTRY$ = MID$
             (ENTRY$,2): GOTO 51340
```

```
51330    IF PLACE% >= TXTSIZE% THEN ENTRY$ = LEFT$ (ENTRY$,TXTSIZE% -
            1):PLACE% = PLACE% - 1: GOTO 51340
51335    ENTRY$ = LEFT$ (ENTRY$,(PLACE% - 1)) +
            MID$ (ENTRY$,PLACE% + 1)
51340    GOSUB 52660                             ' PRINT NEW STRING
51345    GOSUB 52500                             ' PRINT INVERSE
51350    RETURN
51355    '
51360    ' *******************************
51365    '
51370    ' TOGGLE THE INSERT MODE
51375    '
51380    IF INSERT% = 1 THEN INSERT% = 0: RETURN    ' TURN IT OFF
51385    INSERT% = 1                             ' TURN IT ON
51390    RETURN
51395    ' *******************************
51400    '
51405    ' INSERT A CHARACTER
51410    '
51415    '
51420    ' IS IT THE FIRST CHARACTER?
51425    IF PLACE% = 1 THEN ENTRY$ = " " + ENTRY$:
            GOTO 51440
51430    ' INSERT IN THE MIDDLE
51435    ENTRY$ = LEFT$ (ENTRY$,PLACE% - 1) + " "
            + MID$ (ENTRY$,PLACE%)
51440    GOSUB 52660                             ' PRINT THE FIELD
51445    GOSUB 52570                             ' REPOSITION CURSOR
51450    RETURN
51455    '
51460    '  ************************************
51465    '
51470    ' LEFT ARROW
51475    '
51480    GOSUB 52570                             ' DISPLAY NORMAL
51485    IF PLACE% > 1 THEN PLACE% = PLACE% - 1    ' MOVE LEFT ONE
51490    IF PLACE% < FRONT% THEN FRONT% = PLACE%
            : GOSUB 52660                        ' REDISPLAY LINE
51495    GOSUB 52500                             ' DISPLAY INVERSE
51500    RETURN
51505    '
51510    '  ********************************
51515    '

51520    ' RIGHT ARROW
```

```
51525    '
51530    IF MID$ (ENTRY$,PLACE%,1) = "" THEN
            RETURN
51535    GOSUB 52570                               ' DISPLAY AS NORMAL
51540    IF PLACE% < MAXSIZE% THEN PLACE% =
            PLACE% + 1
51545    IF (PLACE% + COL% - FRONT%) > 78 THEN
            FRONT% = PLACE% - 78 + COL% : GOSUB
            52660                                  ' REDISPLAY
51550    GOSUB 52500                               ' DISPLAY AS INVERSE
51555    RETURN
51560    '
51565    ' ****************************
51570    '
51575    ' SKIP TO NEXT WORD
51580    '
51585    '
51590    IF PLACE% = > TXTSIZE% THEN RETURN        ' ALREADY AT END
51595    GOSUB 52570                               ' REMOVE CURSOR
51600    PLACE% = PLACE% + 1                       ' LOOK FOR FIRST SPACE
51605    IF PLACE% = TXTSIZE% THEN GOTO 51630
51610    IF MID$ (ENTRY$,PLACE%,1) <> " " THEN
            GOTO 51600                             ' IS IT A SPACE?
51615    PLACE% = PLACE% + 1                       ' MOVE RIGHT ONE
51620    IF PLACE% = TXTSIZE% THEN GOTO 51630
51625    IF MID$ (ENTRY$,PLACE%,1) = " " THEN
            GOTO 51615                             ' SKIP OVER SPACES
51630    IF (PLACE% + COL% - FRONT%) > 78 THEN
            FRONT% = PLACE% - 78 + COL% : GOSUB
            52660                                  ' REDISPLAY LINE
51635    GOSUB 52500                               ' DISPLAY CURSOR
51640    RETURN
51645    '
51650    ' ****************************
51655    '
51660    ' SKIP TO PREVIOUS WORD
51665    '
51670    IF PLACE% = 1 THEN RETURN                 ' AT THE FRONT ALREADY
51675    GOSUB 52570                               ' REMOVE CURSOR
51680    PLACE% = PLACE% - 1                       ' LOOK FOR SPACE
51685    IF PLACE% = 1 THEN GOTO 51715            ' FORCE MOVE AT LEAST
                                                     ONE SPACE
51690    IF MID$ (ENTRY$,PLACE%,1) = " "
            THEN GOTO 51680                        ' SKIP OVER GROUP OF
                                                     SPACES
```

```
51695    PLACE% = PLACE% - 1
51700    IF PLACE% = 1 THEN GOTO 51715
51705    IF MID$ (ENTRY$,PLACE%,1) <> " " THEN          'IS IT A SPACE?
             GOTO 51695
51710    PLACE% = PLACE% + 1                            ' POSITION OVER FIRST
                                                          LETTER

51715    IF PLACE% < FRONT% THEN FRONT% = PLACE%
             : GOSUB 52660                              ' REDISPLAY LINE
51720    GOSUB 52500                                    ' DISPLAY THE CURSOR
51725    RETURN
51730    '
51735    ' ****************************
51740    ' ERASE TO END OF LINE
51745    '
51750    ' PRESERVE DELETED PIECE BEFORE
             DESTRUCTION
51755    IF PLACE% = 1 THEN PRESERVE$ = ENTRY$ :
             ENTRY$ = "" : GOTO 51770                   ' ERASE WHOLE LINE
51760    PRESERVE$ = MID$(ENTRY$,PLACE%)               ' SAVE THE END
51765    ENTRY$ = LEFT$ (ENTRY$,PLACE% - 1)
51770    GOSUB 52660                                    ' PRINT THE FIELD
51775    GOSUB 52500                                    ' DISPLAY THE CURSOR
51780    RETURN
51785    '
51790    ' **********************************
51795    '
51800    ' SKIP TO END OF LINE
51805    '
51810    GOSUB 52570                                    ' MOVE THE CURSOR
51815    PLACE% = LEN (ENTRY$) + 1
51820    IF PLACE% > MAXSIZE% THEN PLACE% =
             MAXSIZE%                                   ' DO NOT GO PAST END
51825    IF (PLACE% + COL%) > 79 THEN FRONT% =
             PLACE% - 78 + COL% : GOSUB 52660           ' REDISPLAY THE LINE
51830    GOSUB 52500                                    ' SHOW THE CURSOR
51835    RETURN
51840    '
51845    ' ************************
51850    '
51855    ' SKIP TO FRONT OF THE LINE
51860    '
51865    GOSUB 52570                                    ' REMOVE THE CURSOR
51870    PLACE% = 1                                     ' RESET THE POINTERS
51875    FRONT% = 1
51880    GOSUB 52660                                    ' REDISPLAY THE LINE
```

```
51885    GOSUB 52500                              ' DISPLAY THE CURSOR
51890    RETURN
51895    '
51900    '
51905    '
51910    ' DELETE NEXT WORD AND REDISPLAY
51915    '
51920    IF PLACE% > LEN(ENTRY$) OR LEN(ENTRY$)
             = 0 THEN RETURN                      ' DONE YET?
51925    IF MID$(ENTRY$,PLACE%,1) <> " "
             THEN GOSUB 51300 : GOTO 51920        ' DELETE ONE
                                                      CHARACTER AT A TIME
51930    IF PLACE% > LEN(ENTRY$) OR LEN(ENTRY$)
             = 0 THEN RETURN                      ' ERROR TEST
51935    IF MID$(ENTRY$,PLACE%,1) = " " THEN
             GOSUB 51300                          ' REMOVE TRAILING
                                                      SPACES
51940    RETURN
51945    '
51950    '
51955    '
51960    ' TAB KEY
51965    '
51970    GOSUB 52570                              ' REMOVE CURSOR
51975    PLACE% = (INT(PLACE%/8) + 1) * 8         ' SLIDE THE CURSOR
                                                      RIGHT
51980    IF PLACE% > MAXSIZE% THEN PLACE% =
             MAXSIZE%                             ' CAN'T GO PAST END
                                                      OF LINE
51985    IF (PLACE% + COL% - FRONT%) > 79 THEN
             FRONT% = PLACE% - 79 + COL%          ' ADJUST FOR WINDOW
51990    IF PLACE% > LEN(ENTRY$) THEN ENTRY$ =
             ENTRY$ + SPACE$(PLACE% -
             LEN(ENTRY$))                         ' ADD SPACES TO END
51995    GOSUB 52660                              ' REDISPLAY THE LINE
52000    GOSUB 52500                              'SHOW CURSOR
52005    RETURN
52010    '
52015    '
52020    ' RESTORE DELETE BUFFER
52025    '
52030    ' INSERT IF LINE NOT BLANK OTHERWISE
             EQUATE TO PRESERVE$
52035    IF LEN(ENTRY$) = 0 THEN ENTRY$ =
             PRESERVE$ : GOTO 52045               ' NOTHING THERE
```

```
52040     IF PLACE% = 1 THEN ENTRY$ = PRESERVE$ +
             ENTRY$ ELSE ENTRY$ =
             LEFT$(ENTRY$,PLACE% - 1) +
             PRESERVE$ + MID$(ENTRY$,PLACE%)
52045     GOSUB 52660                               ' REDISPLAY LINE
52050     GOSUB 52500                               ' SHOW CURSOR
52055     RETURN
52060     '
52065     '
52070     '
52075     ' RESTORE ORIGINAL ENTRY$
52080     '
52085     ENTRY$ = ORG.ENTRY$
52090     GOSUB 51855                               ' REDISPLAY AND JUMP
                                                       TO FRONT OF TEXT
52095     RETURN
52100     '
52105     '
52110     '
52500     ' DISPLAY THE CHARACTER IN HIGH
             INTENSITY (SET TO LINE NUMBER
             52500)
52505     ' THIS GIVES THE ILLUSION OF CURSOR
             MOVEMENT
52510     '
52515     LOCATE ROW%,(COL% + PLACE% - FRONT%)     ' POSITION CURSOR
52520     COLOR 31,0                                ' HIGH INTENSITY
                                                       BLINKING
52525     XX$ = MID$(ENTRY$,PLACE%,1)              ' MOVE FOR THE NEXT IF
52530     IF XX$ = "" OR XX$ = " " THEN XX$ = " "  ' SHOW UNDERLINE FOR
                                                       SPACE
52535     PRINT XX$;                                ' PRINT THE INVERSE
52540     COLOR 7,0                                 ' RESTORE TO NORMAL
                                                       VIDEO
52545     LOCATE ROW%,(COL% + PLACE% -
             FRONT%)
                                                    ' REPOSITION THE
                                                       CURSOR
52550     RETURN
52555     '
52560     ' *********************
52565     '
52570     ' POSITION AND DISPLAY NORMAL
52575     '
52580     LOCATE ROW%,(COL% + PLACE% - FRONT%)
52585     XX$ = MID$(ENTRY$,PLACE%,1)              ' PRINT ONE LETTER
```

```
52590    IF XX$ = "" THEN XX$ = FILL$              ' IF NULL THEN MAKE IT
                                                       A SPACE
52595    PRINT XX$;
52600    '
52605    LOCATE ROW%,(COL% + PLACE% -              ' REPOSITION THE
            FRONT%)                                    CURSOR
52610    RETURN
52615    '
52620    ' ****************************
52625    '
52630    ' ENTRY POINT FOR EXIT ROUTINES
52635    '
52640    FRONT% = 1                                ' MAKE SURE CURSOR IS
                                                       AT FRONT
52645    IF PLACE% > 79 - COL% THEN PLACE% = 79 -
            COL%                                   ' IN CASE OFF SCREEN
52650    '
52655    '
52660    ' DISPLAY TEXT$
52665    ' FILL$ IS THE FILL CHARACTER
52670    ' TXTSIZE% IS THE LENGTH OF ENTRY$
52675    ' MAXSIZE% IS THE MAXIMUM ALLOWED
            LENGTH
52680    '
52685    '
52690    TXTSIZE% = LEN (ENTRY$)                   ' HOW LONG IS THE
                                                       CURRENT FIELD?
52695    '
52700    ' IS ENTRY$ TOO LONG?
52705    '
52710    IF TXTSIZE% > MAXSIZE% THEN ENTRY$ =
            LEFT$ (ENTRY$,MAXSIZE%):TXTSIZE% =
            MAXSIZE%
52715    '
52720    ' POSITION THE CURSOR
52725    '
52730    LOCATE ROW%,COL%                          ' ROW POSITION
52735    '
52740    ' PRINT THE TEXT
52745    '
52750    IF MAXSIZE% > 79 - COL% THEN X = (79 -
            COL%) ELSE X = MAXSIZE%
52755    PRINT MID$(ENTRY$,FRONT%,X);             ' NO LINE FEED
52760    '
52765    ' PRINT THE FILL CHARACTER
```

```
52770    '
52775    IF (TXTSIZE% - FRONT%) > X THEN RETURN      ' NO FILL$ TO PRINT
52780    FOR XX = (TXTSIZE% - FRONT%) TO (X - 2)
52785      PRINT FILL$;
52790    NEXT XX
52795    RETURN                                      ' ALL DONE
52800    '
52805    ' *********************
52810    '
60000    ' STANDARD ERROR PROCESSING ROUTINE
60005    '
60010    X = ERR                                     ' ERROR NUMBER
60015    Y = ERL                                     ' LINE NUMBER OF ERROR
60020    RESUME 60025
60025    KEY OFF                                     ' TURN OFF SO WE CAN
                                                       USE 25TH LINE
60030    LOCATE 25,1                                 ' POSITION CURSOR ON
                                                       25TH LINE
60035    PRINT "ERROR ";X;" ON LINE ";Y
60040    BEEP                                        ' RING THE BELL
60045    END                                         ' THAT'S ALL FOLKS
60050    '
60055    '
60060    '
```

SCREEN TEXT EDITOR

INTRODUCTION

In the previous chapter we created a line editor capable of editing a single line of text. Often, however, it is necessary to enter and edit a paragraph or more of text. In this chapter we will develop a screen text editor that will enable us to enter and edit multiple pages. This program will be developed in two parts. The first part is the actual text editor, which can be added to your own programs. The second part provides disk input/output capability. By combining both parts, you will have a stand-alone, text-editing, and program-development system.

Design

This program is going to be a multipurpose text editor. Not only do we want to be able to edit text as part of a program, but we also want to develop a stand-alone text editor that can be used for writing letters or computer programs. Thus our program supports both purposes.

Another feature of the program is the ability to output text to a printer. Combined with the program developed in Chapter 7, this program will be able to use the many special features of your printer, such as different character fonts and bold printing. See your printer manual for the special codes it requires.

In the second half of this chapter, we provide the capability to print, load, save, auto number, or quit.

Building the Program

The heart of the text editor is the line editor developed in Chapter 2. To build the screen text editor, start with a copy of the line editor program from Chapter 2 and add the additional program lines presented in this chapter. We recommend that you start with a new diskette that holds a copy of the program from Chapter 2 and add the new program lines to this diskette. Be sure to make backups at each stage of entry and each time you successfully complete a test point.

User Features

This subroutine (made up of a collection of subroutines) is a free-form full-screen text editor. By adding this editor to your programs, you will enable your users to enter and edit large blocks of text instead of being restricted to single-line entries. This editor is powerful yet easy to use. Figure 3.1 shows the available features.

These features are implemented using the IBM function keys and special keys. Wherever appropriate (or possible), we use the keys as labeled by IBM. Naturally you can change the key assignments to be compatible with the word processor or any program you use regularly.

FIG. 3.1   Text Editor Features

Enter (carriage return)	Advance cursor to front of next line.
Down arrow	Move cursor down one line.
Up arrow	Move cursor up one line.
Page down	Advance cursor down 24 lines.
Page up	Move cursor up 24 lines.
Home page	Return to first line of text.
Last page	Advance to last page of text.
Insert line	Insert blank line.
Delete line	Delete current line.
Split line	Divide current line. Text to right of cursor moved to next line.
Concatenate line	Add next line to end of current line.
Wraparound	Word wraparound.
Move block	Move block of text.
Copy block	Duplicate block of text.
Delete block	Erase block of text.
Save block	Write block of text to diskette.

Programmer Features

This subroutine is easy for the programmer to use. The text is kept in a string array. The calling program must tell the editor how large the array is, what line in the array to begin editing on, and the number of array lines that contain text.

Part 1: TEXT EDITOR PROGRAM

The flowchart for the basic text editor is shown in Figure 3.2. This flowchart shows that the calling program defines the starting conditions; then the text editor displays a screen of text and edits a line of

FIG. 3.2   Text editor flowchart

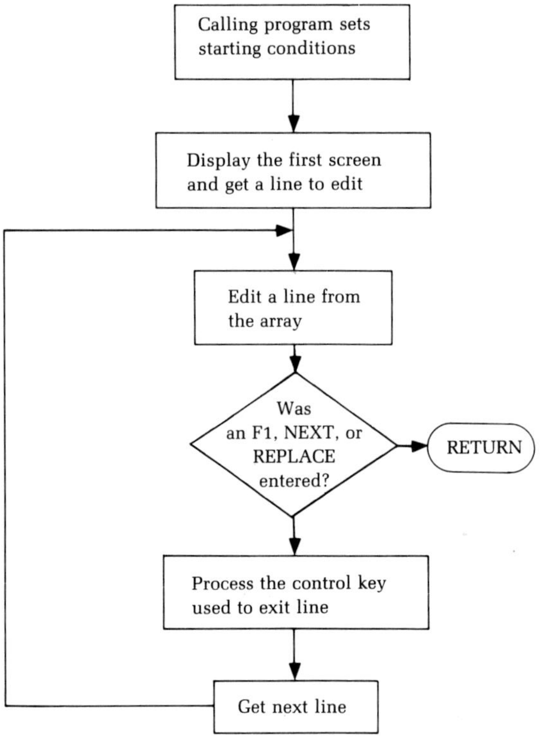

Calling program sets
starting conditions

Display the first screen
and get a line to edit

Edit a line from
the array

Was
an F1, NEXT, or
REPLACE
entered?

RETURN

Process the control key
used to exit line

Get next line

text. After the line has been edited, the program tests to see if the user is done. If the user is not done, the text editor processes the next positioning command.

The program corresponding to the flowchart in Figure 3.2 is as follows.

```
42000      ' TEXT EDITOR
42005      '
42010      ' VARIABLE DEFINITION
42015      ' LROW% STARTING ROW NUMBER
42020      ' LCOL% STARTING COL NUMBER
42025      ' LINES$( ) TEXT ARRAY
```

```
42030      ' LAST% DIMENSIONS OF TEXT ARRAY
42035      ' MLINES% LARGEST LINE USED IN ARRAY
42040      ' LINES% CURRENT LINE BEING EDITED
42045      ' FIRST% LINE AT TOP OF SCREEN
42050      GOSUB 42790                              ' DISPLAY THE SCREEN
42055      '
42060      ' ENTRY FOR NO REDISPLAY
42065      '
42070      FILL$ = " "                              ' DEFINE THE FILL
                                                        CHARACTER
42075      MASK$ = "N"                              ' SET FOR TEXT EDITOR
42080      ROW% = LROW%                             ' START AT LAST ROW
42085      COL% = LCOL%                             ' START AT LAST COL
42090      '
42095      ' TOP OF EDIT LOOP
42100      CTRL% = 0                                ' CLEAR THE EXIT FLAG
42105      ENTRY$ = LINES$(LINES%)                  ' PUT CURRENT LINE INTO
                                                        LINE EDITOR
42110      IF PLACE% > LEN (ENTRY$) THEN
               PLACE% = LEN (ENTRY$) + 1            ' ASSIGN PLACE% HERE
42115      IF PLACE% = 0 THEN PLACE% = 1            ' NULL LINE
42120      IF PLACE% > 79 - COL% THEN FRONT% =
               PLACE% - 40 : GOSUB 52660            ' CENTER IF OFF RIGHT END
                                                        SEARCH AND REPLACE
                                                        NEED THIS
42125      GOSUB 50160                              ' EDIT THE TEXT BUT DO NOT
                                                        REDISPLAY ENTRY$
42130      IF HELP% <> 0 THEN HELP$ =
               "CHAP3B.HLP" : GOSUB 48000 :
               GOTO 42000                           ' PROCESS HELP REQUEST
42135      LINES$(LINES%) = ENTRY$                  ' SAVE THE EDITED LINE
42140      ' TEST FOR ESC, F1, NEXT OR REPLACE
42145      IF (CTRL% >= 27) AND (CTRL% <= 29)
               THEN LROW% = ROW%:LCOL% = COL%:
               RETURN                               ' BACK TO CALLER
42150      ON CTRL% GOSUB 42170,42210,42265,42615,42655,42720,
               42435,42510,42380,42315,43210,43370,43165,43505
42155      GOTO 42095
42160      ' ****************************************
42165      '
```

The following subsections describe various aspects of the text editor program.

Explanation of Variables

The text editor program requires only a few more variables than the line editor. LROW% (line 42080) and LCOL% (line 42085) set the screen starting position. The first time the text editor is called, these variables are set to 1.

The text to be edited is contained in array LINES$( ) (see line 120). The calling program must either clear (equate to nulls) or fill in the array with text before it calls the text editor. LAST% is the dimension of the array LINES$. For example, LINES$ is dimensioned by the statement DIM LINES$(LAST%), (line 115).

DIM   The DIMension statement is used to allocate space for an array.

EXAMPLE

```
DIM A(12)
```

This command provides for elements in the array A from position 0 through 12.

MLINES% is the number of array elements used. For instance, if the array is dimensioned to 100, but only the first 23 lines contain information, then MLINES% is set equal to 23 and LAST% is equal to 100. If the array is blank and contains no text, then MLINES% is set equal to 1.

LINES% is the number of the line currently being edited. The calling program must set it equal to 1 if there is nothing in the array or if editing is to begin on line 1, the first line. If editing is not to begin on the first line, then LINES% is set equal to the line number to be edited. For example, if editing is to begin on line 25, set LINES% equal to 25.

FIRST% is the number of the line to appear at the top of the screen. Normally FIRST% will start with the same value as LINES%.

Explanation of the Program

The text editor routine displays the current screen, keeps track of the cursor's position, and processes the exiting commands. The text editor enters the line editor routine at line 50160 (see line 42125 of the text editor program). We enter the line editor at this point because the text editor does not need to have the line editor redisplay the text before or after editing. You must remember to be careful when editing subroutines, like the line editor, that have multiple-entry points. You do not want to introduce an error by changing the operation of an entry point.

PLACE% is used by the line editor to mark the current character being edited. Setting PLACE% equal to 1 will cause the cursor to start cursor to start at the beginning of the line. In the text editor, PLACE% is set equal to 1 when a carriage return is entered, and it is not changed when an up or down arrow is entered. The up and down motions look nicer, and it is more convenient for the user if the cursor stays in the current column position as the cursor is moved through the text. If PLACE% is larger than the length of the line the cursor is moving to, PLACE% is set equal to the length of the new line so that editing may begin at the end of the new line.

Miscellaneous Subroutines

There are two subroutines that are used here but explained elsewhere in the book. The help system (GOSUB 48000) is from Chapter 4 and the error-processing routine (GOSUB 60000) was described in Chapter 2.

In this chapter we do not use the actual help subroutine; rather we include a few lines to simply hold its place in the program. You should add the complete subroutine once you have completed Chapter 4.

The two subroutines follow.

```
48000    ' RESERVED FOR HELP SUBROUTINE CHAPTER 4
48005    '
48010    RETURN
```

```
48015     '
48020     '
48025     '

60000     ' STANDARD ERROR PROCESSING ROUTINE
60005     '
60010     X = ERR                              'ERROR NUMBER
60015     Y = ERL                              ' LINE NUMBER OF
                                                   ERROR
60020     RESUME 60025
60025     KEY OFF                              ' TURN OFF SO WE CAN
                                                   USE 25TH LINE
60030     LOCATE 25,1                          ' POSITION CURSOR
                                                   ON 25TH LINE
60035     PRINT "ERROR ";X;" ON LINE ";Y
60040     BEEP                                 ' RING THE BELL
60045     END                                  ' THAT'S ALL FOLKS
60050     '
60055     '
60060     '
```

Explanation of Screen Display Subroutine

The screen display subroutine (line 42050, GOSUB 42790) clears the screen by using the CLS command and then uses a FOR–NEXT loop to display the text array, starting with text line FIRST%.

CLS The CLS command clears the text area and moves the cursor to the upper-left corner of the screen.

The program for the screen display routine is as follows:

```
42790     ' DISPLAY THE CURRENT SCREEN
42795     '
42800     CLS                                  ' CLEAR THE SCREEN
42805     FOR X = 1 TO 24
42810        Z = FIRST% + X - 1
42815        LOCATE X,1                        ' POSITION THE CURSOR
42820        IF LEN(LINES$(Z)) > 78 THEN PRINT
          LEFT$(LINES$(Z),78); ELSE PRINT
          LINES$(Z);                           ' IF IT FITS PRINT IT
```

```
42825   NEXT X
42830   RETURN
42835   ' *********************************
42840   '
```

TEST POINT

Before testing the screen display routine, you will need to enter a test routine plus a temporary program line:

```
42057 END
```

Since we do not want to proceed past this subroutine, this temporary line will cause execution to stop after the screen is displayed. If you now enter

```
RUN (CR)
```

the screen should clear, and the program will stop with the cursor on the last line.

If this routine has worked so far, add some more temporary program lines:

```
100         '
110         ' SCREEN EDITOR TEST ROUTINE
120         '
130         DIM LINES$(50)                     ' DEFINE SCREEN ARRAY
140         LAST% = 50                         ' NUMBER OF TEXT LINES
150         MLINES% = 0                        ' INITIALIZE VARIABLES
160         ANUM% = 0
170         ROW% = 1
180         COL% = 1
190         LINES% = 1
200         FIRST% = 1
202         FOR X = 1 TO 50
204         LINES$(X) = "THIS IS LINE NUMBER "+
                STR$(X)
206         NEXT X
210         '
220         ' LEAVE A GAP HERE
```

```
230        '
240        GOSUB 41000                    ' CALL THE EDITOR
250        END
```

These lines fill the array with text. Enter

```
RUN (CR)
```

and you should now see the text for lines 2 through 24 displayed. The text for line 1 scrolled off the top of the screen because of the END statement on line 42057.

After the screen display section is tested, line 41057 is no longer needed. Delete it and add

```
42137      END
```

You can now test the line editor as part of the screen editor. Enter

```
RUN (CR)
```

and the screen should clear, the text in the first 24 lines should be displayed, and the cursor should be positioned on the first line over the L. Edit this line and the program will stop after ENTER is pressed.

After you are satisfied that everything is working, delete line 42137.

SCREEN EDITING COMMANDS

The screen editor requires several new commands to be added to the line editor routine. These characters will set the CTRL% variable. Recall that if CTRL% is not 0, the line editor will return to the calling program. In this case the caller is the text editor program. After the line editor returns, the text editor saves the edited line and processes the CTRL% command.

The new characters and commands, shown in Figure 3.3 are to be added to the line editor. A keyboard overlay for the function keys is shown in Figure 3.4. Make a copy on heavy bond paper, cut it out, and place it over the function keypad for your convenience.

FIG. 3.3   Command Summary Table

Enter (carriage return)	Advance cursor to front of next line.
Down arrow	Move cursor down one line.
Up arrow	Move cursor up one line.
Page down	Advance cursor down 24 lines.
Page up	More cursor up 24 lines.
Home	Return to first line of text.
Control home	Advance cursor to last page of text.
F1	Exit the Editor.
Shift F1	HELP.
F3	Insert blank line.
Shift F3	Delete current line.
F4	Divide current line. Text to right of cursor moved to next line.
Shift F4	Concatenate lines.
F5	Mark start of block.
Shift F5	Mark end of block.
F6	Move block to cursor.
Shift F6	Save block to diskette.
F7	Duplicate block at cursor.
Shift F7	Delete block.
F8	Advance cursor to new occurence.
Shift F8	Replace old phrase with new phrase.
F9	Word wrap toggle.

FIG. 3.4   Keyboard overlay. Copy this figure, cut out the figure, and place it over the function keys on your keyboard.

Help	Restore
Exit Mode	Del Word
Del Line	Conc Line
Insert Line	Split Line
Block End	Block Save
Block Start	Block Move
Block Delete	Replace
Block Copy	Next
Word Wrap	

Basic Business Subroutines, IBM PC

The program for these commands is inserted directly into the line editor program.

The program lines for implementing the new commands are as follows.

```
50333    IF MASK$ = "N" THEN GOSUB 50550 :
            RETURN                              ' AUTO NUMBER
50550    ' TEXT EDITOR MASK
50555    '
50560    IF LEN(ENTRY$) >= WRAPSIZE% AND
            PLACE% >= WRAPSIZE% THEN GOSUB
            42940 : RETURN                      ' WRAP AROUND TEST
50565    IF A.KEY% <> 32 OR ANUM% = 0 OR PLACE%
            <> 1 OR LEN(ENTRY$) > 0 THEN GOSUB
            50900 : RETURN                      ' WHEN NOT TO ADD
                                                  NUMBER
50570    ' AUTO NUMBERING ON AND IN FIRST
            CHARACTER
50575    ENTRY$ = MID$(STR$(ANUM%),2)          ' REMOVE SPACE DUE TO
                                                  STR$()
50580    ENTRY$ = ENTRY$ + SPACE$(8 -
            LEN(ENTRY$))                        ' INDENT
50585    ANUM% = ANUM% + 5
50590    PLACE% = LEN (ENTRY$)
50595    GOSUB 52660                            ' PRINT ENTRY$
50600    GOSUB 52500                            ' CURSOR DISPLAY
50605    RETURN
50610    ' ********************************
50615    '
50620    '
51191    IF A.KEY% = 361 THEN CTRL% = 8        ' F3 INSERT LINE
51192    IF A.KEY% = 362 THEN GOSUB 43090 :
            RETURN                              ' F4 SPLIT LINE
51193    IF A.KEY% = 363 THEN MARK.START% =
            LINES% : RETURN                     ' F5 SET START MARK
51194    IF A.KEY% = 364 THEN CTRL% = 13       ' F6 MOVE BLOCK
51196    IF A.KEY% = 365 THEN CTRL% = 11       ' F7 COPY BLOCK
51197    IF A.KEY% = 366 THEN CTRL% = 28       ' F8 NEXT FIELD
51198    IF A.KEY% = 367 THEN GOSUB 42905 :
            RETURN                              ' F9 WORD WRAP TOGGLE
51206    IF A.KEY% = 371 THEN CTRL% = 4        ' HOME
51207    IF A.KEY% = 372 THEN CTRL% = 3        ' UP ARROW
51208    IF A.KEY% = 373 THEN CTRL% = 5        ' PG UP
51221    IF A.KEY% = 380 THEN CTRL% = 2        ' DOWN ARROW
51222    IF A.KEY% = 381 THEN CTRL% = 6        ' PG DOWN
51231    IF A.KEY% = 386 THEN CTRL% = 7        ' SHIFT F3 DELETE LINE
51232    IF A.KEY% = 387 THEN CTRL% = 10       ' SHIFT F4 PACK LINE
51233    IF A.KEY% = 388 THEN MARK.END% =
            LINES% : RETURN                     ' SHIFT F5 BLOCK END
```

```
51234   IF A.KEY% = 389 THEN CTRL% = 14        ' SHIFT F6 SAVE BLOCK
                                                    TO DISK
51236   IF A.KEY% = 390 THEN CTRL% = 12        ' SHIFT F7 DELETE BLOCK
51237   IF A.KEY% = 391 THEN CTRL% = 29        ' SHIFT F8 REPLACE
51266   IF A.KEY% = 419 THEN CTRL% = 9         ' CTRL HOME LAST PAGE
52638   IF FRONT% = 1 AND ORG.ENTRY$=ENTRY$
            THEN GOSUB 52570 : RETURN           ' LINE UNCHANGED SO DO
                                                    NOT PRINT
```

In the following subsections we create and test the programs for new commands.

Moving Down a Line

Two different keys can be used to move down a line: the down arrow or the ENTER key. The down arrow will keep the cursor in the same column on the screen. ENTER acts as a carriage return on a typewriter and will move the cursor to the first character of the next line. Many word processors insert a blank line when the ENTER key is pressed, which we find to be annoying. We prefer to insert blank lines as a separate command. You can change this, however, if you want to be compatible with your word processor.

Several boundary conditions must be treated here. LINES% cannot be larger then LAST%, since LAST% is the array dimension. If LINES% becomes larger than MLINES% (the value of the last used line in the array), then MLINES% must be incremented.

As an added feature this routine allows lines to be split and continued to the next line. To be consistent with the IBM Basic Compiler, we use an underscore as the continuation character. If a continuation character has been used and the next line is blank, editing begins at the first TAB stop on the new line. This last feature is especially convenient if a BASIC program is being written. Indenting the line will make it stand out from the rest of the text. A nonblank line is not indented because that means that the user is editing existing text.

Finally, we test to determine whether we are on the bottom line of the screen. If we are, then the screen must be moved up by calling the page scroll subroutine.

The following routines move the cursor down a line.

```
42170      ' CARRIAGE RETURN
42175      '
42180      PLACE% = LEN(WRAP$) + 1                    ' POSITION AT FRONT OR
                                                        END IF WRAP
42185      WRAP$ = ""                                 ' RESET FOR NEXT TIME
42190      GOSUB 42210                                ' LINE FEED
42195      RETURN
42200      ' ***********************************
42205      '
42210      ' LINE FEED
42215      '
42220      IF LINES% = LAST% THEN RETURN              ' MAX NO MORE LINES LEFT
42225      LINES% = LINES% + 1
42230      IF LINES% > MLINES% THEN MLINES% =
               LINES%                                 ' INC LARGEST LINE
                                                        COUNTER
42235      ROW% = ROW% + 1
42240      IF ROW% > 24 THEN ROW% = 12 : X = 13 :
               Y = 0 : GOSUB 42740                    ' SKIP HALF PAGE
42245      IF (RIGHT$(ENTRY$,1) = "_") AND
               (LEN(LINES$(LINES%)) = 0) THEN
               PLACE% = 1 : LINES$(LINES%) =
               SPACE$(8)                              ' ADD OFFSET
42250      RETURN
42255      ' ***********************************
42260      '
```

TEST POINT

After typing in the program, enter RUN (CR). Once the screen is
displayed, press ENTER and the cursor should move to line 2. Now
edit line 2 and press the down arrow. If there is no text on the next
line, the cursor drops down to line 3 and moves to the first column. If
there is text on the next line, then the cursor stays in the same column (assuming the length of line 3 is greater than or equal to the
length of line 2). The page-scrolling test will have to be done after you
have entered that routine (which is presented in a later subsection).

Moving Up a Line

The up arrow moves the cursor up one line. To move up a line, we
decrement both LINES% and ROW% by one. As in moving down a

line, we must also test a number of boundary conditions. LINES% must be greater than 0. IF ROW% becomes equal to 0, we have gone past the top of the screen, and the screen must be rolled down a line. Rolling down a line is done by telling the page scroll subroutine to move up one line.

The following routine moves the cursor up a line.

```
42265      ' UP ARROW
42270      '
42275      IF LINES% = 1 THEN RETURN                    ' AT TOP ALREADY
42280      LINES% = LINES% - 1
42285      ROW% = ROW% - 1
42290      IF ROW% < 1 THEN ROW% = 12 : X = 12 : Y =
               0 : GOSUB 42675                          ' SKIP HALF PAGE
42295      RETURN
42300      '
42305      ' * * * * * * * * * * * * * * * * * * * * * * * * * * * * * * * *
42310      '
```

Instead of scrolling just one line up or down, you may wish to scroll half a page, or 12 lines. To do this, you will have to adjust both ROW% and LINES%. Some users may be annoyed that the screen refreshes every time it scrolls one line. Others may be annoyed that the cursor jumps half a page. Your implementation is a matter of personal preference.

TEST POINT

Execute the program you have so far, and after the screen has displayed, press the ENTER key a few times to move the cursor down the screen. Now press the up arrow and move back up one line. Edit this line and enter another up arrow. Next, press ENTER and return to the line just edited. It should contain the text you edited. Before proceeding to the next section, continue to check to make sure everything is working correctly. Move the cursor up and down several times and edit several lines. Also try some of the previous commands.

Scroll Up a Page

To move up one page of text, we press the PAGE UP key. In the routine that follows, FIRST% and LINES% are decremented, and the text window is moved up. If entered while already on the first page of text, the cursor will move to the top row on the screen.

The scrolling-up routine is as follows.

```
42655     ' SCROLL UP A PAGE
42660     '
42665     X = 24                             ' JUMP A FULL PAGE
42670     Y = X                              ' OFFSET POINTER
42675     ' ENTRY POINT FOR ROLL UP
42680     IF FIRST% <= X THEN GOSUB
              42845:ROW% = 1: GOSUB
              42790: RETURN                  ' JUMP TO TOP OF FIRST PAGE
42685     FIRST% = FIRST% - X                ' MOVE THE TOP LINE
42690     LINES% = LINES% - Y                ' CHANGE THE ARRAY POINTER
42695     GOSUB 42790                        ' DISPLAY THE SCREEN
42700     RETURN
42705     '
42710     ' *****************************************
42715     '
```

TEST POINT

Enter 30 lines of text. Move the cursor down to the second page, and then press PAGE UP to scroll up one page. Test all the functions as you did for moving the cursor up one line. Now verify that when the up arrow is pressed while on the first line of the screen, the screen text is scrolled down one line.

Scroll Down a Page

To move down a page of text, press the PAGE DOWN key. In large documents it is necessary to jump up and down through the text 24 lines at a time instead of one at a time.

The scroll-down subroutine increments FIRST% and LINES% and then redisplays the screen. The boundary conditions occur at the bottom line on a screen and the last page. The variable X is used to set the number of lines to be scrolled. For a full page, scroll X is set equal to 24. The single-line scroll sets X equal to 1, and a half-page scroll would set X equal to 12. If the cursor is already on the last page of text, then it will move to the last line; otherwise, it will remain on the same row on the screen and the text will move one page.

The scrolling-down routine is as follows.

```
42720      ' SCROLL DOWN A PAGE
42725      '
42730      X = 24                                           ' JUMP A FULL
                                                                PAGE
42735      Y = X                                            ' OFFSET POINTER
42740      ' ENTRY POINT FOR ROLL DOWN
42745      IF MLINES% < = 24 THEN LINES% =
              MLINES%:ROW% = MLINES%: RETURN                ' ON FIRST PAGE
42750      IF FIRST% + X > MLINES% THEN FIRST% =
              MLINES% - 23:LINES% =
              MLINES%:ROW% = 24: GOTO 42765                 ' BOTTOM
42755      FIRST% = FIRST% + X
42760      LINES% = LINES% + Y
42765      GOSUB 42790                                      ' DISPLAY THE
                                                                SCREEN
42770      RETURN
42775      '
42780      ' ******************************************
42785      '
```

TEST POINT

Scroll down a page, and then perform the same tests you performed for scrolling up a page.

Jump to the Home Page

To return to the first, or home page, press HOME. This feature comes in handy, for example, when you are proofreading a document. Jumping to the first page is done by setting all of the pointers equal to 1 and then displaying the screen.

The program for returning to the home page is as follows.

```
42615   ' GOTO THE HOME PAGE
42620   '
42625   GOSUB 42845                 ' RESET THE POINTERS
42630   GOSUB 42790                 ' SHOW THE SCREEN
42635   RETURN                      ' A OK
42640   '
42645   ' **********************************
42650   '
42845   ' CLEAR EVERYTHING
42850   '
42855   LINES% = 1                  ' CURRENT LINE NUMBER
42860   FIRST% = 1                  ' TOP LINE ON THE SCREEN
42865   LROW% = 1                   ' START ON FIRST LINE
42870   LCOL% = 1
42875   ROW% = 1
42880   COL% = 1
42885   RETURN
42890   ' **********************************
42895   '
42900   '
```

TEST POINT

To test the routine for jumping to the home page, advance the cursor down several pages, and then press HOME to jump back to the first page. Test some of the previous commands, and do some editing to make sure everything is still working correctly.

Jump to the Last Page

Control Home advances the cursor to the last page. When editing a document, it is very convenient to be able to jump directly to the end of the document instead of stepping 24 lines at a time.

The following subroutine jumps to the last page of text.

```
42380    ' JUMP TO LAST PAGE
42385    '
42390    FIRST% = MLINES% - 23              ' FIND THE LINE
                                              AT THE TOP OF
                                              THE SCREEN
42395    IF FIRST% < 1 THEN FIRST% = 1      ' CANNOT HAVE
                                              LINE LESS
                                              THAN 1
42400    LINES% = FIRST%
42405    ROW% = 1
42410    COL% = 1
42415    GOSUB 42790                        ' DISPLAY THE
                                              SCREEN
42420    RETURN
42425    ' ************************************
42430    '
```

TEST POINT

Execute the program and enter Control Home. The last page of the text should be displayed, and the cursor should be on the top line of the screen.

The F1 Key

The F1 key is used to exit the text editor subroutine and return to the calling program. (This will be the command area of Part 2.)

On-Line Help

The HELP system is presented in Chapter 4, but we have included this routine to reserve a location for it. The shift F1 key is used to request HELP. The HELP subroutine will be at line 48000. The reserved lines are:

```
48000    ' RESERVED FOR HELP SUBROUTINE CHAPTER 4
48005    '
48010    RETURN
48015    '
48020    '
48025    '
```

Inserting a Blank Line

Function key F3 is used to insert a blank line. Line 51191 sets CTRL%
to 8 when key F3 is pressed. To insert a blank line, we split the array
at the current line number and move all the text on higher line numbers down one line. After the array has been moved, the current line
becomes the blank line, MLINE% is incremented, and the screen is
redisplayed.

The following routine is used to insert a blank line.

```
42510    ' INSERT A BLANK LINE
42515    '
42520    GOSUB 42550                                 ' DO THE INSERT
42525    LINES$(LINES%) = ""
42530    GOSUB 42790                                 ' REDISLAY SCREEN
42535    RETURN
42540    '
42545    '
42550    ' INSERT A LINE
42555    '
42560    IF MLINES% >= LAST% THEN MSG$ = "TEXT
            ARRAY FULL." : GOSUB 43045 : RETURN      ' OVERFLOW
42565    MLINES% = MLINES% + 1
42570    IF LINES% = 1 THEN Y = 2 ELSE Y = LINES%    ' SET COUNTER
42575    FOR X = MLINES% TO Y STEP - 1
42580    LINES$(X) = LINES$(X - 1)                    ' MOVE TEXT DOWN A LINE
42585    NEXT X
42590    RETURN
42595    '
42600    '
            ********************************
42605    '
```

This is really two subroutines. There are two subroutines because several other subroutines need to insert blank lines (block copy and block move) but do not need to redisplay the screen after every inserted line. The first routine begins at line 42510 and the second at line 42550. The second routine inserts a blank line into the text. The first routine calls the second (line 42520) and then redisplays the screen.

TEST POINT

There are two special boundary conditions that must be tested for at this point. These occur when inserting on either the first or the last line of the array.

Enter RUN (CR) and the cursor will appear on line 1. You can test the first boundary condition by pressing F3. The screen should clear, and all the lines should be redisplayed but shifted down one line. The first line should be blank. Now move the cursor to the last line and press F3.

Displaying Messages

The previous subroutine, for inserting a blank line, uses another subroutine (GOSUB 43045) to display an error message when the text array is full (line 42560). This subroutine prints the text in MSG$ on the 25th line of the screen, clears the remainder of the 25th line, and pauses, before returning, to allow the user time to read the message. The program is:

```
43045    ' DISPLAY MESSAGE MSG$ ON 25TH LINE
43050    '
43055    LOCATE 25,1
43060    X = LEN(MSG$)                          ' CLEAR LINE AFTER MSG$
                                                   WITH SPACES
43065    IF X >= 79 THEN PRINT LEFT$(MSG$,79);
         ELSE PRINT MSG$;SPACE$(79-X);
```

```
43070    FOR X = 1 TO 1000              ' PAUSE TO ALLOW USER
                                          TIME TO READ MESSAGE

43075    NEXT X
43080    RETURN
43085     '
43090     '
43095     '
```

TEST POINT

Thus far, inserting a blank line is the only routine to use the display
message subroutine. The message routine is called when the array is
full. In order to test the message routine we can either enter 50 lines
of text (our current array size, line 130) or we can change line 140 to

```
140 LAST% = 5
```

and then enter 6 lines of text. We choose to use the latter test and
modify line 140 rather than attempt to enter too many lines.

  After you test this subroutine, remember to change line 140 back
to

```
140 LAST% = 50
```

Deleting a Line

To delete a line of text, press shift F3. To delete a line, we split the
array at the current line number, and all the text on the higher line
numbers is moved up one line. MLINES% is decremented, and what
had been the last line is erased.

  The deleted line is stored in PRESERVE$ and can be restored us-
ing shift F2. This feature can be used to move a single line of text or
to duplicate a line several times. (Delete the line, reposition the cursor
to the new location, and then press shift F2 and F3 each time you
want a copy.)

  The program for deleting a line is as follows.

```
42435       ' DELETE A LINE
42440       '
42445       PRESERVE$ = LINES$(LINES%)            ' SAVE FOR POSSIBLE RESTORE
42450       IF MLINES% = 1 THEN LINES$(1) =
              "": GOTO 42485                      ' ONLY ONE LINE
42455       IF LINES% = MLINES% THEN ROW% =
              ROW% - 1:LINES% = LINES% -
              1: GOTO 42475                        ' LAST LINE IN TEXT
42460       FOR X = LINES% TO MLINES% - 1
42465       LINES$(X) = LINES$(X + 1)
42470       NEXT X
42475       LINES$(MLINES%) = ""
42480       IF MLINES% > 1 THEN MLINES% = MLINES% - 1
42485       GOSUB 42790                            ' DISPLAY SCREEN
42490       RETURN
42495       '
42500       ' ********************************
42505       '
```

TEST POINT

Boundary conditions occur on the first and last lines of the text, and so tests are performed to detect these conditions.

Enter RUN (CR) and then press shift F3. The screen should clear and show what appears to be lines 2 through 25 but are now really lines 1 through 24. Now move the cursor to the last line of the text. Press shift F3 and the last line should disappear. Try this again and verify that you can still edit and move the cursor.

Splitting a Line

Sometimes a line needs to be divided, with the text to the right of the cursor deleted from the current line and placed on the next line. The F4 key and the following routine are used to do this.

```
43100       ' SPLIT THIS LINE
43105       '
43110       LINES% = LINES% + 1
43115       GOSUB 42550                            ' INSERT A BLANK LINE
```

```
43120    LINES$(LINES%) =
           MID$(ENTRY$,PLACE%)              ' MOVE END TO NEXT LINE
43125    LINES% = LINES% - 1                ' RESTORE LINE POINTER
43130    CTRL% = 1                          ' MARK AS ENTER
43135    IF PLACE% > 1 THEN ENTRY$ =
           LEFT$(ENTRY$,PLACE%-1) ELSE
           ENTRY$ = ""                      ' REDEFINE THIS LINE
43140    GOSUB 42790                        ' REDISPLAY SCREEN
43145    RETURN
43150    '
43155    '
43160    '
```

This routine first inserts a blank line using the line insert routine (line 43115). It then places the text to the right of the cursor into the new line and removes it from the original line. Finally, it redisplays the screen and returns.

TEST POINT

Enter several lines of text, move the cursor to the middle of one of the lines, and press F4. The line should split. Repeat this on the first, last, and middle lines, on a blank line, and at the end of a line.

Concatenating Two Lines

Shift F4 concatenates (combines) two lines of text into one. The routine that follows combines two lines and then deletes the second line from the array.

If we are on the last line, there is nothing to concatenate; this condition is the only special one. NOTE: If the new line is too long, it will be truncated by the line editor and some text will be lost.

The following program combines two lines.

```
42315    ' PACK TWO LINES
42320    '
42325    IF LINES% = MLINES% THEN RETURN    ' AT THE END
```

```
42330    LINES$(LINES%) = LINES$(LINES%) +
            LINES$(LINES% + 1)                        ' PACK THE LINES
42335    IF LINES% = MLINES% THEN GOTO 42355     ' LAST LINE
42340    FOR X = LINES% + 1 TO MLINES% - 1
42345    LINES$(X) = LINES$(X + 1)                    ' MOVE LINE UP ONE
42350    NEXT X
42355    LINES$(MLINES%) = " "                        ' CLEAR THE LAST LINE
42360    MLINES% = MLINES% - 1                        ' REDUCE MAX LINE BY ONE
42365    GOSUB 42790
42370    RETURN
42375    '
```

TEST POINT

To test the concatenating feature, press shift F4 while on the first line.
The screen should clear, and the line should contain the original line
plus the second line. The remainder of the text lines will move up one
line. If you jump to the last line, you can test the boundary condition
of concatenating a blank line.

Setting Block Markers

Several commands require that you identify the beginning and ending
lines of a block of text (note that you cannot take a partial line unless
you first split the line). These commands are COPY, MOVE, DELETE,
and SAVE BLOCK.

To set the beginning marker, move the cursor to the first line of
text you wish to include in the block, and then press the F5 key. Now
move the cursor to the last line of interest, and press shift F5. This
sets the block markers.

The variables MARK.START% and MARK.END% are set in lines
51193 and 51233 that were previously entered.

Save Block of Text to Diskette

Occasionally it is necessary to extract part of one document for use
in another document. This subroutine provides a convenient way to
do this.

After the block markers are set, the shift F6 key is pressed. Then the program requests a file name, writes the block to diskette, and returns. The program listing follows:

```
43505    ' SAVE BLOCK TO DISK
43510    '
43515    SAV.ROW% = ROW%                          ' SAVE FOR RETURN
43520    SAV.COL% = COL%                          ' DITTO
43525    ROW% = 25                                ' ACCEPT FILE NAME ON
                                                      25TH LINE
43530    COL% = 30
43535    LOCATE 25,1
43540    PRINT "SAVE IN FILE: ";
43545    ENTRY$ = "TEMP.TXT"                      ' DEFAULT FILE NAME
43550    GOSUB 50000                              ' CALL LINE EDITOR
43555    MSG$ = ""                                ' CLEAR 25TH LINE
43560    GOSUB 43045                              ' DO IT
43565    IF CTRL% = 27 OR LEN(ENTRY$) = 0 THEN
             GOTO 43600                           ' ESC OR ERROR
43570    OPEN ENTRY$ FOR OUTPUT AS #2
43575    IF MARK.END% < MARK.START% THEN SWAP
             MARK.END%,MARK.START%
43580    FOR X = MARK.START% TO MARK.END%         ' WRITE TO DISK
43585    PRINT#2,LINES$(X)
43590    NEXT X
43595    CLOSE#2
43600    ROW% = SAV.ROW%
43605    COL% = SAV.COL%
43610    PLACE% = 1
43615    RETURN
43620    '
43625    '
43630    '
```

Notice that the program provides a default file named TEMP.TXT, and uses the line editor to accept a different name. If the user presses F1 (to abandon) or deletes the entire name, the subroutine exits and nothing is saved. It is a good practice always to allow a consistent, nondestructive escape path for your users. We try to use the F1 key as the quit, exit, or abandon key.

TEST POINT

Enter several lines of text, mark off the block, and press the shift F6 key. Repeat this test at the beginning, the middle, and the end of a large document.

Copy a Block of Text

A word processor would be incomplete if it did not have the capability to copy or duplicate blocks of text.

Before a block can be copied, we must be able to tell the computer where the block begins and ends. We use the F5 key to set the beginning of the block and shift F5 to set the end of the block. This is done by moving the cursor to the beginning line of the block and pressing F5 and then moving the cursor to the end line and pressing shift F5. This method is also used for the MOVE, DELETE, and SAVE commands.

Once the block ends are set, the user moves the cursor to the line where the copy is to go and then presses the F7 key. The program then inserts enough lines for the copy and does the copy.

The program to do this is:

```
43210    ' COPY BLOCK AND REDISPLAY SCREEN
43215    '
43220    GOSUB 43250                               ' COPY THE BLOCK
43225    GOSUB 42790                               ' REDISPLAY THE SCREEN
43230    RETURN
43235    '
43240    '
43245    '
43250    ' COPY A BLOCK OF TEXT
43255    IF MARK.END% = 0 OR MARK.START% = 0 THEN
            RETURN                                 ' ERROR
43260    ' ADJUST BLOCK MARKERS IF NECESSARY
43265    IF MARK.END% < MARK.START% THEN SWAP
            MARK.END%,MARK.START%                  ' START AT TOP
43270    X = MARK.END% - MARK.START% + 1           ' NUMBER OF LINES TO
                                                     COPY
43275    IF MLINES% + X > LAST% THEN MSG$ = "TEXT
```

```
              ARRAY FULL." : GOSUB 43045 : RETURN    ' MEMORY OVERFLOW
43280    MLINES% = MLINES% + X                        ' INCREMENT THE ARRAY
                                                         SIZE

43285    MSG$ + ""                                    ' CLEAR MEANS COPY OK
43290    IF LINES% = 1 THEN Y = 2 ELSE Y = LINES%
43295    FOR Z = MLINES% TO Y+X STEP -1               ' MOVE THE LINES DOWN
43300    LINES$(Z) = LINES$(Z-X)
43305    NEXT Z
43310    '
43315    ' ADJUST IF COPY IS TO LINE ABOVE BLOCK
43320    '
43325    IF MARK.START% >= Y THEN MARK.START% =
             MARK.START% + X                          ' ADJUST FOR INSERT
43330    IF MARK.END% >= Y THEN MARK.END% =
             MARK.END% + X                            ' DITTO
43335    FOR Z = 0 TO X - 1                           ' NOW COPY
43340    LINES$(Y + Z) =
             LINES$(MARK.START% + Z)
43345    NEXT Z
43350    RETURN
43355    '
43360    '
43365    '
```

TEST POINT

Enter several lines of text and set the beginning and ending markers.
Move the cursor to the destination and press the F7 key. Try this at
the beginning and the end of the text, with the end marks reversed
(end at the top).

Delete a Block of Text

When a large block of text needs to be removed, it is easier to use a
block-delete routine than to delete one line at a time.

The block-marker keys (F5 and shift F5) define the block, and the
shift F7 key is used to delete the block.

The routine compresses the array, clears the lines at the end of
the array, and resets the block marker variables. It is divided into two
parts: One does the deleting, and the other redisplays the screen. This

was done in case you want to delete a block but not redisplay the screen.

The listing is:

```
43370     ' DELETE BLOCK AND REDISPLAY SCREEN
43375     '
43380     GOSUB 43410                          ' DELETE THE BLOCK
43385     GOSUB 42790                          ' REDISPLAY THE SCREEN
43390     RETURN
43395     '
43400     '
43405     '
43410     ' DELETE A BLOCK OF TEXT
43415     IF MARK.START% = 0 OR MARK.END% = 0
              THEN RETURN                       ' MARKS NOT SET
43420     ' ADJUST MARKS SO MARK.START IS LESS
              THAN MARK.END
43425     IF MARK.END% < MARK.START% THEN SWAP
              MARK.END%,MARK.START%              ' START AT TOP
43430     X = MARK.END% - MARK.START% + 1
43435     FOR Z = MARK.END%+1 TO MLINES%        ' REMOVE THE BLOCK
43440     LINES$(Z-X) = LINES$(Z)
43445     NEXT Z
43450     FOR Z = (MLINES% - X + 1) TO MLINES%  ' CLEAR OLD LINES AT
                                                     END
43455     LINES$(Z) = ""
43460     NEXT Z
43465     MLINES% = MLINES% - X                 ' DECREMENT SIZE
                                                     COUNTER
43470     IF LINES% > MLINES% THEN LINES% =
              MLINES%                            ' CORRECT IF AT END
43475     MARK.START% = 0                       ' CLEAR THE MARKERS
43480     MARK.END% = 0
43485     RETURN
43490     '
43495     '
43500     '
```

TEST POINT

Enter several lines of text, mark the ends of the block, and delete the block by pressing the shift F7 key. Repeat at the beginning, the middle, and the end of the text.

Move a Block of Text

This subroutine uses the F6 key and portions of the COPY and DE-LETE subroutines. COPY is called first to duplicate the text at the new location, and then the DELETE routine is called to erase the original lines and redisplay the screen.

The MOVE subroutine is:

```
43165     ' MOVE A BLOCK OF TEXT
43170     '
43175     GOSUB 43250                          ' FIRST COPY THE BLOCK
43180     IF LEN(MSG$) = 0 THEN GOSUB 43410    ' IF OK THEN DELETE IT
43185     GOSUB 42790                          ' REDISPLAY THE SCREEN
43190     RETURN
43195     '
43200     '
43205     '
```

TEST POINT

Enter several lines of text and mark off the block. Position the cursor and press F6. Test this routine at both ends of the text and in the middle.

Word Wrap

Word wrap is a feature common to most word processors. When word wrap is turned on, the program senses when too much text has been entered on a line and automatically moves the last full word of text to the next line. Word wrapping allows the user to enter continuously text without having to be concerned about typing past the right edge of the screen.

In this text editor, when word wrap is on, the program will wrap at column 75 (line 42915). In other words, if the user enters more than 75 characters on a line the program will move the cursor and the last word to the next text line. When word wrap is off, the user can enter up to 250 characters on a line; when the right side of the screen is reached, the line editor will slide the text to the left.

Word wrapping requires several subroutines. The first toggles word wrap on and off (GOSUB 42905 and line 51198). The second subroutine (GOSUB 42940) does the splitting of the original line and the insertion of a blank line if necessary. It is called by a line to be added to the line editor (line 50560).

These routines are:

```
42905      ' TOGGLE WORD WRAP
42910      '
42915      IF WRAPSIZE% <> MAXSIZE% THEN
               WRAPSIZE% = MAXSIZE% ELSE
               WRAPSIZE% = 75                        ' SET SCREEN WRAP LINE
                                                         LENGTH
42920      RETURN
42925      '
42930      '
42935      '
42940      ' END OF LINE WORD WRAP SUBROUTINE
42945      '
42950      X = TXTSIZE% - 1
42955      IF MID$(ENTRY$,X,1) = " " THEN
               GOTO 42975                            ' SEARCH FOR SPACE
42960      X = X - 1                                 ' RIGHT TO LEFT SEARCH
42965      IF X = 0 THEN MSG$ = "NO WORD WRAP,
               NO BLANK ON LINE." : GOSUB
               43045 : RETURN                        ' ERROR
42970      GOTO 42955                                ' NOT AT FRONT SO KEEP
                                                         LOOKING
42975      WRAP$ = MID$(ENTRY$,X+1) + A.KEY$         ' GET THE LAST WORD
42980      LINES$(LINES%) =
               LEFT$(ENTRY$,X)                       ' TRUNCATE ORIGINAL LINE
42985      ENTRY$ = LINES$(LINES%)                   ' RESET ENTRY$
42990      LINES% = LINES% + 1                       ' STEP TO NEXT LINE
42995      IF LEN(LINES$(LINES%)) > 0 THEN
               GOSUB 42550                           ' INSERT BLANK LINE
43000      LINES$(LINES%) = WRAP$                    ' SET TO WRAP AROUND
43005      LINES% = LINES% - 1
43010      CTRL% = 1                                 ' MARK AS ENTER KEY
43015      PLACE% = 1
43020      GOSUB 42790                               ' REDISPLAY THE SCREEN
43025      RETURN
```

```
43030    '
43035    '
43040    '
```

TEST POINT

There are two boundary conditions: entering text at the end of the document and entering text in the middle of the document. First, press F9 and turn word wrap on; then enter several lines of text. The line should split as you try to type text past the edge of the screen. Next, move the cursor to the middle of the text and type. When the edge of the screen is reached, the line should split and a new line inserted after it. Finally, press F9 again and verify that word wrap is turned off.

SUMMARY OF PART 1

We have now created a simple text editor. This subroutine can be used as part of a larger program. There are countless applications where such a text editor can be used.

PART 2: COMPLETE TEXT EDITOR PROGRAM

The previous subroutines will edit text. It is up to the program that calls the text-editing subroutines to load or save the information edited by the user. In this section we add these routines to the text editor to make a stand-alone screen-text editor. We call this program the Complete Text Editor.

For a stand-alone text editor, we need to be able to send text to the printer, load and save text files to and from the diskette, or to quit and forget everything entered. These features are included in our program and are presented in detail in this part of the chapter. The following is a list of these additional commands and their explanations.

The commands consist of a complete word followed, in some commands, by a diskette file name or number. The command words are shown in Figure 3.5.

For example, to load and then edit a text file called Sales Letter, the user would enter

FIG. 3.5   Command Words

LOAD FN	Load diskette file called FN.
FILES	Display diskette directory.
SAVE FN	Save text to diskette file called FN.
DONE FN	Save text as FN and then QUIT.
PACK FN	Concatenate and save text file and then QUIT.
AUTO #	Turn auto line numbering on or off.
AUTO	Turn auto line numbering off.
EDIT #	Edit the text starting at line #.
F1 key	Return to current page in text editor.
PRINT	Print text file.
FORMAT	Pack and print text file.
CLEAR	Erase all text.
SEARCH field	Find field in text.
REPLACE field A> field B	At user option, replace field A with field B wherever found in text.
GLOBAL field A> field B	Same as replace except automatically replaces all occurrences.
WRAP	Toggle word wrap feature.
QUIT	Return to BASIC and clear the array.

        LOAD SALES LETTER

After the file is loaded, the user could enter either

        EDIT 1 or F1

to begin editing on line 1.

The flowchart for the complete text editor is shown in Figure 3.6. When a valid command is entered, the editor will execute the command and return to the command screen to await another command.

FIG. 3.6   Flowchart for the complete text editor

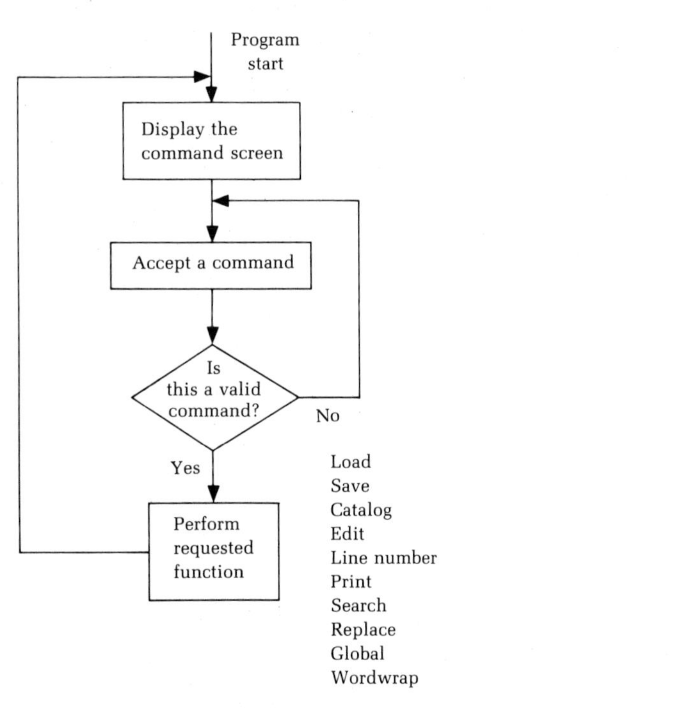

COMMAND DISPLAY AND PROCESSOR ROUTINE

The rather lengthy program listing that follows is the command display and processor routine. The display gives information on the current status of the text being edited and a HELP screen illustrating the available commands.

Before the display is shown, a FRE() command is executed. If there is a lot of text in the editor, this command can take several seconds to execute. The FRE() command is valuable for two reasons: First, it tells the user how much memory is available to accept additional text; second, it does some housekeeping of the memory for you.

The number of lines used and the auto line-numbering values, if any, are shown in the command area of the program. In addition, an explanation of the commands is displayed.

FRE (A$) The FRE(A$) command returns the amount of memory available to the user in characters or bytes. FRE(A$) performs the housekeeping task of clearing unused values from memory, freeing that space for current use.

BASIC automatically executes this command whenever memory becomes too full. Occasionally you may notice that a program has an unusual and unexplained delay; it is BASIC cleaning up memory.

Why, you may ask, does BASIC need to clean up memory? This is a result of the design of IBM BASIC. String variables are assigned new memory area whenever they are changed. The old area becomes unused (but not erased), and the memory becomes full. BASIC keeps track of this and does the cleanup automatically—unless we use FRE(A$).

The line editor is used to accept a command from the user. We have chosen to spell out the words completely and not abbreviate the commands; however, you have the option of adding abbreviations for the commands.

After a command is executed, the command screen is redisplayed and another command is accepted. Notice in the listing that follows that some of the commands return to line 40070 and some to line 40365, which is a branch to 40075. If the command just executed affects the amount of free memory, then another FRE(A$) command needs to be executed; otherwise, no FRE(A$) command is needed. As mentioned above, the FRE(A$) command can take some time to execute if there is a lot of text, and so we do not want to use the command unnecessarily and slow the program down unnecessarily.

The complete text editor line numbering begins with number 40000. Lines 100–130 initialize the text array and some constants. It is convenient to place initialization routines at the beginning of the program listing so that you always know where to find them.

The program listing for the command display and processor is as follows.

```
100       ' CHAPTER 3 - FULL SCREEN EDITOR
105       '
110       ON ERROR GOTO 60000              ' STANDARD ERROR
                                             PROCESSING
115       LAST% = 1000                     ' NUMBER OF LINES OF
                                             TEXT
120       DIM LINES$(LAST%)                ' TEXT ARRAY. NOTE:
                                             COMPILER REQUIRES
                                             NUMBER
125       '
130       '
40000     ' EDITOR * COMPLETE TEXT EDITOR WITH
            COMMAND AREA
40005     '
40010     ' USES THE LINE EDITOR WITH A FEW
            ADDITIONAL EXIT KEYS
40015     '
40020     ' COMMAND AREA ROUTINE
40025     '
40030     MLINES% = 1                      ' SET THE MAX LINE
                                             COUNTER
40035     GOSUB 42845                      ' CLEAR VARIABLES
40040     KEY OFF
40045     FOR X = 1 TO 10
40050     KEY X,""                         ' CLEAR THE FUNCTION
                                             KEYS
40055     NEXT X
40060     MAXSIZE% = 250                   ' MAXIMUM LINE LENGTH
```

```
40065    WRAPSIZE% = MAXSIZE%                              ' START WITH WORD WRAP
                                                               OFF
40070    FX = FRE(ENTRY$)                                  ' CLEAR THE MEMORY
40075    CLS
40080    PRINT "EDITOR COMMAND AREA FREE"; FX              ' TITLE AND FREE MEMORY
40085    PRINT "LINES USED ";MLINES%;" ON LINE
             ";LINES%;
40090    IF ANUM% > 0 THEN PRINT "AUTO ";ANUM%;
40095    IF WRAPSIZE% <> MAXSIZE% THEN PRINT
             " WORD WRAP";
40100    PRINT : PRINT
40105    PRINT ">";
40110    PRINT
40115    PRINT
40120    PRINT "LOAD NAME      LOAD A TEXT FILE            CLEAR ERASE
                                                               MEMORY"
40125    PRINT "FILES         DISPLAY DISK
                                 DIRECTORY"
40130    PRINT
40135    PRINT "EDIT ##       EDIT LINE NUMBER            SEARCH FIELD"
40140    PRINT "F1            EDIT CURRENT LINE NUMBER     REPLACE FIELD>
                                                             FIELD"
40145    PRINT "                                          GLOBAL FIELD>
                                                             FIELD"
40150    PRINT "AUTO ##       AUTO LINE NUMBER"
40155    PRINT "AUTO          TURN OFF LINE               WRAP      TOGGLE
                                 NUMBERING                    WORD WRAP"
40160    PRINT
40165    PRINT "SAVE NAME     SAVE THE TEXT FILE"
40170    PRINT "DONE NAME     SAVE AND EXIT TO
                                 BASIC"
40175    PRINT "PACK NAME     PACK, SAVE AND EXIT"
40180    PRINT
40185    PRINT "PRINT         PRINT TEXT FILE"
40190    PRINT "FORMAT        PACK AND PRINT TEXT
                                 FILE"
40195    PRINT
40200    PRINT "QUIT          ABANDON AND EXIT TO BASIC"
40205    MASK$ = "a"                                       ' SET THE MASK
40210    ENTRY$ = ""                                       ' CLEAR IT
40215    ROW% = 4                                          ' COMMAND INPUT LINE
40220    COL% = 3
40225    PLACE% = 1                                        ' EDITOR SETS PLACE%
40230    FILL$ = " "
```

```
40235    GOSUB 50105                              ' ENTER LINE EDITOR AT
                                                    HELP%=0 LINE

40240    IF HELP% <> 0 THEN HELP$ =
         "CHAP3A.HLP" : GOSUB 48000 : GOTO
         40060                                    ' PROCESS HELP REQUEST
                                                    THEN REDISPLAY
40245    IF CTRL% = 27 THEN ENTRY$ = "EDIT"       ' F1 MEANS EDIT TEXT
40250    X = INSTR(1,ENTRY$," ")                  'LOOK FOR END OF
                                                    COMMAND
40255    IF X = 0 THEN X = LEN(ENTRY$)
40260    IF X = 0 THEN GOTO 40075                 ' NOTHING IN ENTRY$
40265    FOR Y = 1 TO X                           ' FORCE THE COMMAND
                                                    INTO UPPER CASE
40270            Z = ASC(MID$(ENTRY$,Y,1))        ' GET ONE LETTER
40275            IF Z >= 97 AND Z <= 122 THEN
                    MID$(ENTRY$,Y,1) =
                    CHR$(Z-32)                     ' SHIFT THE CASE
40280    NEXT Y
40285    IF LEFT$(ENTRY$,4) = "AUTO" THEN
            GOSUB 40380 : GOTO 40365              ' AUTO NUMBER
40295    IF LEFT$(ENTRY$,4) = "EDIT" OR CTRL% =
            27 THEN GOSUB 40430: GOTO 40070       ' EDIT THE TEXT
40300    IF LEFT$(ENTRY$,4) = "DONE" THEN GOTO
            40645                                  ' SAVE AND END
40305    IF LEFT$(ENTRY$,4) = "LOAD" THEN
            GOSUB 40490: GOTO 40070               ' LOAD FILE
40310    IF LEFT$(ENTRY$,5) = "FILES" THEN
            GOSUB 40905 : GOTO 40365              ' DISPLAY A DIRECTORY
40315    IF LEFT$(ENTRY$,4) = "SAVE" THEN
            GOSUB 40730 : GOTO 40365              ' SAVE THE TEXT
40320    IF LEFT$(ENTRY$,4) = "PACK" THEN
            GOSUB 40680 : CLS : END               ' PACK,SAVE,EXIT
40325    IF LEFT$(ENTRY$,5) = "PRINT" THEN
            PRT% = 1: GOSUB 40730 : GOTO 40365    ' PRINT AS IS
40330    IF LEFT$(ENTRY$,6) = "FORMAT" THEN
            PRT% = 1: GOSUB 40680: CLS : END      ' PACK PRINT AND EXIT
40335    IF LEFT$(ENTRY$,6) = "SEARCH" THEN
            REPLACE% = 0 : GOSUB 41085 : GOTO
            40365                                  ' SEARCH FOR FIELD
40340    IF LEFT$(ENTRY$,7) = "REPLACE" THEN
            REPLACE% = 1 : GOSUB 41085 :
            REPLACE% = 0 : GOTO 40365             ' REPLACE STRINGS
40345    IF LEFT$(ENTRY$,6) = "GLOBAL" THEN
            GOSUB 40975 : GOTO 40365              ' GLOBAL EXCHANGE
```

```
40350    IF LEFT$(ENTRY$,5) = "CLEAR" THEN
             CLEAR : GOTO 100                          ' CLEAR MEMORY
40355    IF LEFT$(ENTRY$,4) = "WRAP" THEN
             GOSUB 42905                                ' GOTO 40340 ' WORD
                                                                WRAP TOGGLE
40360    IF LEFT$(ENTRY$,4) = "QUIT" THEN CLS :
             END                                        ' CLEAR AND QUIT
40365    GOTO 40075                                     ' TRY AGAIN
40370    ' ***********************************************
```

Various aspects of the command display routine are described in the subsections that follow.

TEST POINT

After RUN (CR) is entered, the screen should clear, the command area should be displayed, and the cursor should be positioned next to the > symbol. The editor is now waiting for a command. The only command that can be executed at this time is QUIT. Try it to verify that at least this command works. As you can see from line 40360, QUIT clears the screen and stops execution.

The Edit Command

The EDIT command, or the F1 key, is used to toggle between the command area and the text editor. The F1 key is used to be consistent with using the F1 key to exit the text editor. The EDIT command has two modes: with or without a line number. If the user knows which line number is to be edited, then EDIT ## is used, where ## is the line to be edited. If the current text window is desired, the user does not need to enter a line number.

The program detects which method is used by checking the length of the command entered. If it is four characters long, then only EDIT has been entered. If it is longer than four characters, a number must be extracted from ENTRY$. This number is extracted by using a VAL() command. If the value (line number) does not fall within the range of line numbers available, then the user is returned to the command area and gets to try again.

VAL() The VAL() command searches the assigned string for a numerical value and returns that value.

EXAMPLE

```
5000    HAZEL$="AGE 12"
5100    NUMBER=VAL(MID$(HAZEL$,4))
5200    PRINT NUMBER
RUN
12
```

In this example we extract a value from the string HAZEL$ with VAL(), starting at character position 4 (use of MID$).

The EDIT command routine is as follows.

```
40430      ' EDIT THE TEXT
40435      '
40440      IF LEN (ENTRY$) = 4 THEN GOSUB
               42000: RETURN                    ' START AT CURRENT LINE NUMBER
40445      FIRST% = VAL (MID$
               (ENTRY$,5))                       ' LINE NUMBER USER WANTS TO
                                                   EDIT
40450      IF FIRST% < 1 THEN FIRST% = 1
40455      LINES% = FIRST%
40460      LROW% = 1                            ' START AT TOP LINE
40465      LCOL% = 1                            ' START IN FIRST COLUMN
40470      GOSUB 42000                          ' TEXT EDITOR
40475      RETURN
40480      ' *********************************
40485      '
```

TEST POINT

After the EDIT command routine is entered, you will be able to move back and forth between the command area and the editor. Either enter EDIT (CR) or press the F1 key. The screen should clear, and you should be able to enter and edit text. Use the F1 key when you wish to exit the editor and return to the command area. Once in the command area, press the F1 key again to be sure that the editor returns the correct display. You are rapidly approaching an operational text-editing system.

Text-Saving and Printing Subroutine

Other important capabilities are saving and printing the text that has been entered or edited. This subroutine utilizes two flag variables to allow the saving and printing functions to be combined. The commands implemented in this subroutine are SAVE, DONE, PACK, PRINT, and FORMAT.

OPEN   The OPEN command is used to open files for output or disk access. The OPEN command has many options, and so we suggest you review your BASIC manual for a detailed definition. When using text files, the OPEN statement is always used in combination with either INPUT # C,A$ or PRINT # C,A$, where C is the "channel number" of the opened file and A$ is the string variable to be read or written to diskette.

It is also possible to open a communications port on your serial interface board. The IBM BASIC is designed to support printing to a parallel printer port using the LPRINT statement; but if we wish to print directly to a printer connected to a serial port, then we must open the port.

EXAMPLE

```
OPEN "CHAP7.RPT" FOR OUTPUT AS #1
```

will allow you to print data to a file named CHAP7.RPT.

```
OPEN "COM1:1200,N,8,1,CS10000,DS,LF" FOR OUTPUT AS #1
```

will allow you to send data to a serial printer connected to com port 1.

The text-saving or printing routine that follows allows text to be saved or printed in two different formats. In the first format the text is saved or printed exactly as it looks on the screen. In the second format the continuation symbols are removed, and the text is saved or printed in packed, or concatenated, form. For the second format the text array (LINES$) is processed looking for an _ (underscore) symbol as the last character of a line. When an _ is found, the current line and the next line are combined, or concatenated. After the entire array is processed, it is written to diskette using the same routine used by the first save format.

The underscore symbol is used as the continuation line symbol within the text editor. When you are typing a long piece of text within the editor, you can use an underscore as the last character on a line to continue the text to the next line. The PACK command later removes the underscore symbols and saves the text.

When two lines are concatenated, all leading spaces in the second line are removed. The leading spaces are there to indent the text and make it more legible. If you want spaces at this point in the concatenated line, they must be added in front of the underscore symbol.

After all the text has been written to the diskette or the printer, it is necessary to CLOSE the file. Closing the file must be done to ensure that the text has actually been written to the disk. When a line is printed or written to diskette, BASIC does not immediately put it on the diskette. The text first goes to a temporary storage location in memory (commonly called a *buffer*). This buffer is 512 bytes long; which is equivalent in size to one sector on the disk. Rather than write the text to the disk at every PRINT command (which is time-consuming), BASIC waits until the buffer is full before it writes. This feature is included for efficiency; it is done automatically as data are sent to or retrieved from the disk. (See the BASIC manual for the full explanation of buffering.)

What happens if the buffer is not completely filled and nothing else is to be sent to the diskette? Well, BASIC waits for you to finish filling the buffer, not realizing that you are done. If the computer is turned off, that last partial buffer will never make it to the diskette. The CLOSE command is used to tell the computer that you have finished using that diskette file and to write the final buffer to diskette.

CLOSE   The CLOSE command forces the remaining characters in the

file buffer to diskette. There are two modes: with and without a
file number. With a file number, only that file is closed. Without
a file number, all files are closed.

EXAMPLE

```
5000    OPEN ENTRY$ FOR OUTPUT AS #1
5100    CLOSE #1
```

The following subroutine saves text on a diskette.

```
40645    ' SAVE TEXT AND END
40650    '
40655    GOSUB 40730                              ' SAVE THE TEXT
40660    CLS
40665    END
40670    ' ***********************************
40675    '

40680    ' CONCATENATE AND SAVE FILE
40685    '
40690    Y = 0
40695    FOR X = 1 TO MLINES%
40700        Y = Y + 1
40705        LINES$(Y) = LINES$(X)                ' PACK THE ARRAY
40710        IF RIGHT$ (LINES$(X),1) =
                "_" THEN GOSUB 40860: GOTO 40715
40715    NEXT X
40720    MLINES% = Y                              ' NEW MAX LINE COUNT
40725    '
40730    ' SAVE THE TEXT
40735    '
40740    ENTRY$ = MID$(ENTRY$,6)                  ' GET THE FILE NAME
40745    IF LEN(ENTRY$) = 0 THEN ENTRY$ =
                FILE.NAME$                        ' USE LOAD NAME
40750    IF LEN(ENTRY$) = 0 THEN PRINT
                CHR$(7) : ENTRY$ = "TEMP.TXT"     ' TEMP NAME
40755    '
40760    '
40765    '                                        '
40770    '                                        '
```

```
40775      IF PRT% > 0 THEN GOTO 40820        ' PRINT IT DON'T WRITE
                                                  TO DISK
40780      OPEN ENTRY$ FOR OUTPUT AS #1       ' OPEN IT SO WE CAN KILL
                                                  IT
40785      CLOSE #1
40790      KILL ENTRY$                        ' ERASE THE FILE
40795      OPEN ENTRY$ FOR OUTPUT AS #1
40800      '
40805      '
40810      '
40815      '
40820      FOR X = 1 TO MLINES%
40825      IF PRT% = 0 THEN PRINT#1,LINES$(X)
              ELSE LPRINT LINES$(X)            ' FOR BOTH SAVE AND
                                                  PRINT WITH COMM PORT
40830      NEXT X
40835      IF PRT% > 0 THEN PRT% =
              0 :LPRINT CHR$(12)               ' SET CRT AND FORM FEED
40840      CLOSE #1
40845      RETURN
40850      ' *******************************
40855      '
40860      ' CONCATENATE IT
40865      IF MID$ (LINES$(X + 1),1,1) = " " THEN
              LINES$(X + 1) = MID$ (LINES$(X +
              1),2): GOTO 40865                ' STRIP SPACES
40870      XX = LEN (LINES$(Y)) - 1
40875      LINES$(Y) = LEFT$ (LINES$(Y),XX) +
              LINES$(X + 1)                     ' STRIP '_' AND PACK
40880      X = X + 1
40885      IF RIGHT$ (LINES$(Y),1) = "_" THEN
              GOTO 40860                        ' CONTINUE PACKING IF
                                                  NECESSARY
40890      RETURN
40895      '
40900      ' *********************************
```

TEST POINT

This test is the first part of a two-part test. (The second part occurs
after the next subsection.) Edit some text, and then save it by entering
SAVE TEST.TXT (CR). At this point, to determine what was written

to diskette, you will have to exit the program and BASIC (do not forget to save the program) and, once in DOS, enter

```
TYPE TEST.TXT (CR)
```

The file should appear just as you entered it.

Text-Loading Subroutine

Text is written as a sequential text file by using a PRINT statement. In contrast, an INPUT command is used to read the text file.
The following routine reads or loads text into the editor.

```
40490     ' LOAD A TEXT FILE
40495     '
40500     ENTRY$ = MID$(ENTRY$,6)
40505     IF LEN(ENTRY$) = 0 THEN RETURN         ' THE USER FORGOT THE
                                                       NAME
40510     FILE.NAME$ = ENTRY$                    ' SAVE FOR LATER USE
40515     ' LOOK UP THE FILE ON THE DISK FIRST
40520     ON ERROR GOTO 40590                    ' SET ALTERNATIVE ERROR
                                                       POINT
40525     OPEN ENTRY$ FOR INPUT AS #1
40530     ON ERROR GOTO 60000                    ' RESTORE NORMAL ERROR
                                                       POINT
40535     IF MLINES% >= LAST% THEN MSG$ =
              "TEXT ARRAY FULL." : GOSUB
              43045 : GOTO 40575                  ' OVERFLOW OF MEMORY
40540     IF LINES% < MLINES% THEN GOSUB
              42550                               ' INSERT BLANK LINE FIRST
40545     LINE INPUT#1, LINES$(LINES%)           ' FETCH A LINE FROM THE
                                                       DISK
40550     IF EOF(1) THEN GOTO 40575              ' ALL DONE
40555     LINES% = LINES% + 1
40560     IF LINES% >= MLINES% THEN MLINES% = MLINES% + 1
40565     IF MLINES% >= LAST% THEN MSG$ =
              "TEXT ARRAY FULL." : GOSUB
              43045 : GOTO 40575                  ' OVERFLOW OF MEMORY
40570     GOTO 40540
40575     CLOSE #1
40580     GOSUB 42845                            ' RESET ALL THE POINTERS
40585     RETURN
```

```
40590      '
40595      RESUME 40600                          ' CLEAR THE ERROR FLAG
                                                   AND CONTINUE
40600      ON ERROR GOTO 60000                   ' RESTORE ERROR
                                                   PROCESSING TO NORMAL
                                                   LINE
40605      MSG$ = "FILE " + ENTRY$ + " NOT FOUND."
40610      GOSUB 43045                           ' DISPLAY ERROR MSG
40615      RETURN
40620      '
40625      '
40630      ' *********************************
40635      '
40640      '
```

This routine first verifies that the requested file is on diskette.
IBM BASIC has the annoying habit of giving you a system error if it is
told to open a nonexistant file for input. We can, however, use this to
our advantage by creating a file "lookup" routine using the ONERROR
and RESUME statements.

You may recall that at the start of this program (line 110) we
have the command ONERROR GOTO 60000, where 60000 is the beginning of our standard error processing routine. We change this in line
40520 to

```
40520   ONERROR GOTO 40590
```

On the next line (line 40525) we OPEN the file to be loaded. If the file
is there, it is opened and the program proceeds to the next line (line
40530), which again sets the ONERROR condition to line 60000. If,
however, the file to be opened does not exist, then we will have an
error and BASIC will branch to line 40590.

The subroutine at 40590 does several things. First, it clears the error condition by using the RESUME 40600 statement. Second, it sets
the error branch back to 60000 and prints an error message for the
user. Finally, it RETURNS to the main menu.

This technique of anticipating errors and having the program automatically recover can be used in many other ways. This is another
example of a user-friendly feature.

As part of this routine we used a rather unconventional and poor programming technique. We used a GOTO (ONERROR GOTO) to get a program segment that exited with a RETURN. In this case it is not a serious violation, but we have seen this carried to an extreme by others. There are people who use both GOTO and GOSUB to get to the same routine and then use conditionals to decide whether they exit with another GOTO or a RETURN. This is a bad practice; it destroys the program flow and does not allow for predictable operation of the subroutines. Except in rare cases, you should use GOSUB and not GOTO to get to subroutines. It is also a good practice to minimize the number of GOTOs you use because their excessive use makes the program flow difficult to follow and understand.

If the diskette file is being added into the middle of the text array, then the program inserts a new line for each line added. This feature can cause the loading of large files to take a long time because many lines will have to be inserted and the text moved.

After every line is added, the program determines whether the array is full. If full, an error message is printed and the routine exits. Otherwise, the routine proceeds to add the next line.

The EOF (end of file) command is used to test for the end of the diskette file.

TEST POINT

The test here is to load the file saved in the previous test point. To be sure that all the variables are cleared, enter QUIT, RUN the program, and then enter LOAD TEST.TXT (CR). Press F1, and the screen should display the text previously saved. If it does not, determine whether the error occurred in the load or the save routine. Check the save routine first.

Auto Line Numbering

Auto line numbering is a convenience feature for editing BASIC programs with the editor. The routine consists of two sections: the switch section, which turns the line numbering feature on and off, and the actual line-numbering routine.

The AUTO command works differently from the AUTO command in BASIC. In BASIC, line numbering is started by entering AUTO (CR) and is stopped by pressing Control Break. Since we cannot press Control Break (pressing this key combination will stop the program), we must turn line numbering on and off differently. When the AUTO command is entered without a number or with the number 0, then line numbering will be turned off. Otherwise, line numbering will begin with the line number entered.

When line numbering is turned on, the editor calls the numbering routine with every key (see line 50550). The numbering routine tests to see if a space was entered (ASCII value 32) as the first character. If a space was not entered or if numbering is turned off, the key will be accepted as normal and the routine will return to the caller. If a space is entered and line numbering is on, a line is created by using the current line number. Next, the line number is incremented. We prefer to increment by five, but you can select any value. It is not advisable to increment by one unless you write error-free programs.

A new MASK$ character, N, has been added (line 50333) to support auto numbering.

The routine for auto line numbering is as follows.

```
40380     ' SET THE AUTO NUMBER SWITCH
40385     ' FLIP ITS VALUE
40390     '
40395     TXTSIZE% = LEN (ENTRY$)
40400     IF TXTSIZE% = 4 THEN ANUM% = 0: RETURN      ' TURN OFF AUTO NUM
40405     ENTRY$ = MID$ (ENTRY$,5)                    ' GET THE VALUE
40410     ANUM% = VAL (ENTRY$)
40415     RETURN
40420     ' ********************************************
40425     '
```

TEST POINT

In the command area, turn auto line numbering on by using the command

```
AUTO 100 (CR)
```

Press the F1 key to move to the editor. Once in the editor, press the space bar. The number 100 should appear, and the cursor should be positioned at the first tab stop. Enter some text and press ENTER. On the second line, press the space bar again. The number 105 should appear with the cursor at the first tab stop.

To turn auto line numbering off, return to the command area and enter

```
AUTO (CR)
```

Return to the editor and verify that auto numbering has turned off.

Directory

There is nothing more annoying than being in a program and discovering that you have forgotten the name of a file or what diskette is in the disk drive. The FILES command saves time and frustration because it eliminates the need to exit the program to list a directory. This feature is user friendly. The editor uses everything the user enters on the command line as a command. This feature can be used for any diskette. For example, Entering FILES B: will display a directory of drive B.

FILES (DIRECTORY) The FILES command lists diskette directory entries.

The INPUT command at the end of the routine is provided to allow the user time to read the last group of file names.

The FILES routine is as follows.

```
40905    ' CATALOG DISK
40910    '
40915    CLS                                       ' CLEAR SCREEN
40920    X = INSTR(1,ENTRY$,".")                   ' LOOK FOR . IN FILE
                                                     NAME
40925    IF LEN(ENTRY$) > 5 AND X = 0 THEN ENTRY$
            =ENTRY$ + "*.*"                         ' IN CASE THEY FORGOT
40930    IF LEN(ENTRY$) = 5 THEN FILES ELSE
```

```
                FILES MID$(ENTRY$,6)
40935   PRINT
40940   PRINT
40945   INPUT "PRESS ENTER TO CONTINUE
            ";ENTRY$                            ' PAUSE AT BOTTOM
40950   RETURN
40955   ' ********************************
40960   '
40965   '
40970   '
```

TEST POINT

When you type in FILES (CR) from the command area, the current
drive should activate and the directory should appear on the screen.
Try this again using another diskette-drive name.

Search and Replace

These functions are so closely related they are combined into one
large routine. The flowchart for them is shown in Figure 3.7.

The SEARCH command looks for the desired field, beginning at
the cursor's position in the text file. The REPLACE command first
does a SEARCH, and if a match is found, it pauses to give the user
the option of changing the field or not. For both commands, the F8
key is used to advance the cursor to the next match.

The program is:

```
41085   ' THE SEARCH AND REPLACE ROUTINES
41090   '
41095   '
41100   X = INSTR(8,ENTRY$,">")                 ' NEEDED FOR REPLACE
41105   IF X = 0 AND REPLACE% = 1 THEN MSG$ =
            "MISSING > SYMBOL IN REPLACE" :
            GOSUB 43045 : RETURN                 ' TEST FOR ERROR AND
                                                   DISPLAY MESSAGE
41110   IF REPLACE% = 0 THEN SEARCH$ =
            MID$(ENTRY$,8) ELSE SEARCH$ =
            MID$(ENTRY$,9,(X-9)) : REPLACE$ =
```

```
                   MID$(ENTRY$,X+1)                    ' SET UP SEARCH AND
                                                         REPLACE
41115    REPLEN% = LEN(SEARCH$)                        ' FOR REPLACE USE
41120    PASS% = 0                                     ' MARK AS IN COMMAND
                                                         AREA

41125    '
41130    ' ENTRY POINT FOR NEXT REQUEST
41135    '
41140    GOSUB 41290                                   ' SEARCH FORWARD FOR
                                                         MATCH

41145    IF SEARCH% = 0 THEN MSG$ = "NO MATCH
            FOUND." : GOSUB 43045 : GOSUB
            42845 : RETURN                             ' EXIT
41150    '
41155    ' IF A MATCH IS FOUND THEN WE NEED TO
            DISPLAY THE SCREEN AND EDIT IT.
41160    '
41165    PLACE% = SEARCH%                              ' POSITION OVER MATCH
41170    FRONT% = 1                                    ' RESET JUST IN CASE
41175    IF (LINES% <= FIRST% + 23) AND (PASS% <>
            0) THEN LROW% = LINES% - FIRST%
            + 1 : GOSUB 42060 : GOTO 41235            ' ON CURRENT SCREEN
                                                         ALLOW EDIT
41180    '
41185    ' NOT ON CURRENT SCREEN SO REDISPLAY

41190    '
41195    FIRST% = LINES% - 4                           ' PUT LINE OF INTEREST
                                                         NEAR TOP
41200    IF FIRST% < 1 THEN FIRST% = 1                 ' ERROR CHECK
41205    LROW% = LINES% - FIRST% + 1
41210    LCOL% = 1
41215    PASS% = 1                                     ' MARK THAT SCREEN
                                                         DISPLAYED
41220    GOSUB 42000                                   ' REDISPLAY AND EDIT
41225    '
41230    ' RETURNS HERE AFTER EDIT IF ESC, NEXT OR
            REPLACE KEYS ARE STRUCK
41235    '
41240    IF CTRL% = 27 THEN GOSUB 42845 : RETURN       ' WANT TO GO TO COMMAND
                                                         AREA
41245    IF CTRL% = 28 THEN LINES% =LINES% + 1 :
            GOTO 41130                                 ' NEXT KEY SEARCH
41250    ' HERE IF CTRL% = 29, REPLACE KEY
```

FIG. 3.7 Flow chart for Search and Replace Routines

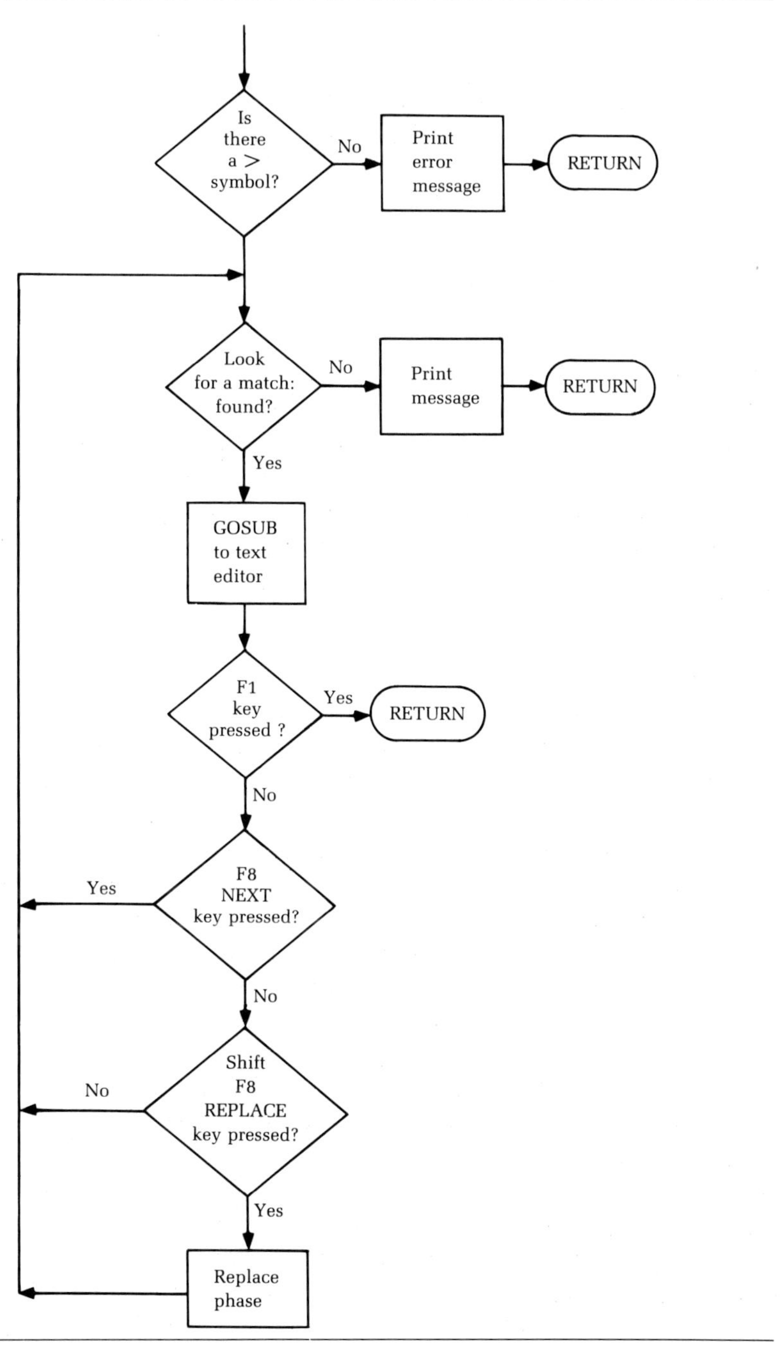

```
41255    IF SEARCH%=1 THEN LINES$(LINES%) =
            REPLACE$ +
            MID$(LINES$(LINES%),SEARCH% +
            REPLEN%) ELSE LINES$(LINES%) =
            LEFT$(LINES$(LINES%),SEARCH%-1) +
            REPLACE$ +
            MID$(LINES$(LINES%),SEARCH% +
            REPLEN%)                                ' DO REPLACEMENT
41260    ENTRY$ = LINES$(LINES%)                    ' REDISPLAY FIELD
41265    GOSUB 52660                                ' DISPLAY ENTRY$
41270    LINES% = LINES% + 1                        ' STEP TO NEXT LINE FOR
                                                        SEARCH
41275    GOTO 41130                                 ' SEARCH FOR NEXT MATCH
41280    '
41285    '
41290    ' SEARCH FOR A STRING
41295    '
41300    IF LINES% > MLINES% THEN SEARCH% = 0 :
            RETURN                                  ' ALL DONE
41305    SEARCH% =
            INSTR(1,LINES$(LINES%),SEARCH$)         ' LOOK FOR THE STRING
41310    IF SEARCH% <> 0 THEN RETURN                ' FOUND A MATCH
41315    LINES% = LINES% + 1                        ' SKIP TO NEXT LINE
41320    GOTO 41290                                 ' AND CONTINUE SEARCH
41325    '
41330    '
41335    '
```

After a match is found, the routine sets pointers and then does a GOSUB 42000, to the text editor subroutine. Once in the text editor the users are free to do anything they wish. The program will return to this routine after an F1, F8, or shift F8 key is pressed. F1 will cause the SEARCH/REPLACE subroutine to exit to the command area. The F8 key will advance the cursor to the next match. Shift F8 will cause the old field to be replaced with the new field.

TEST POINT

Enter several lines of text and position the cursor on the first line. Press F1 and return to the command area. Now SEARCH for a word or phrase, and press the NEXT key (F8) until no matches are found and the routine returns to the command area. Repeat this, but edit the text and move the cursor before pressing the NEXT key. SEARCH for a field that does not exist. After you verify that SEARCH is working, repeat the above process for REPLACE.

Global

The GLOBAL command is basically the REPLACE command without the user-change option. In other words, GLOBAL will replace all occurrences of a match.

After the SEARCH and REPLACE variables are filled, the SEARCH subroutine (line 41290) is used to find a match. If a match is found, it is replaced and a counter is incremented and displayed for the user's benefit.

Only one occurrence of a match is changed per line. If there is more than one possible match on a line, then only the first one is changed.

The GLOBAL subroutine is:

```
40975     ' GLOBAL SEARCH AND REPLACE ROUTINE
40980     '
40985     Z = 0                                   ' RESET MATCH COUNTER
40990     X = INSTR(8,ENTRY$,">")                 ' LOOK FOR DELIMITER
40995     IF X = 0 THEN RETURN
41000     LOCATE 25,1 : PRINT Z,"MATCHES FOUND.";
41005     SEARCH$ = MID$(ENTRY$,8,(X-8))
41010     REPLACE$ = MID$(ENTRY$,X+1)             ' REPLACEMENT
41015     REPLEN% = LEN(SEARCH$)                  ' SET FOR FUTURE USE
41020     GOSUB 41290                             ' USE SEARCH ROUTINE TO
                                                  '     FIND STRING
41025     IF SEARCH% = 0 THEN FOR X = 1 TO 1000 :
              NEXT : GOSUB 42845 : RETURN         ' PAUSE, RESET POINTERS
                                                  '     AND RETURN
41030     '
41035     ' FOUND A MATCH SO REPLACE IT
41040     '
41045     IF SEARCH%=1 THEN LINES$(LINES%) =
              REPLACE$ +
              MID$(LINES$(LINES%),SEARCH% +
              REPLEN%) ELSE LINES$(LINES%) =
```

```
                    LEFT$(LINES$(LINES%),SEARCH%-1)
                    + REPLACE$ +
                    MID$(LINES$(LINES%),SEARCH% +
                    REPLEN%)                         ' DO REPLACEMENT
41050       Z = Z + 1                                ' INCREMENT CHANGE
                                                       COUNTER
41055       LOCATE 25,1 : PRINT Z;                   ' AND DISPLAY IT
41060       LINES% = LINES% + 1                      ' STEP TO NEXT LINE
41065       GOTO 41020                               ' CONTINUE LOOKING
41070       '
41075       '
41080       '
```

TEST POINT

Enter some duplicate words on several lines of text and position the
cursor at the top of the screen. Exit to the command area and select
the GLOBAL option. Return to the edit area and see if all the variables were correctly replaced. Repeat the process by changing the
field again.

Clear

CLEAR is a simple command that effectively restarts the editor and
erases all the text currently in memory. The entire command is contained in line 40350.

```
40350   IF LEFT$(ENTRY$,1) =
            "CLEAR" THEN CLEAR : GOTO 100      ' CLEAR MEMORY
```

CLEAR CLEAR frees up all memory used for data shortage but does
       not erase the program. After a CLEAR statement is executed, you
       should branch to the beginning of the program to restart and re-
       define all variables and arrays.

Quit

The command QUIT will allow the user to exit the editor without saving any of the edited text. The command is contained in line 40360.

```
40360   IF LEFT$(ENTRY$,1) = "QUIT" THEN CLS : END    ' CLEAR AND QUIT
```

Word Wrap

The WORD WRAP command does the same thing as the F9 key. It toggles word wrapping on and off. The word wrap command lines are contained in 40095 and 40355. Line 40095 prints "WORD WRAP" on the first line of the screen if word wrapping is turned on. Line 40355 calls the word wrap toggle subroutine (GOSUB 42905).

```
40095   IF WRAPSIZE% <> MAXSIZE% THEN PRINT "WORD WRAP";

40355   IF LEFT$(ENTRY$,1) =
            "WRAP" THEN GOSUB 42905    ' WORD WRAP TOGGLE
```

ENHANCEMENTS

Enhancements can be made to this program by implementing either more commands in the command mode or special key commands in the text editor. By looking at some of the word processors on the market, you may find additional features to add. Remember, however, that as more features are added, the amount of memory available for text becomes smaller, and so the size of your largest possible document shrinks.

EDITING PROGRAMS

Working your way through the rest of the book will be much easier. Now you can use the editor, which you just typed in and tested for errors, for the entry of all the subsequent programs.

Keep in mind that the files you type in with the editor are saved as text files. To load a text file into BASIC, use either the commands MERGE or LOAD. During a MERGE or LOAD, BASIC treats each line of the text file as though it were being typed at the keyboard.

Occasionally as a program is loaded, SYNTAX ERROR message will be printed on the screen. This error means that the computer has encountered an illegal command and that this line was not accepted. You will have to correct the line by comparing a listing of the original text file with the accepted program listing.

If you use continuation symbols in your text, then you must save the file by using the PACK command to strip out the continuation symbols. When using PACK, remember to use a file name different from the one used with SAVE; otherwise, you will erase the original unpacked text file.

USER INSTRUCTIONS

The user instructions presented throughout this book are included as examples of simple documentation. As we stated previously, you should always document your programs. As you can see from these examples, even a short set of written instructions can be helpful.

The following sections cover the entry and editing of text, using the command area; creating new documents; saving, loading, and merging documents; searching, replacing, and printing documents.

Entering and Editing Text in the Text Editor

With the text editor you are able to enter and edit text. You may move the cursor up or down from line to line or page to page. You can insert blank lines or delete lines anywhere in the text, and you can enter lines longer than the screen width.

The text editor uses all the commands of the line editor plus several additional ones. The newly added commands and their keys are as follows.

Enter (carriage return)	Advance cursor to front of next line.
Down arrow	Move cursor down one line.
Up arrow	Move cursor up one line.

Page down	Advance cursor down 24 lines.
Page up	Move cursor up 24 lines.
Home	Return to first line of text.
Control home	Advance cursor to last page of text.
F3	Insert blank line.
Shift F3	Delete current line.
F4	Divide current line. Text to right of cursor moved to next line.
Shift F4	Concatenate lines.
F5	Mark start of block.
Shift F5	Mark end of block.
F6	Move block to cursor.
Shift F6	Save block to diskette.
F7	Duplicate block at cursor.
Shift F7	Delete block.
F8	Advance cursor to next occurence.
Shift F8	Replace old phrase with new phrase.
F9	Word wrap toggle.

Command Area

In addition to being able to enter and edit text, the screen editor is capable of loading and saving text to the diskette or sending it to the printer. The commands consist of a complete word followed, in some commands, by a diskette file name.

The command words are as follows.

LOAD FN	Load diskette file called FN.
FILES	Display diskette directory.
SAVE FN	Save text to diskette file called FN.

DONE FN	Save text as FN and then QUIT.
PACK FN	Concatenate and save text file and then QUIT.
AUTO #	Turn auto line numbering on or off.
AUTO	Turn auto line numbering off.
EDIT #	Edit the text starting at line #.
F1 KEY	Return to current page in text editor.
PRINT	Print text file.
FORMAT	Pack and print text file.
CLEAR	Erase all text.
SEARCH field	Find field in text.
REPLACE field A> field B	At user option, replace field A with field B wherever found in text.
GLOBAL field A> field B	Same as replace except automatically replaces all occurrences.
WRAP	Toggle word wrap feature.
QUIT	Return to BASIC and clear the array.

Creating a New Document

To enter a new document, you simply enter either

```
EDIT 1, EDIT or press the F1 key
```

while in the command mode.

You may enter text anywhere on the screen. When the cursor reaches the bottom of the screen, the text will scroll up a line so that you can continue editing without interruption. Also, if you are on the top row of the screen and going up, the text scrolls down a line until you reach the first line of text.

When you finish editing text, press the F1 key to return to the command area.

Saving a Document

There are three different ways to save text. First, you can use the SAVE FN command, where FN is the diskette file name of your choice. This command will save the current text file and return you to the command area. Second, DONE FN will save the text file and return you to BASIC. Finally, PACK FN will concatenate all the continuation lines and save the concatenated file. Once completed, PACK will return you to BASIC.

Here are some examples of how to use these commands.

```
SAVE FRED.LTR
SAVE MAILING.LST

DONE EDITOR.TXT
DONE PRICES.DATE

PACK FRED.PAK
PACK EDITOR.BAS
```

Loading an Existing Document

An existing document or text file is loaded by using the LOAD FN command. For example, to load and then edit an existing text file called PARTS.LST, you enter

```
LOAD PARTS.LST
```

After the file is loaded, enter either

```
EDIT or EDIT 1 or press the F1 key
```

to begin editing the text on line 1.

If you wish to begin editing the document on some line other than line 1, enter

```
EDIT #
```

where # is the number of the line you wish to edit. For example, to begin editing on line 34, enter EDIT 34.

Merging Documents

A text file on the diskette can be merged with text already in memory. This is accomplished by placing the cursor before the line where you want the new text to go. The LOAD command inserts the new text into the existing text, and it does not erase any of the original text. In other words, if you are adding ten new lines, the text after the cursor is moved down ten lines before the new lines are added. For this reason, the LOAD command can sometimes take a long time to finish.

Printing Documents

Any document can be printed by using either the PRINT FN or the FORMAT FN command. The PRINT command will print the document exactly as seen on your screen. The FORMAT command will combine the continuation lines before printing.

COMPLETE SCREEN TEXT EDITOR PROGRAM

Here is the complete screen text editor listing.

```
100      ' CHAPTER 3 - FULL SCREEN EDITOR
105      '
110      ON ERROR GOTO 60000          ' STANDARD ERROR
                                         PROCESSING
115      LAST% = 1000                 ' NUMBER OF LINES OF
                                         TEXT
120      DIM LINES$(LAST%)            ' TEXT ARRAY. NOTE:
                                         COMPILER REQUIRES
                                         NUMBER
125      '
130      '
40000    ' EDITOR * COMPLETE TEXT EDITOR WITH
            COMMAND AREA
```

```
40005    '
40010    ' USES THE LINE EDITOR WITH A FEW
            ADDITIONAL EXIT KEYS
40015    '
40020    ' COMMAND AREA ROUTINE
40025    '
40030    MLINES% = 1                              ' SET THE MAX LINE
                                                     COUNTER
40035    GOSUB 42845                              ' CLEAR VARIABLES
40040    KEY OFF
40045    FOR X = 1 TO 10
40050    KEY X,""                                 ' CLEAR THE FUNCTION
                                                     KEYS
40055    NEXT X
40060    MAXSIZE% = 250                           ' MAXIMUM LINE LENGTH
40065    WRAPSIZE% = MAXSIZE%                     ' START WITH WORD WRAP
                                                     OFF
40070    FX = FRE(ENTRY$)                         ' CLEAR THE MEMORY
40075    CLS
40080    PRINT "Editor Command Area Free ";FX     ' TITLE AND FREE MEMORY
40085    PRINT "LINES USED ";MLINES%;" ON
            LINE ";LINES%;
40090    IF ANUM% > 0 THEN PRINT " AUTO ";ANUM%;
40095    IF WRAPSIZE% <> MAXSIZE% THEN PRINT
            " WORD WRAP";
40100    PRINT : PRINT
40105    PRINT ">";
40110    PRINT
40115    PRINT
40120     PRINT "LOAD NAME     LOAD A TEXT FILE            CLEAR ERASE
                                                            MEMORY"
40125     PRINT "FILES         DISPLAY DISK DIRECTORY
40130     PRINT
40135     PRINT "EDIT ##       EDIT LINE NUMBER            SEARCH FIELD"
40140     PRINT "F1            EDIT CURRENT LINE NUMBER     REPLACE FIELD>
                                                            FIELD"
40145     PRINT "                                          GLOBAL FIELD>
                                                            FIELD"
40150     PRINT "AUTO ##       AUTO LINE NUMBER"
40155     PRINT "AUTO          TURN OFF LINE NUMBERING     WRAP   TOGGLE
                                                            WORD WRAP"
40160     PRINT
40165     PRINT "SAVE NAME     SAVE THE TEXT FILE"
40170     PRINT "DONE NAME     SAVE AND EXIT TO BASIC"
40175     PRINT "PACK NAME     PACK, SAVE AND EXIT"
40180     PRINT
```

```
40185    PRINT "PRINT          PRINT TEXT FILE"
40190    PRINT "FORMAT         PACK AND PRINT TEXT FILE"
40195    PRINT
40200    PRINT "QUIT           ABANDON AND EXIT TO BASIC"

40205    MASK$ = "a"                              ' >SET THE MASK
40210    ENTRY$ = ""                              ' CLEAR IT
40215    ROW% = 4                                 ' COMMAND INPUT LINE
40220    COL% = 3
40225    PLACE% = 1                               ' EDITOR SETS PLACE%
40230    FILL$ = " "
40235    GOSUB 50105                              ' ENTER LINE EDITOR AT
                                                       HELP%=0 LINE
40240    IF HELP% <> 0 THEN HELP$ =
             "CHAP3A.HLP" : GOSUB 48000 : GOTO
             40060                                "PROCESS HELP REQUEST
                                                     THEN REDISPLAY
40245    IF CTRL% = 27 THEN ENTRY$ = "EDIT"       "F1 MEANS EDIT TEXT
40250    X = INSTR(1,ENTRY$," ")                  ' LOOK FOR END OF
                                                     COMMAND
40255    IF X = 0 THEN X = LEN(ENTRY$)
40260    IF X = 0 THEN GOTO 40075                 ' NOTHING IN ENTRY$
40265    FOR Y = 1 TO X                           ' FORCE THE COMMAND
                                                     INTO UPPER CASE
40270    Z = ASC(MID$(ENTRY$,Y,1))                ' GET ONE LETTER
40275    IF Z >= 97 AND Z <= 122 THEN
             MID$(ENTRY$,Y,1) = CHR$(Z-32)         ' SHIFT THE CASE
40280    NEXT Y
40285    IF LEFT$(ENTRY$,4) = "AUTO" THEN
             GOSUB 40380 : GOTO 40365             ' AUTO NUMBER
40290    IF LEFT$(ENTRY$,4) = "PACK" THEN
             GOSUB 40680: CLS : END               ' PACK,SAVE AND QUIT
40295    IF LEFT$(ENTRY$,4) = "EDIT" OR CTRL% =
             27 THEN GOSUB 40430: GOTO 40070      ' EDIT THE TEXT
40300    IF LEFT$(ENTRY$,4) = "DONE" THEN GOTO
             40645 '                              ' SAVE AND END
40305    IF LEFT$(ENTRY$,4) = "LOAD" THEN
             GOSUB 40490: GOTO 40070              ' LOAD FILE
40310    IF LEFT$(ENTRY$,5) = "FILES" THEN
             GOSUB 40905 : GOTO 40365             ' DISPLAY A DIRECTORY
40315    IF LEFT$(ENTRY$,4) = "SAVE" THEN
             GOSUB 40730 : GOTO 40365 :           'SAVE THE TEXT
40320    IF LEFT$(ENTRY$,4) = "PACK" THEN
             GOSUB 40680 : CLS : END              ' PACK,SAVE,EXIT
```

```
40325    IF LEFT$(ENTRY$,5) = "PRINT" THEN
             PRT% = 1: GOSUB 40730 : GOTO 40365         ' PRINT AS IS
40330    IF LEFT$(ENTRY$,6) = "FORMAT" THEN
             PRT% = 1: GOSUB 40680: CLS : END           ' PACK PRINT AND EXIT
40335    IF LEFT$(ENTRY$,6) = "SEARCH" THEN
             REPLACE% = 0 : GOSUB 41085 : GOTO
             40365                                       ' SEARCH FOR FIELD
40340    IF LEFT$(ENTRY$,7) = "REPLACE" THEN
             REPLACE% = 1 : GOSUB 41085 :
             REPLACE% = 0 : GOTO 40365                   ' REPLACE STRINGS
40345    IF LEFT$(ENTRY$,6) = "GLOBAL" THEN
             GOSUB 40975 : GOTO 40365                    ' GLOBAL EXCHANGE
40350    IF LEFT$(ENTRY$,5) = "CLEAR" THEN
             CLEAR : GOTO 100                            ' CLEAR MEMORY
40355    IF LEFT$(ENTRY$,4) = "WRAP" THEN
             GOSUB 42905 ' GOTO 40340                    ' WORD WRAP TOGGLE
40360    IF LEFT$(ENTRY$,4) = "QUIT" THEN CLS :
             END                                         ' CLEAR AND QUIT
40365    GOTO 40075                    ' TRY AGAIN
40370    ' *****************************************
40375    '
40380    ' SET THE AUTO NUMBER SWITCH
40385    ' FLIP ITS VALUE
40390    '
40395    TXTSIZE% = LEN (ENTRY$)
40400    IF TXTSIZE% = 4 THEN ANUM% = 0: RETURN     ' TURN OFF AUTO NUM
40405    ENTRY$ = MID$ (ENTRY$,5)                    ' GET THE VALUE
40410    ANUM% = VAL (ENTRY$)
40415    RETURN
40420    ' *****************************************
40425    '
40430    ' EDIT THE TEXT
40435    '
40440    IF LEN (ENTRY$) = 4 THEN GOSUB 42000:
             RETURN                                   ' START AT CURRENT LINE
                                                      '   NUMBER
40445    FIRST% = VAL (MID$ (ENTRY$,5))             ' LINE NUMBER USER
                                                      '   WANTS TO EDIT
40450    IF FIRST% < 1 THEN FIRST% = 1
40455    LINES% = FIRST%
40460    LROW% = 1                                   ' START AT TOP LINE
40465    LCOL% = 1                                   ' START IN FIRST COLUMN
40470    GOSUB 42000                                 ' TEXT EDITOR
40475    RETURN
```

```
40480    ' ********************************
40485    '
40490    ' LOAD A TEXT FILE
40495    '
40500    ENTRY$ = MID$(ENTRY$,6)
40505    IF LEN (ENTRY$) = 0 THEN RETURN          ' THE USER FORGOT THE
                                                        NAME
40510    FILE.NAME$ = ENTRY$                      ' SAVE FOR LATER USE
40515    ' LOOKUP THE FILE ON THE DISK FIRST
40520    ON ERROR GOTO 40590                      ' SET ALTERNATIVE
                                                        ERROR POINT
40525    OPEN ENTRY$ FOR INPUT AS #1
40530    ON ERROR GOTO 60000                      ' RESTORE NORMAL ERROR
                                                        POINT
40535    IF MLINES% >= LAST% THEN MSG$ = "TEXT
             ARRAY FULL." : GOSUB 43045 : GOTO
             40575                                 ' OVERFLOW OF MEMORY
40540    IF LINES% < MLINES% THEN GOSUB 42550     ' INSERT BLANK LINE
                                                        FIRST
40545    LINE INPUT#1, LINES$(LINES%)             ' FETCH A LINE FROM THE
                                                        DISK
40550    IF EOF(1) THEN GOTO 40575                ' ALL DONE
40555    LINES% = LINES% + 1
40560    IF LINES% >= MLINES% THEN MLINES% =
             MLINES% + 1
40565    IF MLINES% >= LAST% THEN MSG$ = "TEXT
             ARRAY FULL." : GOSUB 43045 : GOTO
             40575                                 ' OVERFLOW OF MEMORY
40570    GOTO 40540
40575    CLOSE #1
40580    GOSUB 42845                              ' RESET ALL THE
                                                        POINTERS
40585    RETURN
40590    '
40595    RESUME 40600                             ' CLEAR THE ERROR FLAG
                                                        AND CONTINUE
40600    ON ERROR GOTO 60000                      ' RESTORE ERROR
                                                        PROCESSING TO
                                                        NORMAL LINE
40605    MSG$ = "FILE " + ENTRY$ + "NOT FOUND."
40610    GOSUB 43045                              ' DISPLAY ERROR MSG
40615    RETURN
40620    '
40625    '
```

```
40630    ' *********************************
40635    '
40640    '
40645    ' SAVE TEXT AND END
40650    '
40655    GOSUB 40730                              ' SAVE THE TEXT
40660    CLS
40665    END
40670    ' *********************************
40675    '
40680    ' CONCATENATE AND SAVE FILE
40685    '
40690    Y = 0
40695    FOR X = 1 TO MLINES%
40700    Y = Y + 1
40705    LINES$(Y) = LINES$(X)                    ' PACK THE ARRAY
40710    IF RIGHT$ (LINES$(X),1) = "_" THEN
             GOSUB 40860: GOTO 40715
40715    NEXT X
40720    MLINES% = Y                              ' NEW MAX LINE COUNT
40725    '
40730    ' SAVE THE TEXT
40735    '
40740    ENTRY$ = MID$(ENTRY$,6)                  ' GET THE FILE NAME
40745    IF LEN(ENTRY$) = 0 THEN ENTRY$ =
             FILE.NAME$                           ' USE LOAD NAME
40750    IF LEN(ENTRY$) = 0 THEN PRINT CHR$(7)
             : ENTRY$ = "TEMP.TXT"                ' TEMP NAME
40755    '
40760    '
40765    '
40770    '
40775    IF PRT% > 0 THEN GOTO 40820              ' PRINT IT DON'T WRITE
                                                    TO DISK
40780    OPEN ENTRY$ FOR OUTPUT AS #1             ' OPEN IT SO WE CAN KILL
                                                    IT
40785    CLOSE #1
40790    KILL ENTRY$                              ' ERASE THE FILE
40795    OPEN ENTRY$ FOR OUTPUT AS #1
40800    '
40805    '
40810    '
40815    '
40820    FOR X = 1 TO MLINES%
```

```
40825    IF PRT% = 0 THEN PRINT#1,LINES$(X)
             ELSE LPRINT LINES$(X)
40830    NEXT X
40835    IF PRT% > 0 THEN PRT% = 0 :LPRINT
             CHR$(12)                                ' SET CRT AND FORM FEED
40840    CLOSE#1
40845    RETURN
40850    ' ***********************************
40855    '
40860    ' CONCATENATE IT
40865    IF MID$ (LINES$(X + 1),1,1) = " " THEN
             LINES$(X + 1) = MID$ (LINES$(X +
             1),2): GOTO 40865                       ' STRIP SPACES
40870    XX = LEN (LINES$(Y)) - 1
40875    LINES$(Y) = LEFT$ LINES$(Y),XX) +
             LINES$(X + 1)                           ' STRIP '_' AND PACK
40880    X = X + 1
40885    IF RIGHT$ (LINES$(Y),1) = "_" THEN
             GOTO 40860                              ' CONTINUE PACKING IF
                                                       NECESSARY
40890    RETURN
40895    '
40900    ' *************************************
40905    ' CATALOG DISK
40910    '
40915    CLS                                         ' CLEAR SCREEN
40920    X = INSTR(1,ENTRY$,".")                     ' LOOK FOR . IN FILE
                                                       NAME
40925    IF LEN(ENTRY$) > 5 AND X = 0 THEN ENTRY$
             =ENTRY$ + "*.*"                         ' IN CASE THEY FORGOT
40930    IF LEN(ENTRY$) = 5 THEN FILES ELSE
             FILES MID$(ENTRY$,6)
40935    PRINT
40940    PRINT
40945    INPUT "PRESS ENTER TO CONTINUE ";
             ENTRY$                                  ' PAUSE AT BOTTOM
40950    RETURN
40955    ' *******************************
40960    '
40965    '
40970    '
40975    ' GLOBAL SEARCH AND REPLACE ROUTINE
40980    '
40985    Z = 0                                       ' RESET MATCH COUNTER
40990    X = INSTR(8,ENTRY$,">")                     ' LOOK FOR DELIMITER
```

```
40995    IF X = 0 THEN RETURN
41000    LOCATE 25,1 : PRINT Z," MATCHES
            FOUND.";
41005    SEARCH$ = MID$(ENTRY$,8,(X-8))
41010    REPLACE$ = MID$(ENTRY$,X+1)         ' REPLACEMENT
41015    REPLEN% = LEN(SEARCH$)              ' SET FOR FUTURE USE
41020    GOSUB 41290                         ' USE SEARCH ROUTINE TO
                                               FIND STRING

41025    IF SEARCH% = 0 THEN FOR X = 1 TO 1000 :
            NEXT : GOSUB 42845 : RETURN       ' PAUSE, RESET
                                               POINTERS AND RETURN

41030    '
41035    ' FOUND A MATCH SO REPLACE IT
41040    '
41045    IF SEARCH%=1 THEN LINES$(LINES%) =
            REPLACE$ + MID$(LINES$(LINES%),
            SEARCH% + REPLEN%) ELSE LINES$(LINES%) =
            LEFT$(LINES$(LINES%),SEARCH%;-1) +
            REPLACE$ + MID$(LINES$(LINES%),
            SEARCH% + REPLEN%)
                                             ' DO REPLACEMENT
41050    Z = Z + 1                           ' INCREMENT CHANGE
                                               COUNTER
41055    LOCATE 25,1 : PRINT Z;              ' AND DISPLAY IT
41060    LINES% = LINES% + 1                 ' STEP TO NEXT LINE
41065    GOTO 41020                          ' CONTINUE LOOKING
41070    '
41075    '
41080    '
41085    ' THE SEARCH AND REPLACE ROUTINES
41090    '
41095    '
41100    X = INSTR(8,ENTRY$,">")             ' NEEDED FOR REPLACE
41105    IF X = 0 AND REPLACE% = 1 THEN MSG$ =
            "MISSING > SYMBOL IN REPLACE" : GOSUB
            43045 : RETURN ' TEST FOR ERROR AND
            DISPLAY MESSAGE
41110    IF REPLACE% = 0 THEN SEARCH$ =
            MID$(ENTRY$,8) ELSE SEARCH$ =
            MID$(ENTRY$,9,(X-9)) : REPLACE$ =
            MID$(ENTRY$,X+1)                  ' SET UP SEARCH AND
                                               REPLACE
41115    REPLEN% = LEN(SEARCH$)              ' FOR REPLACE USE
41120    PASS% = 0                           ' MARK AS IN COMMAND
                                               AREA
```

```
41125    '
41130    ' ENTRY POINT FOR NEXT REQUEST
41135    '
41140    GOSUB 41290                                  ' SEARCH FORWARD FOR
                                                          MATCH

41145    IF SEARCH% = 0 THEN MSG$ = "NO MATCH
             FOUND." : GOSUB 43045 : GOSUB
             42845 : RETURN                           ' EXIT
41150    '
41155    ' IF A MATCH IS FOUND THEN WE NEED TO
             DISPLAY THE SCREEN AND EDIT IT.
41160    '
41165    PLACE% = SEARCH%                             ' POSITION OVER MATCH
41170    FRONT% = 1                                   ' RESET JUST IN CASE
41175    IF (LINES% <= FIRST% + 23) AND (PASS% <> 0)
             THEN LROW% = LINES% - FIRST% + 1 : GOSUB
             42060 : GOTO 41235

                                                      ' ON CURRENT SCREEN
                                                          ALLOW EDIT

41180    '
41185    ' NOT ON CURRENT SCREEN SO REDISPLAY
41190    '
41195    FIRST% = LINES% - 4                          ' PUT LINE OF INTEREST
                                                          NEAR TOP
41200    IF FIRST% < 1 THEN FIRST% = 1                ' ERROR CHECK
41205    LROW% = LINES% - FIRST% + 1
41210    LCOL% = 1
41215    PASS% = 1                                    ' MARK THAT SCREEN
                                                          DISPLAYED

41220    GOSUB 42000                                  ' REDISPLAY AND EDIT
41225    '
41230    ' RETURNS HERE AFTER EDIT IF ESC, NEXT OR
             REPLACE KEYS ARE STRUCK
41235    '
41240    IF CTRL% = 27 THEN GOSUB 42845 : RETURN      ' WANT TO GO TO COMMAND
                                                          AREA

41245    IF CTRL% = 28 THEN LINES%=LINES% + 1 :
             GOTO 41130                               ' NEXT KEY SEARCH
41250    ' HERE IF CTRL% = 29, REPLACE KEY
41255    IF SEARCH%=1 THEN LINES$(LINES%) =
             REPLACE$ +
             MID$(LINES$(LINES%),SEARCH% +
             REPLEN%) ELSE LINES$(LINES%) =
             LEFT$(LINES$(LINES%),SEARCH%-1) +
```

```
                REPLACE$ +
                MID$(LINES$(LINES%),SEARCH% +
                REPLEN%)                          ' DO REPLACEMENT
41260   ENTRY$ = LINES$(LINES%)                   ' REDISPLAY FIELD
41265   GOSUB 52660                               ' DISPLAY ENTRY$
41270   LINES% = LINES% + 1                       ' STEP TO NEXT LINE FOR
                                                      SEARCH
41275   GOTO 41130                                ' SEARCH FOR NEXT MATCH
41280   '
41285   '
41290   ' SEARCH FOR A STRING
41295   '
41300   IF LINES% > MLINES% THEN SEARCH% = 0 :
                RETURN                            ' ALL DONE
41305   SEARCH% =
                INSTR(1,LINES$(LINES%),SEARCH$)   ' LOOK FOR THE STRING
41310   IF SEARCH% <> 0 THEN RETURN               ' FOUND A MATCH
41315   LINES% = LINES% + 1                       ' SKIP TO NEXT LINE
41320   GOTO 41290                                ' AND CONTINUE SEARCH
41325   '
41330   '
41335   '
42000   ' TEXT EDITOR
42005   '
42010   ' VARIABLE DEFINITION
42015   ' LROW% STARTING ROW NUMBER
42020   ' LCOL% STARTING COL NUMBER
42025   ' LINES$( ) TEXT ARRAY
42030   ' LAST% DIMENSIONS OF TEXT ARRAY
42035   ' MLINES% LARGEST LINE USED IN ARRAY
42040   ' LINES% CURRENT LINE BEING EDITED
42045   ' FIRST% LINE AT TOP OF SCREEN
42050   GOSUB 42790                               ' DISPLAY THE SCREEN
42055   '
42060   ' ENTRY FOR NO REDISPLAY
42065   '
42070   FILL$ = " "                               ' DEFINE THE FILL
                                                      CHARACTER
42075   MASK$ = "N"                               ' SET FOR TEXT EDITOR
42080   ROW% = LROW%                              ' START AT LAST ROW
42085   COL% = LCOL%                              ' START AT LAST COL
42090   '
42095   ' TOP OF EDIT LOOP
42100   CTRL% = 0                                 ' CLEAR THE EXIT FLAG
```

```
42105    ENTRY$ = LINES$(LINES%)                           ' PUT CURRENT LINE INTO
                                                             LINE EDITOR
42110    IF PLACE% > LEN(ENTRY$) THEN PLACE% =
             LEN(ENTRY$) + 1                                ' ASSIGN PLACE% HERE
42115    IF PLACE% = 0 THEN PLACE% = 1                      ' NULL LINE
42120    IF PLACE% > 79 - COL% THEN FRONT% =
             PLACE% - 40 : GOSUB 52660                      ' CENTER IF OFF RIGHT
                                                             END SEARCH AND
                                                             REPLACE NEED THIS
42125    GOSUB 50160                                        ' EDIT THE TEXT BUT DO
                                                             NOT REDISPLAY
                                                             ENTRY$
42130    IF HELP% <> 0 THEN HELP$ =
             "CHAP3B.HLP" : GOSUB 43635 : GOTO
             42000                                          ' PROCESS HELP REQUEST
42135    LINES$(LINES%) = ENTRY$                            ' SAVE THE EDITED LINE
42140    ' TEST FOR ESC, F1, NEXT OR REPLACE
42145    IF (CTRL% >= 27) AND (CTRL% <= 29) THEN
             LROW% = ROW%:LCOL% = COL%: RETURN              ' BACK TO CALLER
42150    ON CTRL% GOSUB
             42170,42210,42265,42615,42655,42720,42435,42510,42380,
             42315,43210,43370,43165,43505
42155    GOTO 42095
42160    ' ***************************************
42165    '
42170    ' CARRIAGE RETURN
42175    '
42180    PLACE% = LEN(WRAP$) + 1                            ' POSITION AT FRONT OR
                                                             END IF WRAP
42185    WRAP$ = ""                                         ' RESET FOR NEXT TIME
42190    GOSUB 42210                                        ' LINE FEED
42195    RETURN
42200    ' ******************************************
42205    '
42210    ' LINE FEED
42215    '
42220    IF LINES% = LAST% THEN RETURN                      ' MAX NO MORE LINES
                                                             LEFT
42225    LINES% = LINES% + 1
42230    IF LINES% > MLINES% THEN MLINES% =
             LINES%                                         ' INC LARGEST LINE
                                                             COUNTER
42235    ROW% = ROW% + 1
42240    IF ROW% > 24 THEN ROW% = 12 : X = 13 : Y =
             0 : GOSUB 42740                                ' SKIP HALF PAGE
```

```
42245   IF (RIGHT$(ENTRY$,1) = "_") AND
            (LEN(LINES$(LINES%)) = 0) THEN
            PLACE% = 1 : LINES$(LINES%) =
            SPACE$(8)                                   ' ADD OFFSET
42250   RETURN
42255   ' ********************************
42260   '
42265   ' UP ARROW
42270   '
42275   IF LINES% = 1 THEN RETURN                       ' AT TOP ALREADY
42280   LINES% = LINES% - 1
42285   ROW% = ROW% - 1
42290   IF ROW% < 1 THEN ROW% = 12 : X = 12 : Y = 0
            : GOSUB 42675                               ' SKIP HALF PAGE
42295   RETURN
42300   '
42305   ' ************************************
42310   '
42315   ' PACK TWO LINES
42320   '
42325   IF LINES% = MLINES% THEN RETURN                 ' AT THE END
42330   LINES$(LINES%) = LINES$(LINES%) +
            LINES$(LINES% + 1)                          ' PACK THE LINES
42335   IF LINES% = MLINES% THEN GOTO 42355             ' LAST LINE
42340   FOR X = LINES% + 1 TO MLINES% - 1
42345       LINES$(X) = LINES$(X + 1)                   ' MOVE LINE UP ONE
42350   NEXT X
42355   LINES$(MLINES%) = ""                            ' CLEAR THE LAST LINE
42360   MLINES% = MLINES% - 1                           ' REDUCE MAX LINE BY
                                                          ONE
42365   GOSUB 42790
42370   RETURN
42375   '
42380   ' JUMP TO LAST PAGE
42385   '
42390   FIRST% = MLINES% - 23                           ' FIND THE LINE AT THE
                                                          TOP OF THE SCREEN
42395   IF FIRST% < 1 THEN FIRST% = 1                   ' CANNOT HAVE LINE LESS
                                                          THAN 1
42400   LINES% = FIRST%
42405   ROW% = 1
42410   COL% = 1
42415   GOSUB 42790                                     ' DISPLAY THE SCREEN
42420   RETURN
42425   ' ************************************
```

```
42430    '
42435    ' DELETE A LINE
42440    '
42445    PRESERVE$ = LINES$(LINES%)                      ' SAVE FOR POSSIBLE
                                                             RESTORE
42450    IF MLINES% = 1 THEN LINES$(1) = "":
             GOTO 42485                                   ' ONLY ONE LINE
42455    IF LINES% = MLINES% THEN ROW% = ROW% -
             1:LINES% = LINES% - 1: GOTO 42475            ' LAST LINE IN TEXT
42460    FOR X = LINES% TO MLINES% - 1
42465        LINES$(X) = LINES$(X + 1)
42470    NEXT X
42475    LINES$(MLINES%) = ""
42480    IF MLINES% > 1 THEN MLINES% = MLINES% - 1
42485    GOSUB 42790                                      ' DISPLAY SCREEN
42490    RETURN
42495    '
42500    ' *********************************
42505    '
42510    ' INSERT A BLANK LINE
42515    '
42520    GOSUB 42550                                      ' DO THE INSERT
42525    LINES$(LINES%) = ""
42530    GOSUB 42790                                      ' REDISPLAY SCREEN
42535    RETURN
42540    '
42545    '
42550    ' INSERT A LINE
42555    '
42560    IF MLINES% >= LAST% THEN MSG$ = "TEXT
             ARRAY FULL." : GOSUB 43045 : RETURN          ' OVERFLOW
42565    MLINES% = MLINES% + 1
42570    IF LINES% = 1 THEN Y = 2 ELSE Y = LINES%         ' SET COUNTER
42575    FOR X = MLINES% TO Y STEP -1
42580    LINES$(X) = LINES$(X - 1)                        ' MOVE TEXT DOWN A LINE
42585    NEXT X
42590    RETURN
42595    '
42600    ' *********************************
42605    '
42610    '
42615    ' GOTO THE HOME PAGE
42620    '
42625    GOSUB 42845                                      ' RESET THE POINTERS
42630    GOSUB 42790                                      ' SHOW THE SCREEN
42635    RETURN                                           ' A OK
```

```
42640    '
42645    ' ********************************
42650    '
42655    ' SCROLL UP A PAGE
42660    '
42665    X = 24                                  ' JUMP A FULL PAGE
42670    Y = X                                   ' OFFSET POINTER
42675    ' ENTRY POINT FOR ROLL UP
42680    IF FIRST% <= X THEN GOSUB 42845:ROW% =
             1: GOSUB 42790: RETURN              ' JUMP TO TOP OF FIRST
                                                   PAGE
42685    FIRST% = FIRST% - X                     ' MOVE THE TOP LINE
42690    LINES% = LINES% - Y                     ' CHANGE THE ARRAY
                                                   POINTER
42695    GOSUB 42790                             ' DISPLAY THE SCREEN
42700    RETURN
42705    '
42710    ' ********************************************
42715    '
42720    ' SCROLL DOWN A PAGE
42725    '
42730    X = 24                                  ' JUMP A FULL PAGE
42735    Y = X                                   ' OFFSET POINTER
42740    ' ENTRY POINT FOR ROLL DOWN
42745    IF MLINES% < = 24 THEN LINES% =
             MLINES%:ROW% = MLINES%: RETURN      ' ON FIRST PAGE
42750    IF FIRST% + X > MLINES% THEN FIRST% =
             MLINES% - 23:LINES% = MLINES%:ROW%
             = 24: GOTO 42765                    ' BOTTOM
42755    FIRST% = FIRST% + X
42760    LINES% = LINES% + Y
42765    GOSUB 42790                             ' DISPLAY THE SCREEN
42770    RETURN
42775    '
42780    ' ************************************
42785    '
42790    ' DISPLAY THE CURRENT SCREEN
42795    '
42800    CLS                                     ' CLEAR THE SCREEN
42805    FOR X = 1 TO 24
42810    Z = FIRST% + X - 1
42815    LOCATE X,1                              ' POSITION THE CURSOR
42820    IF LEN(LINES$(Z)) > 78 THEN
             PRINT LEFT$(LINES$(Z),78);
             ELSE PRINT LINES$(Z);              ' IF IT FITS PRINT IT
42825    NEXT X
```

```
42830     RETURN
42835     ' *******************************
42840     '
42845     ' CLEAR EVERYTHING
42850     '
42855     LINES% = 1                              ' CURRENT LINE NUMBER
42860     FIRST% = 1                              ' TOP LINE ON THE
                                                      SCREEN
42865     LROW% = 1                               ' START ON FIRST LINE
42870     LCOL% = 1
42875     ROW% = 1
42880     COL% = 1
42885     RETURN
42890     ' **********************************
42895     '
42900     '
42905     ' TOGGLE WORD WRAP
42910     '
42915     IF WRAPSIZE% <> MAXSIZE% THEN
              WRAPSIZE% = MAXSIZE% ELSE
              WRAPSIZE% = 75                      ' SET SCREEN WRAP LINE
                                                      LENGTH
42920     RETURN
42925     '
42930     '
42935     '
42940     ' END OF LINE WORD WRAP SUBROUTINE
42945     '
42950     X = TXTSIZE% - 1
42955     IF MID$(ENTRY$,X,1) = " " THEN GOTO
              42975                               ' SEARCH FOR SPACE
42960     X = X - 1                               ' RIGHT TO LEFT SEARCH
42965     IF X = 0 THEN MSG$ = "NO WORD WRAP, NO
              BLANK ON LINE." : GOSUB 43045 :
              RETURN                              ' ERROR
42970     GOTO 42955                              ' NOT AT FRONT SO KEEP
                                                      LOOKING
42975     WRAP$ = MID$(ENTRY$,X+1) + A.KEY$       ' GET THE LAST WORD
42980     LINES$(LINES%) = LEFT$(ENTRY$,X)        ' TRUNCATE ORIGINAL
                                                      LINE
42985     ENTRY$ = LINES$(LINES%)                 ' RESET ENTRY$
42990     LINES% = LINES% + 1                     ' STEP TO NEXT LINE
42995     IF LEN(LINES$(LINES%)) > 0 THEN GOSUB
              42550                               ' INSERT BLANK LINE
43000     LINES$(LINES%) = WRAP$                  ' SET TO WRAP AROUND
```

```
43005      LINES% = LINES% - 1
43010      CTRL% = 1                                ' MARK AS ENTER KEY
43015      PLACE% = 1
43020      GOSUB 42790                              ' REDISPLAY THE SCREEN
43025      RETURN
43030      '
43035      '
43040      '
43045      ' DISPLAY MESSAGE MSG$ ON 25TH LINE
43050      '
43055      LOCATE 25,1
43060      X = LEN(MSG$)                            ' CLEAR LINE AFTER MSG$
                                                      WITH SPACES
43065      IF X >= 79 THEN PRINT LEFT$(MSG$,79);
              ELSE PRINT MSG$;SPACE$(79-X);
43070      FOR X = 1 TO 1000                        ' PAUSE TO ALLOW USER
                                                      TIME TO READ MESSAGE
43075      NEXT X
43080      RETURN
43085      '
43090      '
43095      '
43100      ' SPLIT THIS LINE
43105      '
43110      LINES% = LINES% + 1
43115      GOSUB 42550                              ' INSERT A BLANK LINE
43120      LINES$(LINES%) = MID$(ENTRY$,PLACE%)     ' MOVE END TO NEXT LINE
43125      LINES% = LINES% - 1                      ' RESTORE LINE POINTER
43130      CTRL% = 1                                ' MARK AS ENTER
43135      IF PLACE% > 1 THEN ENTRY$ =
              LEFT$(ENTRY$,PLACE%-1) ELSE
              ENTRY$ = ""                           ' REDEFINE THIS LINE
43140      GOSUB 42790                              ' REDISPLAY SCREEN
43145      RETURN
43150      '
43155      '
43160      '
43165      ' MOVE A BLOCK OF TEXT
43170      '
43175      GOSUB 43250                              ' FIRST COPY THE BLOCK
43180      IF LEN(MSG$) = 0 THEN GOSUB 43410        ' IF OK THEN DELETE IT
43185      GOSUB 42790                              ' REDISPLAY THE SCREEN
43190      RETURN
43195      '
43200      '
```

```
43205     '
43210     ' COPY BLOCK AND REDISPLAY SCREEN
43215     '
43220     GOSUB 43250                              ' COPY THE BLOCK
43225     GOSUB 42790                              ' REDISPLAY THE SCREEN
43230     RETURN
43235     '
43240     '
43245     '
43250     ' COPY A BLOCK OF TEXT
43255     IF MARK.END% = 0 OR MARK.START% = 0
             THEN RETURN                           ' ERROR
43260     ' ADJUST BLOCK MARKERS IF NECESSARY
43265     IF MARK.END% < MARK.START% THEN SWAP
             MARK.END%,MARK.START%                 ' START AT TOP
43270     X = MARK.END% - MARK.START% + 1          ' NUMBER OF LINES TO
                                                     COPY
43275     IF MLINES% + X > LAST% THEN MSG% = "TEXT
             ARRAY FULL." : GOSUB 43045 : RETURN   ' MEMORY OVERFLOW
43280     MLINES% = MLINES% + X                    ' INCREMENT THE ARRAY
                                                     SIZE
43285     MSG$ = ""                                ' CLEAR MEANS COPY OK
43290     IF LINES% = 1 THEN Y = 2 ELSE Y = LINES%
43295     FOR Z = MLINES% TO Y+X STEP -1           ' MOVE THE LINES DOWN
43300     LINES$(Z) = LINES$(Z-X)
43305     NEXT Z
43310     '
43315     ' ADJUST IF COPY IS TO LINE ABOVE BLOCK
43320     '
43325     IF MARK.START% >= Y THEN MARK.START% =
             MARK.START% + X                       ' ADJUST FOR INSERT
43330     IF MARK.END% >= Y THEN MARK.END% =
             MARK.END% + X                         ' DITTO
43335     FOR Z = 0 TO X - 1                       ' NOW COPY
43340     LINES$(Y + Z) = LINES$(MARK.
             START% + Z)
43345     NEXT Z
43350     RETURN
43355     '
43360     '
43365     '
43370     ' DELETE BLOCK AND REDISPLAY SCREEN
43375     '
43380     GOSUB 43410                              ' DELETE THE BLOCK
43385     GOSUB 42790                              ' REDISPLAY THE SCREEN
43390     RETURN
```

```
43395    '
43400    '
43405    '
43410    ' DELETE A BLOCK OF TEXT
43415    ' IF MARK.END% = 0 OR MARK.START = 0
             THEN RETURN                            'MARKERS NOT SET
43420    ' ADJUST MARKS SO MARK.START IS LESS
             THAN MARK.END
43425    IF MARK.END% < MARK.START% THEN SWAP
             MARK.END%,MARK.START%                  ' START AT TOP
43430    X = MARK.END% - MARK.START% + 1
43435    FOR Z = MARK.END%+1 TO MLINES%            ' REMOVE THE BLOCK
43440    LINES$(Z-X) = LINES$(Z)
43445    NEXT Z
43450    FOR Z = (MLINES% - X + 1) TO MLINES%      ' CLEAR OLD LINES AT
                                                        END
43455    LINES$(Z) = ""
43460    NEXT Z
43465    MLINES% = MLINES% - X                     ' DECREMENT SIZE
                                                        COUNTER
43470    IF LINES% > MLINES% THEN LINES% =
             MLINES%                                ' CORRECT IF AT END
43475    MARK.START% = 0                           ' CLEAR THE MARKERS
43480    MARK.END% = 0
43485    RETURN
43490    '
43495    '
43500    '
43505    ' SAVE BLOCK TO DISK
43510    '
43515    SAV.ROW% = ROW%                           ' SAVE FOR RETURN
43520    SAV.COL% = COL%                           ' DITTO
43525    ROW% = 25                                 ' ACCEPT FILE NAME ON
                                                        25TH LINE
43530    COL% = 30
43535    LOCATE 25,1
43540    PRINT "SAVE IN FILE: ";
43545    ENTRY$ = "TEMP.TXT"                       ' DEFAULT FILE NAME
43550    GOSUB 50000                               ' CALL LINE EDITOR
43555    MSG$ = ""                                 ' CLEAR 25TH LINE
43560    GOSUB 43045                               ' DO IT
43565    IF CTRL% = 27 OR LEN(ENTRY$) = 0 THEN
             GOTO 43600                             ' ESC OR ERROR
43570    OPEN ENTRY$ FOR OUTPUT AS #2
43575    IF MARK.END% < MARK.START% THEN SWAP
             MARK.END%,MARK.START%
```

```
43580    FOR X = MARK.START% TO MARK.END%          ' WRITE TO DISK
43585    PRINT#2,LINES$(X)
43590    NEXT X
43595    CLOSE#2
43600    ROW% = SAV.ROW%
43605    COL% = SAV.COL%
43610    PLACE% = 1
43615    RETURN
43620    '
43625    '
43630    '
48000    ' RESERVED FOR HELP SUBROUTINE CHAPTER 4
48005    '
48010    RETURN
48015    '
48020    '
48025    '
50333    IF MASK$ = "N" THEN GOSUB 50550 :
             RETURN                                 ' AUTO NUMBER
50550    ' TEXT EDITOR MASK
50555    '
50560    IF LEN(ENTRY$) >= WRAPSIZE% AND
             PLACE% >= WRAPSIZE% THEN GOSUB
             42940 : RETURN                         ' WRAP AROUND TEST
50565    IF A.KEY% <> 32 OR ANUM% = 0 OR PLACE% <
             > 1 OR LEN(ENTRY$) > 0 THEN GOSUB
             50900: RETURN                          ' WHEN NOT TO ADD
                                                        NUMBER
50570    ' AUTO NUMBERING ON AND IN FIRST
             CHARACTER
50575    ENTRY$ = MID$(STR$(ANUM%),2)              ' REMOVE SPACE DUE TO
                                                        STR$()
50580    ENTRY$ = ENTRY$ + SPACE$(8 -
             LEN(ENTRY$))                           ' INDENT
50585    ANUM% = ANUM% + 5
50590    PLACE% = LEN (ENTRY$)
50595    GOSUB 52660                               ' PRINT ENTRY$
50600    GOSUB 52500                               ' CURSOR DISPLAY
50605    RETURN
50610    ' ********************************
50615    '
50620    '
51191    IF A.KEY% = 361 THEN CTRL% = 8            ' F3 INSERT LINE
51192    IF A.KEY% = 362 THEN GOSUB 43090 :
             RETURN                                 ' F4 SPLIT LINE
```

```
51193   IF A.KEY% = 363 THEN MARK.START% =
            LINES% : RETURN                     ' F5 SET START MARK
51194   IF A.KEY% = 364 THEN CTRL% = 13         ' F6 MOVE BLOCK
51196   IF A.KEY% = 365 THEN CTRL% = 11         ' F7 COPY BLOCK
51197   IF A.KEY% = 366 THEN CTRL% = 28         ' F8 NEXT FIELD
51198   IF A.KEY% = 367 THEN GOSUB 42905 :
            RETURN                              ' F9 WORD WRAP TOGGLE
51206   IF A.KEY% = 371 THEN CTRL% = 4          ' HOME
51207   IF A.KEY% = 372 THEN CTRL% = 3          ' UP ARROW
51208   IF A.KEY% = 373 THEN CTRL% = 5          ' PG UP
51221   IF A.KEY% = 380 THEN CTRL% = 2          ' DOWN ARROW
51222   IF A.KEY% = 381 THEN CTRL% = 6          ' PG DN
51231   IF A.KEY% = 386 THEN CTRL% = 7          ' SHIFT F3 DELETE LINE
51232   IF A.KEY% = 387 THEN CTRL% = 10         ' SHIFT F4 PACK LINE
51233   IF A.KEY% = 388 THEN MARK.END% =
            LINES% : RETURN                     ' SHIFT F5 BLOCK END
51234   IF A.KEY% = 389 THEN CTRL% = 14         ' SHIFT F6 SAVE BLOCK
                                                    TO DISK
51236   IF A.KEY% = 390 THEN CTRL% = 12         ' SHIFT F7 DELETE BLOCK
51237   IF A.KEY% = 391 THEN CTRL% = 29         ' SHIFT F8 REPLACE
51266   IF A.KEY% = 419 THEN CTRL% = 9          ' CTRL HOME LAST PAGE
52638   IF FRONT% = 1 AND ORG.ENTRY$=ENTRY$
            THEN GOSUB 52570 : RETURN           ' LINE UNCHANGED SO DO
                                                    NOT PRINT

60000   ' STANDARD ERROR PROCESSING ROUTINE
60005   '
60010   X = ERR                                 ' ERROR NUMBER
60015   Y = ERL                                 ' LINE NUMBER OF ERROR
60020   RESUME 60025
60025   KEY OFF                                 ' TURN OFF SO WE CAN USE
                                                    25TH LINE
60030   LOCATE 25,1                             ' POSITION CURSOR ON
                                                    25TH LINE
60035   PRINT "ERROR ";X;" ON LINE ";Y
60040   BEEP                                    ' RING THE BELL
60045   END                                     ' THAT'S ALL FOLKS
60050   '
60055   '
60060   '
```

ANSWERING USERS' HELP REQUESTS

INTRODUCTION

An on-line help system is one of the most user-friendly features a program can have. A good help system will save everyone involved with the computer time and frustration. Operators not familiar with computers often are afraid of making mistakes or of appearing stupid when they are confused about what the computer wants them to do. With an on-line help system they can ask the computer for assistance as often as needed. They do not have to bother you, and you will not have to answer the same questions over and over. Once again, user-friendly software is programmer friendly.

In this chapter we develop a subroutine to display user-help screens. These screens are kept on diskette and used automatically by the help routine whenever the user has questions.

A help system is easy to implement with the use of our line editor. You may recall that we included a feature in the line editor that sets a variable called HELP% whenever the user presses shift F1. In addition to the line editor and the help subroutines, the help system consists of a series of sequential text files. A separate help screen or text file is used for each help request to be supported.

In your program you must test HELP% after every call to the line editor. If help has been requested (HELP% does not equal 0), then you must call the help subroutine. This subroutine will clear the screen and display the appropriate help file and pause at the bottom of each screen. After reading the help message, the user presses ENTER and the subroutine returns.

Help text files can be entered using the text editor developed in Chapter 3. For a help screen to be useful, it should reference a manual page (you are going to document your program, aren't you?) and provide as much information as possible.

In the following sections this program is developed by first describing the design of the program and then by testing each component subroutine.

Chapter 4 is a stand-alone chapter; it does not need to be merged with any other chapter.

Programmer Features

For help, the programmer needs to pass a file name to the help subroutine, and then the original screen must be restored after the help text has been displayed.

The programmer creates the help text files, which contain information about when to pause, what to display, and what to show as bright, dim, or flashing.

Design and User Features

We want the help subroutine to display a text file that highlights important text and pauses periodically to allow the user time to read the screen. Thus the help system supports bright, dim, and flashing displays and pauses every 22 lines (a full screen) or whenever directed by the text file. A screen is considered full at 22 lines to allow room for one blank line plus the pause line.

The user should be able to terminate the help display and return to the calling program and should be able to control the pace at which the help screen is displayed. These features are included in our help program.

HELP PROGRAM

Figure 4.1 shows the flowchart for the help program. The processing of the screen is straightforward. The file is opened and each line is read and processed. The subroutine is looking for the symbols used to set the intensity or to pause. If such a character is found, then a GOSUB is made to the appropriate subroutine. Regular text is simply printed.

After a screen (22 lines) has been shown, the subroutine pauses and the user is asked, Do you wish more? This message gives the user time to read the screen and an opportunity to stop the help-display process if the question has already been answered. This procedure is repeated until the help file has been shown or the user requests an exit.

You may notice that we tested for a good file name here, just as we did in Chapter 3. The RESUME line number was modified (line 48115) and then the file was opened. If the file had been successfully opened, then the RESUME line number was reset to 60000 (line 48125). The file name error processing routine begins on line 48490.

The following program corresponds to the flowchart in Figure 4.1.

```
48000    ' SHOW HELP * SCREEN DISPLAY ROUTINE
48005    '
48010    '
48015    '
48020    ' DISPLAYS SCREEN AND USES BRIGHT AND DIM CHARACTERS
48025    ' WILL PAUSE WHEN THE SCREEN IS FULL
```

FIG. 4.1   Help screen flowchart

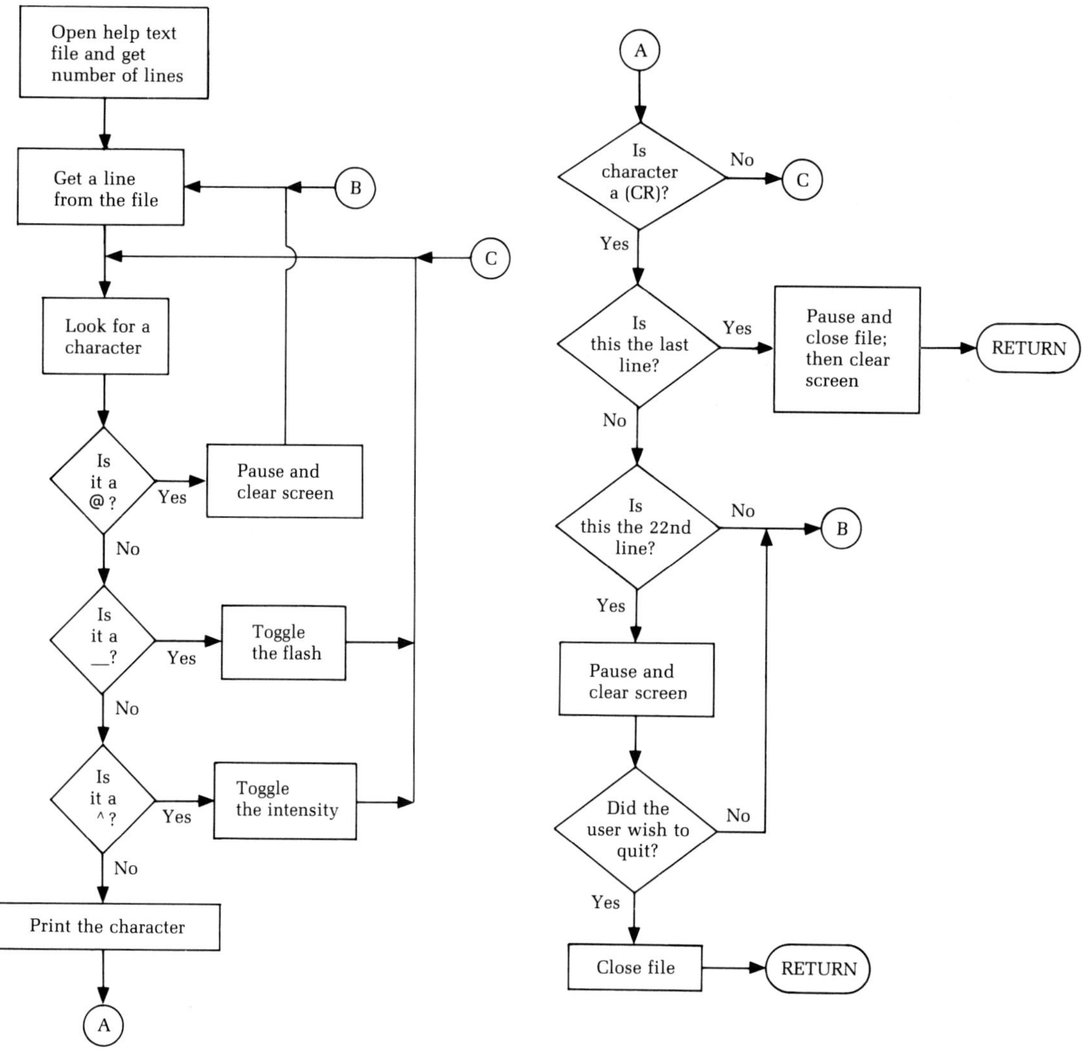

```
48030    ' TO ALLOW THE USER TIME TO READ
48035    '
48040    '
48045    ' IMPORTANT VARIABLES USED:
48050    '    Y              BRIGHTNESS FLAG
48055    '    YY             FLASH FLAG
48060    '    ROW%           TOTAL NUMBER OF LINES DISPLAYED
48065    '    NOPAUSE%  1= DO NOT PAUSE AT END OF PAGE. 0=PAUSE
48070    '
48075    '
48080    ' BRIGHTNESS TOGGLED ON '^' CHARACTER
48085    '
48090    ' FLASH TOGGLED ON '~' CHARACTER
48095    '
48100    ' ***************************************************
48105    HELP% = 1                              ' REQUIRED, BUT CALLER
                                                     MAY NOT HAVE SET
48110    COLOR 7,0                              ' START DIM
48115    ON ERROR GOTO 48490                    ' IN CASE FILE MISSING
48120    OPEN HELP$ FOR INPUT AS #1             ' OPEN THE HELP FILE
48125    ON ERROR GOTO 60000                    ' NORMAL ERROR
                                                     PROCESSING
48130    '
48135    ' CLEAR THE COUNTERS
48140    '
48145    ROW% = 0
48150    Y = 0                                  ' BRIGHTNESS FLAG
48155    YY = 0                                 ' FLASH FLAG
48160    CLS                                    ' CLEAR SCREEN
48165    ' INPUT THE SCREEN
48170    '
48175    IF EOF(1) <> 0 THEN GOTO 48260         ' TEST FOR END OF FILE
48180    LINE INPUT#1,A$                        ' GET A TEXT LINE
48185    IF HELP% = 0 THEN GOTO 48260           ' HELP% = 0 MEANS EXIT
48190    IF A$ = "@" THEN GOSUB 48400 : GOTO
             48175                              ' PAUSE WANTED?
48195    Z = INSTR(1,A$,"^")                    ' LOOK FOR INTENSITY
                                                     TOGGLE
48200    IF Z = 1 THEN GOSUB 48305 : A$ =
             MID$(A$,2) : GOTO 48195            ' TOGGLE IN FIRST
                                                     POSITION
48205    IF Z > 1 THEN PRINT LEFT$(A$,Z-1); :
             GOSUB 48305 : A$ = MID$(A$,Z+1) :
             GOTO 48195                         ' PRINT PARTIAL LINE
```

```
48210    Z = INSTR(1,A$,"~")                        ' LOOK FOR FLASH TOGGLE
48215    IF Z = 1 THEN GOSUB 48350 : A$ =
             MID$(A$,2) : GOTO 48210                 ' TOGGLE IN FIRST
                                                         POSITION
48220    IF Z > 1 THEN PRINT LEFT$(A$,Z-1); :
             GOSUB 48350 : A$ = MID$(A$,Z+1) :
             GOTO 48210                              ' PRINT PARTIAL LINE
48225    PRINT A$                                    ' NO MORE TOGGLES SO
                                                         PRINT REMAINDER
48230    ROW% = ROW% + 1                             ' INCREMENT THIS PAGE
                                                         LINE COUNTER
48235    IF EOF(1) <> 0 OR ROW% = 22 THEN GOSUB
             48400                                   ' GET NEXT LINE
48240    GOTO 48175                                  ' NOT DONE YET
48245    '
48250    ' *****************************
48255    '
48260    ' EXIT POINT WHEN ALL DONE
48265    '
48270    HELP% = 0                                   ' FILE DONE. CLEAR JUST
                                                         TO BE SAFE.
48275    CLOSE#1                                     ' CLOSE THE FILE
48280    COLOR 7,0                                   ' RESTORE DIM DISPLAY
48285    RETURN
48290    '
48295    ' *****************************
48300    '


48490    ' FILE NOT FOUND ERROR
48495    '
48500    RESUME 48505                                ' CLEAN UP ERROR
                                                         ROUTINE
48505    ON ERROR GOTO 60000                         ' NORMAL ERROR ROUTINE
48510    LOCATE 25,1
48515    PRINT HELP$;" NOT FOUND.";                  ' PRINT ERROR MESSAGE
                                                         ON 25TH LINE
48520    BEEP
48525    RETURN                                      ' RETURN TO CALLER
48530    '
48535    '
48540    '
```

Explanation of Variables

Most of the variables used in the help program are the garbage variables Y, Z, XX, and YY. Check to be sure that your calling routine is not also using these variables.

There are two variables that must be set by the calling routine: HELP$ and NOPAUSE%. HELP$ contains the name of the text file to be shown. NOPAUSE% determines whether the pause line is to be printed or ignored. NOPAUSE% is normally set to 0 so that the pause is performed, but occasionally a pause may not be wanted and then NOPAUSE% is set to 1. This subroutine is used in Chapter 5, for example, where a pause is not wanted.

Explanation of Main Help Routine

The help routine is fairly simple: It uses the INSTR statement to search for the symbols used for display and pausing. If it does not find a symbol (INSTR returns a 0), then it prints the entire line. If it does find a symbol, it prints the text to the left of the symbol and then it calls the appropriate display or pause routine. This process is repeated until the entire line is printed and until the remaining lines in the file are printed.

A counter of the number of lines shown (line 48230) on this screen is maintained by the program. When the screen counter reaches 22, or when the end of the text file is reached, the pause subroutine is called and the user is given time to read the screen and the option to exit. After the file has been shown, the screen is cleared and the subroutine returns to the calling program.

TEST POINT

Before this routine can be tested a sample help screen must be created. We suggest that you use the editor to enter the "CHAP8A.HLP" text used in Chapter 8 on page 261.

The following program will test the help routine. It will not pause or change the screen's intensity.

```
100      ' CHAPTER 4 - TEST ROUTINE FOR HELP DISPLAY
105      '
110      KEY OFF                                       ' CLEAR 25TH LINE
115      CLS
120      ON ERROR GOTO 60000                           ' NORMAL ERROR ROUTINE
125      PRINT "CHAPTER 4 HELP SYSTEM SAMPLE
             PROGRAM"
130      HELP% = 1                                     ' TURN HELP FLAG ON
135      PRINT
140      PRINT "ONE SAMPLE IS NAMED: CHAP8A.HLP"
145      PRINT
150      INPUT "ENTER HELP SCREEN NAME: ";HELP$
155      IF LEN(HELP$) = 0 THEN END ELSE GOSUB
             48000                                     ' DISPLAY HELP SCREEN
160      GOTO 100
165      '
170      ' *******************************
175      '
```

PAUSE SUBROUTINE

The pause subroutine is called when a @ symbol is encountered in the help text and automatically at the end of the text file.

When the help text is created, the writer can make the routine pause by placing @ symbols in the body of the text. Pauses improve the readability of the help text by separating topics in the text. For example, the help text may first give a brief explanation of what the user is to do and then give several screens of detailed explanation. If the brief explanation only uses ten lines, it would look awkward and confusing to mix it with the beginning of the following detailed explanation, and so a pause is used to separate the sections. The pause subroutine also gives the user the chance to exit the help system and return to the original screen.

The pause routine looks like this.

```
48400    ' PAUSE AND ASK FOR MORE?
48405    '
48410    '
48415    IF NOPAUSE% > 0 THEN RETURN                   ' PROGRAMMER DOES NOT
                                                          WANT PAUSE
```

```
48420    COLOR 15,0                          ' DO THIS BRIGHT
48425    LOCATE 23,15                        ' PAUSE LINE POSITION
48430    ENTRY$ = ""                         ' MAKE SURE NOTHING
                                                 HERE
48435    INPUT "DO YOU WISH MORE? ",ENTRY$
48440    CLS                                 ' CLEAR THE SCREEN
48445    IF LEFT$(ENTRY$,1) = "N" OR
             LEFT$(ENTRY$,1) = "n" THEN HELP% =
             0 : RETURN                       ' THEY WANT OUT
48450    ROW% = 0                            ' RESET PAGE LINE
                                                 COUNTER
48455    IF Y <> 0 THEN Y = 0 : GOSUB 48305  ' RETURN TO ORIGINAL
                                                 CONDITION
48460    IF YY <> 0 THEN YY = 0 : GOSUB 48350 ' RETURN TO ORIGINAL
                                                 CONDITION
48465    RETURN                              ' GET NEXT LINE
48470    '
48475    ' *****************************
48480    '
48485    '
```

If NOPAUSE% is greater than 0, then this whole routine is ignored and a pause is not allowed. If the user responds N to the question Do you wish more?, then the program sets HELP% equal to 0.
This zero tells the line-processing section that the user wants to exit,
and it will CLOSE the help file and return to the calling routine.

TEST POINT

Execute the program; it should pause at the end of the help screen.
Next, edit the help file and add a few pause symbols and verify that
it pauses.

CHANGING THE SCREEN INTENSITY

The help text is normally displayed in low intensity. This enables us
to use high intensity to highlight important information. This feature
enhances the overall quality and appearance of the help screens.

The ^ symbol is used to mark the beginning and the end of the
text to be shown highlighted. Whenever this symbol is encountered,

the current state of brightness is reversed. In other words, if the display is in the dim condition and a ^ is encountered, then the high-intensity command (COLOR 15) is given and a flag is set as a reminder that bright is on. When the next ^ is encountered, a COLOR 7 command is given and the flag is reset to 0. This technique allows an individual letter, a word, or the entire text to be highlighted.

EXAMPLE


```
THIS IS A ^TEST^
```


This statement results in the word *TEST* being shown highlighted.

If you are using a color graphics adapter, you could do the highlighting using colors instead. This can be very effective, and with a little experimentation you should be able to determine which color combinations are the most pleasing to your eye.

The program listing for controlling brightness is as follows.

```
48305   ' TOGGLE BRIGHTNESS
48310   '
48315   IF Y > 0 THEN Y = 0 : COLOR 7 , 0 : RETURN      ' CLEAR TO DIM
48320   COLOR 15                                        ' TURN BRIGHT ON
48325   Y = 1                                           ' SET FLAG
48330   RETURN
48335   '
48340   ' ****************************
48345   '
```


TEST POINT

Edit the help text and add some ^ symbols for highlighting. Then execute the program; the highlighting should appear and the program should pause at the bottom of the screen.

BLINKING DISPLAY

In addition to changing the intensity, the program can also make the display blink. This can be used to draw attention to particularly important information. This feature, however, should be used sparingly, because there is nothing more annoying than a screen that is full of blinking text.

The ~ symbol is used to mark the beginning and the end of the blinking text field. As with the intensity subroutine, single letters, a word, or the entire text can be made to blink.

The blink subroutine follows.

```
48350   ' FLASHING VIDEO
48355   '
48360   IF YY > 0 THEN YY = 0 : COLOR 7 , 0 : RETURN    ' FLASHER ON TURN OFF
48365   YY = 1                                          ' SET FLAG
48370   COLOR 31,0                                       ' TURN FLASHER ON
48375   RETURN
48380   '
48385   ' ******************************
48390   '
48395   '
```

COLOR 31,0 is used to turn blinking on. COLOR 7,0 is used to turn it off. Therefore, after a blinking field is printed, the display returns to low intensity. If the display is in high intensity before the blinking is turned off, then you will have to use another ^ after blinking to return the display to high intensity.

ERROR PROCESSING

This program uses the standard error processing routine first seen in Chapter 1. It is repeated here for convenience.

```
60000   ' STANDARD ERROR PROCESSING ROUTINE
60005   '
60010   X = ERR                              ' GET ERROR NUMBER
```

```
60015    Y = ERL                                   ' GET LINE NUMBER
60020    RESUME 60025
60025    KEY OFF                                   ' TURN OFF SO WE CAN
                                                       USE 25TH LINE
60030    LOCATE 25,1                               ' DISPLAY ON 25TH LINE
60035    PRINT "ERROR ";X;" ON LINE NUMBER";Y
60040    BEEP                                      ' RING THE BELLS
60045    END                                       ' THAT'S ALL FOLKS
60050    '
60055    '
60060    '
```

USER INSTRUCTIONS

The following sections contain the user instructions for the help system. Please add this to your user's manual.

Requesting Help

If you have questions about what information is to be entered or how to respond to a particular request from the computer, help can be requested by pressing shift F1. If the computer can help you in this section, it will clear the screen and display a help message.

Periodically, and at the end of the message, the computer will pause and ask,

```
Do you wish more?
```

If you press a Y and then ENTER, or if you simply press ENTER, then more text will be displayed if it is available. If you press an N and then ENTER or if the end of the help text has been reached, then the computer will redisplay the original screen and you may continue processing.

If the help message does not answer your questions, refer to the manual or contact the system operator.

COMPLETE HELP PROGRAM

Here is the complete listing of the help program.

```
100        ' CHAPTER 4 - TEST ROUTINE FOR HELP DISPLAY
105        '
110        KEY OFF                                  ' CLEAR 25TH LINE
115        CLS
120        ON ERROR GOTO 60000                      ' NORMAL ERROR ROUTINE
125        PRINT "CHAPTER 4 HELP SYSTEM SAMPLE PROGRAM"
130        HELP% = 1                                ' TURN HELP FLAG ON
135        PRINT
140        PRINT "ONE SAMPLE IS NAMED: CHAP8A.HLP"
145        PRINT
150        INPUT "ENTER HELP SCREEN NAME: ";HELP$
155        IF LEN(HELP$) = 0 THEN END ELSE GOSUB
              48000                                 ' DISPLAY HELP SCREEN
160        GOTO 100
165        '
170        ' ********************************
175        '

48000      ' SHOW HELP * SCREEN DISPLAY ROUTINE
48005      '
48010      '
48015      '
48020      ' DISPLAYS SCREEN AND USES BRIGHT AND DIM CHARACTERS
48025      ' WILL PAUSE WHEN THE SCREEN IS FULL
48030      ' TO ALLOW THE USER TIME TO READ.
48035      '
48040      '
48045      ' IMPORTANT VARIABLES USED:
48050      '           BRIGHTNESS FLAG
48055      '           FLASH FLAG
48060      '           TOTAL NUMBER OF LINES DISPLAYED
48065      '           1=DO NOT PAUSE AT END OF PAGE. 0=PAUSE
48070      '
48075      '
48080      ' BRIGHTNESS TOGGLED ON '^' CHARACTER
48085      '
48090      ' FLASH TOGGLED ON '~' CHARACTER
48095      '
48100      ' ***********************************************************
```

```
48105     HELP% = 1                              ' REQUIRED, BUT CALLER
                                                     MAY NOT HAVE SET
48110     COLOR 7,0                              ' START DIM
48115     ON ERROR GOTO 48490                    ' IN CASE FILE MISSING
48120     OPEN HELP$ FOR INPUT AS #1             ' OPEN THE HELP FILE
48125     ON ERROR GOTO 60000                    ' NORMAL ERROR
                                                     PROCESSING

48130     '
48135     ' CLEAR THE COUNTERS
48140     '
48145     ROW% = 0
48150     Y = 0                                  ' BRIGHTNESS FLAG
48155     YY = 0                                 ' FLASH FLAG
48160     CLS                                    ' CLEAR SCREEN
48165     ' INPUT THE SCREEN
48170     '
48175     IF EOF(1) <> 0 THEN GOTO 48260         ' TEST FOR END OF FILE
48180     LINE INPUT#1,A$                        ' GET A TEXT LINE
48185     IF HELP% = 0 THEN GOTO 48260           ' HELP% = 0 MEANS EXIT
48190     IF A$ = "@" THEN GOSUB 48400 : GOTO
             48175                               ' PAUSE WANTED?
48195     Z = INSTR(1,A$,"^")                    ' LOOK FOR INTENSITY
                                                     TOGGLE
48200     IF Z = 1 THEN GOSUB 48305 : A$ =
             MID$(A$,2) : GOTO 48195             ' TOGGLE IN FIRST
                                                     POSITION
48205     IF Z > 1 THEN PRINT LEFT$(A$,Z-1); :
             GOSUB 48305 : A$ = MID$(A$,Z+1) :
             GOTO 48195                          ' PRINT PARTIAL LINE
48210     Z = INSTR(1,A$,"~")                    ' LOOK FOR FLASH TOGGLE
48215     IF Z = 1 THEN GOSUB 48350 : A$ =
             MID$(A$,2) : GOTO 48210             ' TOGGLE IN FIRST
                                                     POSITION
48220     IF Z > 1 THEN PRINT LEFT$(A$,Z-1); :
             GOSUB 48350 : A$ = MID$(A$,Z+1) :
             GOTO 48210                          ' PRINT PARTIAL LINE
48225     PRINT A$                               ' NO MORE TOGGLES SO
                                                     PRINT REMAINDER
48230     ROW% = ROW% + 1                        ' INCREMENT THIS PAGE
                                                     LINE COUNTER
48235     IF EOF(1) <> 0 OR ROW% = 22 THEN GOSUB
             48400                               ' GET NEXT LINE
48240     GOTO 48175                             ' NOT DONE YET
48245     '
48250     ' ****************************
```

```
48255    '
48260    ' EXIT POINT WHEN ALL DONE
48265    '
48270    HELP% = 0                              ' FILE DONE. CLEAR JUST
                                                    TO BE SAFE.
48275    CLOSE#1                                ' CLOSE THE FILE
48280    COLOR 7,0                              ' RESTORE DIM DISPLAY
48285    RETURN
48290    '
48295    ' ***************************
48300    '
48305    ' TOGGLE BRIGHTNESS
48310    '
48315    IF Y > 0 THEN Y = 0 : COLOR 7,0 : RETURN     ' CLEAR TO DIM
48320    COLOR 15                               ' TURN BRIGHT ON
48325    Y = 1                                  ' SET FLAG
48330    RETURN
48335    '
48340    ' ***************************
48345    '
48350    ' FLASHING VIDEO
48355    '
48360    IF YY > 0 THEN YY = 0 : COLOR 7,0 :
             RETURN                             ' FLASHER ON TURN OFF
48365    YY = 1                                 ' SET FLAG
48370    COLOR 31,0                             ' TURN FLASHER ON
48375    RETURN
48380    '
48385    ' *******************************
48390    '
48395    '
48400    ' PAUSE AND ASK FOR MORE?
48405    '
48410    '
48415    IF NOPAUSE% > 0 THEN RETURN            ' PROGRAMMER DOES NOT
                                                    WANT PAUSE
48420    COLOR 15,0                             ' DO THIS BRIGHT
48425    LOCATE 23,15                           ' PAUSE LINE POSITION
48430    ENTRY$ = ""                            ' MAKE SURE NOTHING
                                                    HERE
48435    INPUT "DO YOU WISH MORE? ",ENTRY$
48440    CLS                                    ' CLEAR THE SCREEN
48445    IF LEFT$(ENTRY$,1) = "N" OR
             LEFT$(ENTRY$,1) = "n" THEN HELP% =
             0 : RETURN                         ' THEY WANT OUT
```

```
48450    ROW% = 0                                    ' RESET PAGE LINE
                                                         COUNTER
48455    IF Y <> 0 THEN Y = 0 : GOSUB 48305         ' RETURN TO ORIGINAL
                                                         CONDITION
48460    IF YY <> 0 THEN YY = 0 : GOSUB 48350       ' RETURN TO ORIGINAL
                                                         CONDITION
48465    RETURN                                      ' GET NEXT LINE
48470    '
48475    ' *****************************
48480    '
48485    '
48490    ' FILE NOT FOUND ERROR
48495    '
48500    RESUME 48505                                ' CLEAN UP ERROR
                                                         ROUTINE
48505    ON ERROR GOTO 60000                         ' NORMAL ERROR ROUTINE
48510    LOCATE 25,1
48515    PRINT HELP$;" NOT FOUND.";                  ' PRINT ERROR MESSAGE
                                                         ON 25TH LINE
48520    BEEP
48525    RETURN                                      ' RETURN TO CALLER
48530    '
48535    '
48540    '

60000    ' ERROR PROCESSING ROUTINE
60005    '
60010    X = ERR                                     ' GET ERROR NUMBER
60015    Y = ERL                                     ' GET LINE NUMBER
60020    RESUME 60025
60025    KEY OFF                                      ' TURN OFF SO WE CAN USE
                                                         25TH LINE
60030    LOCATE 25,1                                  ' DISPLAY ON 25TH LINE
60035    PRINT "ERROR ";X;" ON LINE
            NUMBER ";Y;CHR$(7);                       ' RING MY BELLS
60040    END
60045    '
60050    '
60055    '
```

A DATA ENTRY SCREEN PROCESSOR

INTRODUCTION

Two of the most time-consuming problems encountered when you are developing a program are data entry screens and printed reports. The layout, verification, and modification of these items take up a significant portion of your time. These two functions, however, really represent the finished product. They are what the user actually sees and interacts with.

Users can appreciate this interface with the computer, and it is this input/output—data entry screens and printed reports—that forms their image of the computer, the program, and you. No matter how much energy you put into creating a solution to a problem, the user only sees as far as the input/output. They do not care how flexible you made the program, how easy it is to maintain, or how much thought you put into it. They only care about how readable, presentable, and understandable the input/output is.

As a programmer, you have two choices: You can accept this fact and give the users whatever they want, or you can give them what you think they need and deal with their complaints. We naturally believe in following the path of least resistance, and so this chapter is about a user-friendly data entry screen processor that is also very programmer friendly. Chapter 7 will deal with the task of putting the output information on paper.

Many users view the computer and the data entry screens as barriers between them and their getting a job done. The screens and their logical flow can make the use of the program an enjoyable, productive task—or an unpleasant chore. The data entry screen is where most of the input errors occur. Thus it is particularly important that this part of your program be understandable, predictable, and forgiving.

In this chapter we design and develop a data entry screen program that incorporates both the line editor from Chapter 2 and the help system from Chapter 4. This program is a good example of how to build programs from pieces previously created. In the following subsections we complete the design and develop, test, and document this program.

Design

We want the data entry system to be easy for the user to work with. We also want it to be flexible and easy to modify, without seriously impacting the existing program.

Building the Program

The data entry program builds on the routines that have been developed in previous chapters. The routines of this chapter will be combined with those of Chapters 2 and 4 by using the Merge command in IBM BASIC.

Here is the method to use to build the data entry system:

1. Start with a fresh, formatted diskette.

2. Using PC DOS, transfer a copy of the program from Chapter 2 to the new diskette. Then, using the Merge command, add the program from Chapter 4 to the diskette. Do not forget to delete the test routines for these two chapters.

3. Using the screen editor from Chapter 3, type in the program presented in this chapter and save it with the merged copy of Chapters 2 and 4.

User Features

The line editor is used in the data entry system so that all those wonderful editing features, particularly the ability to edit existing data, are available to the user. The entry system allows the user to move up and down through the fields, editing and making corrections. Before exiting the screen, the user is given the chance to verify and correct entries. All of the editing is done without excessive keystrokes or the implication that the user does not know how to operate the computer. (As mentioned earlier, it is never good practice to have the computer program talk down to the user.)

One nice feature of the data entry system is the use of original, or default, values. You may recall that the line editor can either accept new information or be started with an initial value. This feature is used to allow default values for every field in the data entry screen. For example, if the user is entering new data, all the data fields are blank. However, if the user is editing existing data, then he or she can go directly to the field of interest and modify it. In contrast, the INPUT statement does not allow the display of a default value, nor does it allow the user to edit an existing value.

Programmer Features

The programmer's goal is to minimize the amount of work that has to be done to create and modify screens. It is rather pointless and very boring to keep writing the same type of program over and over again. Therefore we want to write one routine, give it the data, and have it process and return the user input without having to worry about the display or the editing. Our data entry system includes these features.

For each data entry screen, the programmer must create two small subroutines plus the text of the data entry screen.

The data screen processor edits data stored as a string array. For each screen the programmer must write one routine to load the data into the string array and another routine to retrieve the edited data from the array.

The data entry screen is made up of the text describing what information is desired plus data fields. (Recall that a field is what we call each piece of information that the user will be entering.) A field's data type, screen position, and length, along with all the general screen text, is stored in a sequential text file (created by using the screen text editor of Chapter 3).

The data entry program also loads and displays the screen. As it is displaying the screen, it extracts each field's characteristics. After it has displayed the text portion of the screen, it displays the original, or default, values of each of the fields and then begins editing in the first field. The program performs these steps for every screen in the program. As a result there is no duplicated effort and every screen is of a consistent, high quality.

CREATING A DATA ENTRY SCREEN

The data entry screen processor uses both the line editor and the help subroutines. As mentioned earlier, the line editor is more flexible than the INPUT statement. The help subroutine, with a few additional program lines, is used to display the screen text and process the input-mask information. By using the help subroutine, you can have highlighted areas, and you do not duplicate the program lines necessary to display the screen text. Thus you are in the position of being able to implement help with all of your screens without having to do anything special with the programs.

When using the help subroutine, you can utilize ^ (intensity) and ~ (blinking) symbols to highlight areas of special interest. For example, displaying the title of the screen in high intensity by enclosing it in ^ symbols is a nice touch. Be careful not to overuse these features though; overuse can make the screens appear cluttered and cause confusion.

In addition to containing the text the user is to see, the data screen contains information defining where variables are to be accepted and what their masks will be. For this feature the data mask is enclosed between < and > symbols ("less than" and "greater than"). For example, if a ten-character alphanumeric field is desired, it is represented as

```
<a 10>.
```

Text entry begins at the < symbol. (The < and > symbols will not appear on the screen.) As an example, Figure 5.1 illustrates a sample screen for a mailing list program.

Using the text editor, the screen can easily be set up as you wish it to appear. This method is easier and faster than the trial-and-error approach necessary when using PRINTs, LOCATEs, and INPUTs. If the appearance of a screen changes and the variables used are not changed, then there will be no changes required in the BASIC program. You merely edit the screen, and the next time the screen is used, it will be the new screen.

FIG. 5.1   Sample data entry screen layout (as typed)

```
                    ^NAME AND ADDRESS^
        1. NAME                  <A 20>
        2. TITLE                 <A 20>
        3. ADDRESS               <a 20>
        4. CITY                  <a 20>
        5. STATE                 <A 2>
        6. ZIP CODE              <# 5>
        7. TELEPHONE             <A 25>
```

This technique also allows you to easily print copies of the screens so that they can be used as part of the specifications for the project or as part of the user's manual. Even if you have not created as many data entry screens as we have, you can appreciate the ease and flexibility this procedure gives you in creating screens. Having them automatically processed is an added bonus.

SAMPLE VARIABLE-EXCHANGE ROUTINE

The variables used for the example in Figure 5.1 would have names like NAME$, ADDRESS$, ZIP, and so on. A general-purpose screen editor cannot use these exact names but must work with a string array. So the array LINES$() is used for this purpose. In order for the data screen processor to use actual data, the data variables must be exchanged with the string array variables before and after the data entry screen is processed. Two exchange subroutines are required for each screen. One moves the data from the actual variables into the string array, and the other moves the edited string array values back into the actual variables. For example, the following routine moves the data for Figure 5.1 from the variables into the string array.

```
1000   ' ASSIGN DATA SCREEN DEFAULT VALUES
1005   '
1010   LINES$(1) = PERSON$
1015   LINES$(2) = TITLE$
1020   LINES$(3) = ADDRESS$
1025   LINES$(4) = CITY$
1030   LINES$(5) = STATE$
1035   LINES$(6) = MID$(STR$(ZIP),2)        ' REMOVE FIRST SPACE SINCE
                                                        POSITIVE
1040   LINES$(7) = TELE$
1045   RETURN
1050   '
1055   '
1060   '
```

After the data have been edited and the user exits the data entry screen, the following routine is used to exchange the string array with the actual variables.

```
2000   ' EXTRACT VALUES FROM DATA SCREEN ARRAY
2005   '
2010   PERSON$ = LINES$(1)
2015   TITLE$ = LINES$(2)
2020   ADDRESS$ = LINES$(3)
2025   CITY$ = LINES$(4)
2030   STATE$ = LINES$(5)
2035   ZIP = VAL(LINES$(6))
2040   TELE$ = LINES$(7)
2045   RETURN
2050   ' *******************************************
2055   '
2060   '
```

Except for a few minor changes, which are noted in the next section, these routines (plus the data entry screen processor) are all that you have to write to process the screen of Figure 5.1.

DATA ENTRY PROGRAM

The flowchart for the data entry screen processor is shown in Figure 5.2. The basic steps are as follows:

1. Display the data entry screen with the help screen processor.
2. Load the string edit array with the starting, or default, values and show the default values.
3. Edit the data.
4. Save the edited values and test to see if help has been requested.
5. If help was requested, first show the help screen and then redisplay the original data entry screen.
6. If help was not requested, then return to the calling program.

Various aspects of the data screen entry processor are discussed in the following subsections. The following program listing corresponds to the flowchart in Figure 5.2.

FIG. 5.2   Flowchart for data entry screen processor

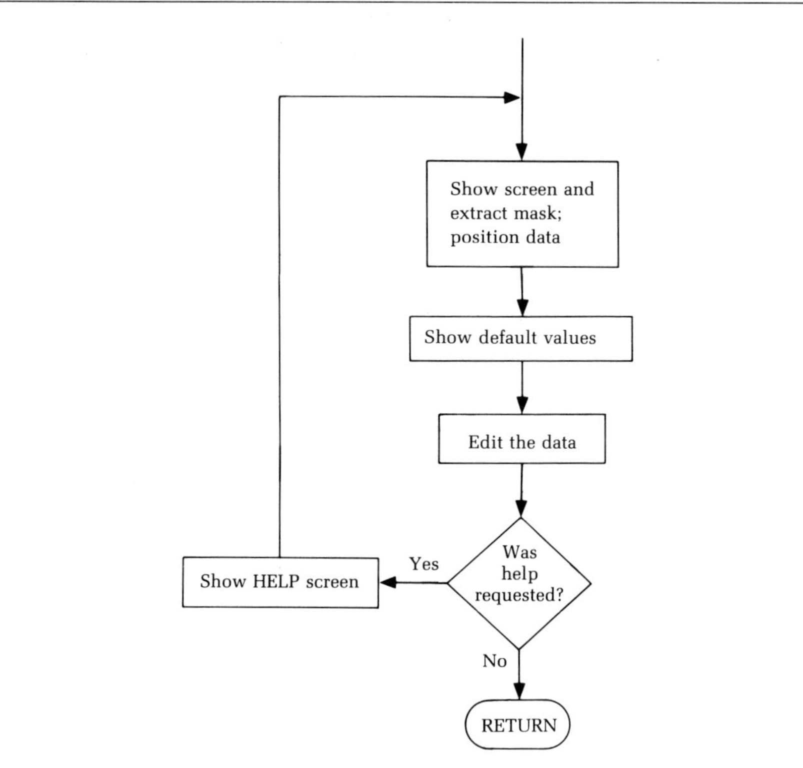


```
44000    ' DATA ENTRY * SCREEN PROCESSOR
44005    '
44010    '
44015    '
44020    ' DISPLAYS SCREEN, LOADS MASK
             DATA
44025    ' DISPLAYS DEFAULT VALUES
44030    ' EDITS AND SAVES VALUES
44035    '
44040    ' VARIABLES USED:
44045    '    LINES$()   HOLDS EDIT DATA
44050    '    ITEMS%     NUMBER TO EDIT
44055    '    SROW%()    FIELD ROW NUMBER
44060    '    SCOL%()    FIELD COL NUMBER
```

```
44065    '    SMASK$()   FIELD MASK$
44070    '    SMAX%()    FIELD LENGTH
44075    '    IMAGE$     NAME OF SCREEN
44080    '    LINES%     CURRENT LINE BEING EDITED
44085    '
44090    '
44095    '
44100    '
44105    '    EDIT A DATA SCREEN
44110    '
44115    '    SHOW THE DATA SCREEN
44120    '
44125    ITEMS% = 0                          ' CLEAR NUMBER OF ITEMS
44130    NOPAUSE% = 1                        ' INFORM HELP SCREEN NOT TO
                                               PAUSE
44135    COL% = 1                            ' RESET POSITION COUNTER
44140    HELP$ = IMAGE$ + ".IMG"             ' NAME OF SCREEN FILE
44145    GOSUB 48000                         ' SHOW SCREEN
44150    NOPAUSE% = 0                        ' RESET TO ALLOW PAUSE
44155    GOSUB 44305                         ' SHOW DEFAULT VALUES
44160    GOSUB 44385                         ' EDIT DATA
44165    IF HELP% = 0 THEN RETURN            ' ALL DONE SO EXIT
44170    HELP$ = IMAGE$ + ".HLP"             ' CREATE HELP FILE NAME FOR
                                               THIS SCREEN
44175    GOSUB 48000                         ' SHOW HELP
44180    GOTO 44000                          ' START OVER
44185    '
44190    ' ****************************
44195    '
44200    '
```

Explanation of the Program

The name of the screen to be processed is passed to the subroutine in
the variable IMAGE$. The subroutine adds the extension .IMG to IM-
AGE$ for the screen name and .HLP for the screen's help file.

If the user requests help, line 44170 creates the help file name and
line 44175 calls the help subroutine. We are adopting the convention
of adding .HLP to the end of the screen name to create the screen's
help text name. For example, if the data entry screen name is MAIL,

then the help text will have the name MAIL.HLP. If you choose to use a different convention, modify line 44170.

Explanation of Variables

NOPAUSE% (line 44130) and HELP$ (line 44140) are used by the help subroutine to display the screen. If NOPAUSE% is equal to 1, then the help routine will not ask "Do you wish more?" at the end of the file.

The data entry program contains several arrays that must be dimensioned before they are used. In the test routine (presented in the next section) they are dimensioned on lines 125 through 145. The arrays are as follows.

```
125   DIM LINES$(LAST%)     ' DIMENSION ALL THE ARRAYS
130   DIM SROW%(LAST%)
135   DIM SCOL%(LAST%)
140   DIM SMASK$(LAST%)
145   DIM SMAX%(LAST%)
```

LAST% is the dimension of all the arrays; it is the maximum number of fields allowed. LINES$() holds the values of the fields being edited. SROW%() and SCOL%() contain the screen coordinates of each field. SMASK$() is the data entry mask, and SMAX%() is the length of each field.

CHANGES TO THE HELP SUBROUTINE

Three lines must be added to the help subroutine so that it can process the field masks or definitions. These lines are:

```
48222   COL% = INSTR(1,A$,"<")        ' LOOK FOR DATA SCREEN MASK
48223   IF COL% > 0 THEN GOSUB 44205  ' CALL DATA ENTRY SYSTEM
48232   COL% = 1                      ' RESET COLUMN COUNTER
```

These lines recognize the < symbol and set the screen column position counter, COL%.

A < symbol is used to mark the beginning of a field definition. When it is encountered, a branch is made to a subroutine that sets the field parameters, GOSUB 44205.

SUBROUTINE FOR SETTING THE FIELD PARAMETERS

The field parameter routine sets the screen row and column coordinates and the edit mask for the field. It does this by finding the > symbol that marks the end of the mask and then it extracts the mask type and length. The program listing follows.

```
44205   ' SET FIELD PARAMETERS
44210   '
44215   IF COL% > 1 THEN PRINT LEFT$(A$,COL% -
           1);                                  ' PRINT TEXT
44220   ITEMS% = ITEMS% + 1                     ' INC FIELD COUNTER
44225   SMASK$(ITEMS%) = ""                     ' CLEAR IT
44230   SROW%(ITEMS%) = ROW% + 1                ' CURRENT ROW NUMBER
44235   SCOL%(ITEMS%) = COL%                    ' CURRENT COLUMN
                                                    NUMBER

44240   Z = COL% + 1
44245   SMASK$(ITEMS%) = MID$(A$,Z,1)           ' GET ONE CHARACTER
44250   X = INSTR(Z,A$,">")                     ' LOOK FOR END OF MASK
44255   IF X = 0 THEN SMAX%(ITEMS%) = 20 ELSE
           SMAX%(ITEMS%) = VAL(MID$(A$,Z+1,X
           -Z-1))                               ' GET LENGTH
44260   IF LEN(A$) > X + 1 THEN A$ = SPACE$(X - Z
           + 2) + MID$(A$,X+1) ELSE A$ = ""     ' PREPARE TO PRINT
44265   RETURN
44270   ' ****************************
44275   '
```

In the above program, four arrays plus one counter are used to contain the field parameters. In lines 44230 and 44235 the integer arrays SROW%() and SCOL%() contain the starting screen coordinates for the fields. These arrays will be assigned to ROW% and COL% when the line editor routine is called. SMASK$() in line 44225 is a string array used to contain the mask for the fields. MASK$ will be set from this array. SMAX%() (line 44255) contains the length of the field. Finally, ITEMS% (line 44220) is used to count the number of fields on the screen. ITEMS% is incremented by one as each field is processed. You may have noticed that ITEMS% is reset to 0 before the screen display subroutine is called.

TEST POINT

At this point you should have entered all the programs presented thus far. Now enter the following program and the data screen shown in Figure 5.1 (saved as CHAP5.IMG). After you enter RUN (CR), this screen should be displayed. The program will stop on line 44155 because the default display routine has not been entered yet.

The following test routine has been designed for only ten fields. It will display the results of the editing. The first time the program is run, the data screen will be blank; the second and subsequent times it will display as defaults the values of the previous edit session.

The test routine is as follows.

```
100       ' CHAPTER 5 - TEST PROGRAM FOR DATA SCREEN PROCESSOR
105       '
110       '
115       ON ERROR GOTO 60000                    ' NORMAL ERROR
                                                     PROCESSING ROUTINE
120       LAST% = 10
125       DIM LINES$(LAST%)                      ' DIMENSION ALL THE
                                                     ARRAYS
130       DIM SROW%(LAST%)
135       DIM SCOL%(LAST%)
140       DIM SMASK$(LAST%)
145       DIM SMAX%(LAST%)
150       KEY OFF                                ' TURN FUNCTION KEYS
                                                     OFF
155       FOR X = 1 TO 10                        ' CLEAR THEM JUST IN
                                                     CASE
160           KEY X,""
165       NEXT X
170       IMAGE$ = "CHAP5"
175       GOSUB 1000                             ' SET UP LINES$() FOR
                                                     DATA ENTRY ROUTINE
180       GOSUB 44000                            ' DATA ENTRY ROUTINE
185       GOSUB 2000                             ' RESTORE VARIABLES
                                                     FROM LINES$()
```

```
190        CLS
195        PRINT "NAME      ",PERSON$
200        PRINT "TITLE     ",TITLE$
205        PRINT "ADDRESS ",ADDRESS$
210        PRINT "CITY      ",CITY$
215        PRINT "STATE     ",STATE$
220        PRINT "ZIP CODE",ZIP
225        PRINT "TELEPHONE",TELE$
230        LOCATE 23,1
235        INPUT "PRESS ENTER TO CONTINUE ";A$
240        GOTO 170
245        '
250        '
```

DISPLAYING THE ORIGINAL VALUES

After the text is displayed and LINES$() has been loaded with the original, or default, values, subroutines GOSUB 44305 displays the values. By displaying the default values, the user is presented with a complete picture of the current data. This technique is better than the method of serially showing and editing one field at a time. By being shown all the information at once, the user has a better understanding of what is being requested.

The display routine uses a FOR–NEXT loop to position the cursor [using the values in SROW%() and SCOL%()] and then prints the default value in LINES$(). The program listing follows.

```
44305      ' SHOW DEFAULT VALUES
44310      '
44315      PLACE% = 1
44320      FRONT% = 1
44325      FILL$ = "."                   ' SET FOR DISPLAY ROUTINE
44330      FOR Z = 1 to ITEMS%
44335          ROW% = SROW%(Z)           ' CURSOR POSITIONING
44340          COL% = SCOL%(Z)
44345          MAXSIZE% = SMAX%(Z)
44350          ENTRY$ = LINES$(Z)
44355          GOSUB 52660               ' DISPLAY THE DATA
44360      NEXT Z
```

```
44365    RETURN
44370    '
44375    ' ****************************
44380    '
```

TEST POINT

After the display subroutine is entered, the program should display the screen and stop at line 44160. Since values have not been assigned to LINES$(), no default will be shown.

EDITING SUBROUTINE

Once the screen text and the default values are displayed, all that remains is to edit the individual fields. The line editor is used because it allows editing in an existing field and offers cursor controls not available with INPUT. Two program lines need to be added to process the up and down arrows. We use the F1 key as the exit key in the programs in this book.

```
51207  IF A.KEY% = 372 THEN CTRL% = 3    ' UP ARROW (SAME AS CHAP 3)
51221  IF A.KEY% = 380 THEN CTRL% = 2    ' DOWN ARROW (SAME AS CHAP 3)
```

Figure 5.3 is a flowchart of the field-editing subroutine, which follows.

```
44385    ' EDIT THE DATA FIELDS
44390    '
44395    LINES% = 1                    ' START IN DATA FIELD
44400    ENTRY$ = LINES$(LINES%)       ' FIELD
44405    ROW% = SROW%(LINES%)          ' ROW
44410    COL% = SCOL%(LINES%)          ' COL
44415    MASK$ = SMASK$(LINES%)        ' MASK
44420    MAXSIZE% = SMAX%(LINES%)      ' FIELD LENGTH
44425    GOSUB 50000                   ' EDIT FIELD
44430    LINES$(LINES%) = ENTRY$       ' SAVE THE EDITED DATA
                                         FIELD
44435    IF HELP% > 0 THEN RETURN      ' HELP REQUESTED IN THE
                                         FIELD
```

```
44440   IF (CTRL% = 3) AND (LINES% > 1) THEN
             LINES% = LINES% - 1: GOTO 44400        ' UP ARROW
44445   IF CTRL% = 3 THEN GOTO 44400                ' UP ARROW BUT ALREADY
                                                      AT TOP
44450   IF CTRL% = 27 THEN GOTO 44465              ' F1 SO GO TO BOTTOM
44455   IF LINES% < ITEMS% THEN LINES% = LINE%
             + 1: GOTO 44400                         ' MOVE DOWN A LINE
44460   '
44465   ' VERIFY ENTRIES
44470   '
44475   LOCATE 24,10                                ' GOTO BOTTOM
44480   COLOR 15,0                                  ' HI INTENSITY
44485   PRINT "CHANGE WHICH ITEM?";
44490   MASK$ = "#"                                 ' ALLOW UP TO 99 FIELDS
44495   MAXSIZE% = 2
44500   ENTRY$ = "0"                                ' DEFAULT
44505   ROW% = 24
44510   COL% = 40
44515   GOSUB 50000                                 ' EDIT DATA
44520   COLOR 7,0                                   ' LOW INTENSITY
44525   IF CTRL% = 3 THEN LINES% = ITEMS% : GOTO
             44400                                   ' UP ARROW
44530   LINES% = VAL(ENTRY$)                        ' LINE TO EDIT
44535   IF LINES% = 0 THEN RETURN                   ' ALL DONE WITH THIS
                                                      SCREEN
44540   IF (LINES% < = ITEMS%) AND (LINES% > 0)
             THEN GOTO 44400                         ' EDIT THE REQUESTED
                                                      FIELD
44545   GOTO 44465                                  ' BAD ENTRY
44550   '
44555   ' ****************************
44560   '
```

Editing begins at the first field, and LINES% (line 44395) is used to
mark the field being edited. Next, the variables required for the line
editor and ENTRY$ are set. After editing, the contents of ENTRY$ are
returned to LINES$(). Then the program determines if the user entered
an up arrow, a F1, or requested help. If none of these requests was
made, then the program assumes the down arrow or ENTER key was
pressed and steps to the next field.

After the last field has been edited, or a F1 has been pressed, the
user is asked,

```
Change which item?
```

FIG. 5.3   Flowchart for field-editing routine

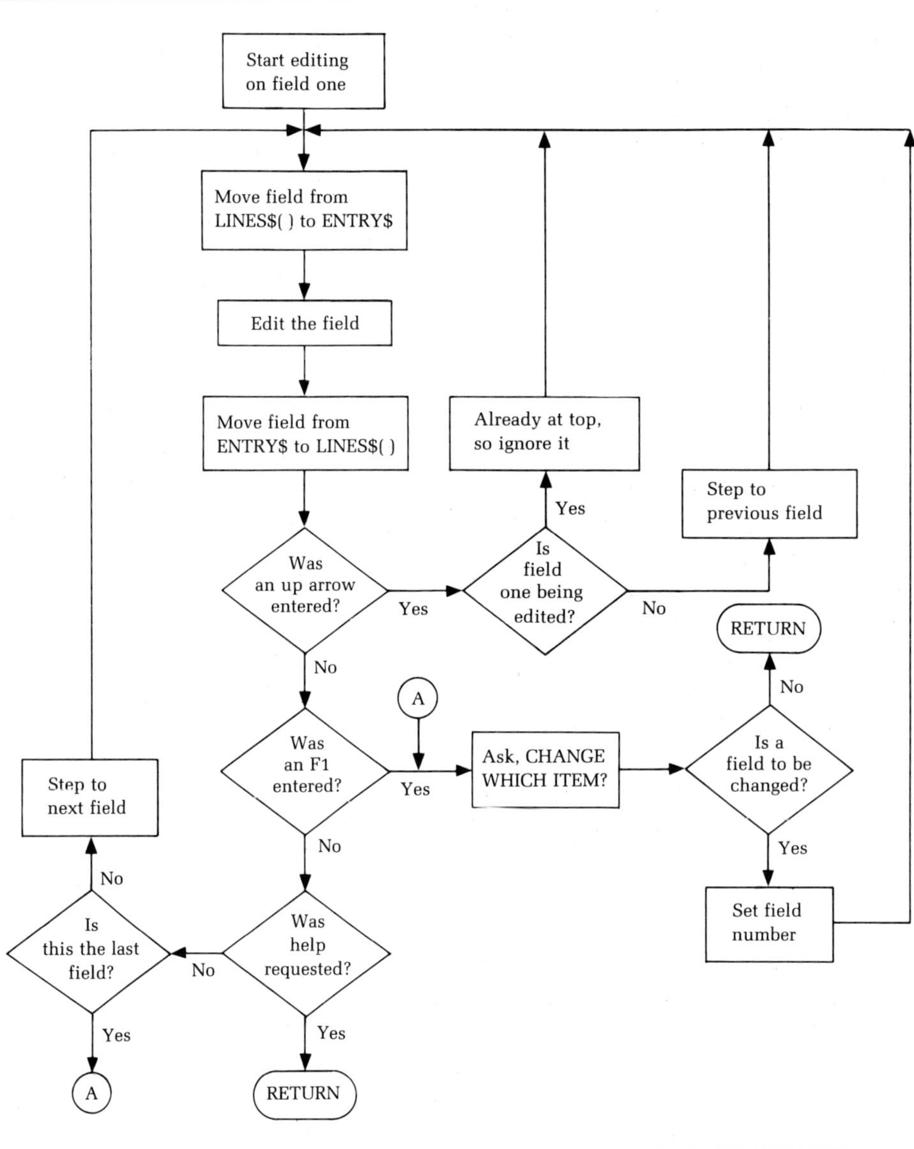

If either 0 (CR) or the ENTER key is pressed, then the editing is completed and the program returns to the calling program. Otherwise, the cursor is moved to the field requested.

The up arrow and F1 keys are user-friendly, labor-saving features. The user does not have to press ENTER for every field on the screen just to get to the Changes line; similarly, the up arrow will move the cursor up a field. You may have noticed that the user can enter an up arrow on the Changes line to move to the previous field. It is often easier to enter several up arrows than to find and enter a field number.

TEST POINT

The data entry system is now complete. You will now want to test the up arrow and F1 keys. Also verify that a field number can be entered on the Changes line and the field edited.

After ENTER is pressed on the Changes line, the test routine will pause and display: Press ENTER to continue. Press ENTER and the program will branch to the beginning of the data entry screen. When the data entry screen is again displayed, the values you just entered should be printed as the new defaults.

Before the help feature can be tested, a help file named CHAP5.HLP will have to be created. Naturally this file can be created by using the text editor from Chapter 3 and can contain any of the help features developed in Chapter 4. After the help screen is displayed, the screen should be cleared and the entry screen redisplayed.

ADDITIONAL OPTION

The editing subroutine begins editing on the first field. You may wish to begin editing with the Changes line instead. When you are editing a blank screen with no defaults, then you will want to begin editing at field one; but when you are editing existing data, it is convenient to begin editing at the Changes line.

This option can be implemented by changing line 44160 to branch optionally to either lines 44385 or 44465. For example, you could use

```
44160 ON EDITSTART% GOSUB 44385,44465
```

where EDITSTART% equals 1 to start in field one and 2 to start on the Changes line.

ERROR PROCESSING

This program uses the standard error processing routine first seen in Chapter 1. It is repeated here for convenience.

```
60000    ' STANDARD ERROR PROCESSING ROUTINE
60005    '
60010    X = ERR                                  ' GET ERROR NUMBER
60015    Y = ERL                                  ' GET LINE NUMBER
60020    RESUME 60025
60025    KEY OFF                                  ' TURN OFF SO WE CAN USE
                                                      25TH LINE
60030    LOCATE 25,1                              ' DISPLAY ON 25TH LINE
60035    PRINT "ERROR ";X;"ON LINE NUMBER";Y
60040    BEEP                                     ' RING THE BELLS
60045    END                                      ' THAT'S ALL FOLKS
60050    '
60055    '
60060    '
```

USER INSTRUCTIONS

The following subsections contain the user instructions for the data entry system. Please add these to your user's manual.

Entering and Editing Data

All data entry screens function in the same manner. They all have features that make it easier for you to edit and change data. The data entry screen consists of three parts: (1) the text used to describe the screen; (2) the data fields; that is, the actual data you can edit; and (3) a line at the bottom of the screen that asks

```
Change which item?
```

This is referred to as the Changes line.

In addition to all the editing capabilities described in the line editor chapter, you can move up and down through the fields or jump directly to the bottom of the screen to the Changes line.

Editing a Field

Whenever a field is being edited, its current value is shown. If you do not wish to change the field, then press ENTER or the down arrow and the cursor will move to the next field. If you do wish to change a field, then just change it by using the various editing commands. Remember that the field is accepted exactly as you see it, and so do not leave out or forget anything.

Moving Between Fields

If you are in a field and wish to go to the next field, press ENTER or the down arrow key. If you wish to go to the previous field, then press the up arrow. You may step up and down through the fields as often as necessary to edit them.

How to Exit the Data Entry Screen

When you wish to stop editing and go to the Changes line, either step down through the fields by pressing ENTER or jump across all the fields directly to the Changes line by pressing the F1 key.

Change Which Item?

The question, Change which item?, is asked at the bottom of every data entry screen. To edit a field, enter its number and then press EN-TER. The program will jump to the field requested.

The up arrow can also be used to step up from the Changes line, one field at a time, to the field you wish to change.

If you do not wish to make any corrections, press ENTER and the program will proceed.

Help Requests

To request help, press shift F1 and a help screen will be displayed. After the help text has been displayed, the original screen will be displayed and the data edited.

COMPLETE DATA ENTRY SCREEN PROGRAM

The complete listing of the data entry program is as follows.

```
100        ' CHAPTER 5 - TEST PROGRAM FOR DATA SCREEN PROCESSOR
105        '
110        '
115        ON ERROR GOTO 60000              ' NORMAL ERROR PROCESSING
                                              ROUTINE
120        LAST% = 10
125        DIM LINES$(LAST%)                ' DIMENSION ALL THE ARRAYS
130        DIM SROW%(LAST%)
135        DIM SCOL%(LAST%)
140        DIM SMASK$(LAST%)
145        DIM SMAX%(LAST%)
150        KEY OFF                          ' TURN FUNCTION KEYS OFF
155        FOR X = 1 TO 10                  ' CLEAR THEM JUST IN CASE
160           KEY X, ""
165        NEXT X
170        IMAGE$ = "CHAP5"
175        GOSUB 1000                       ' SET UP LINES$( ) FOR DATA
                                              ENTRY ROUTINE
```

```
180        GOSUB 44000                        ' DATA ENTRY ROUTINE
185        GOSUB 2000                         ' RESTORE VARIABLES FROM
                                                  LINES$()
190        CLS
195        PRINT "NAME        ",PERSON$
200        PRINT "TITLE       ",TITLE$
205        PRINT "ADDRESS     ",ADDRESS$
210        PRINT "CITY        ",CITY$
215        PRINT "STATE       ",STATE$
220        PRINT "ZIP CODE    ",ZIP
225        PRINT "TELEPHONE ",TELE$
230        LOCATE 23,1
235        INPUT "PRESS ENTER TO CONTINUE ";A$
240        GOTO 170
245        '
250        '

1000       ' ASSIGN DATA SCREEN DEFAULT VALUES
1005       '
1010       LINES$(1) = PERSON$
1015       LINES$(2) = TITLE$
1020       LINES$(3) = ADDRESS$
1025       LINES$(4) = CITY$
1030       LINES$(5) = STATE$
1035       LINES$(6) = MID$(STR$(ZIP),2)       ' REMOVE FIRST SPACE SINCE
                                                  POSITIVE
1040       LINES$(7) = TELE$
1045       RETURN
1050       '
1055       '
1060       '

2000       ' EXTRACT VALUES FROM DATA SCREEN ARRAY
2005       '
2010       PERSON$ = LINES$(1)
2015       TITLE$ = LINES$(2)
2020       ADDRESS$ = LINES$(3)
2025       CITY = LINES$(4)
2030       STATE$ = LINES$(5)
2035       ZIP = VAL(LINES$(6))
2040       TELE$ = LINES$(7)
2045       RETURN
2050       ' ********************************************
2055       '
2060       '
```

```
44000      ' DATA ENTRY * SCREEN PROCESSOR
44005      '
44010      '
44015      '
44020      ' DISPLAYS SCREEN, LOADS MASK DATA
44025      ' DISPLAYS DEFAULT VALUES
44030      ' EDITS AND SAVES VALUES
44035      '
44040      ' VARIABLES USED:
44045      '    LINES$()        HOLDS EDIT DATA
44050      '    ITEMS%          NUMBER TO EDIT
44055      '    SROW%()         FIELD ROW NUMBER
44060      '    SCOL%()         FIELD COL NUMBER
44065      '    SMASK$()        FIELD MASK$
44070      '    SMAX%()         FIELD LENGTH
44075      '    IMAGE$          NAME OF SCREEN
44080      '    LINES%          CURRENT LINE BEING EDITED
44085      '
44090      '
44095      '
44100      '
44105      ' EDIT A DATA SCREEN
44110      '
44115      ' SHOW THE DATA SCREEN
44120      '
44125      ITEMS% = 0                        ' CLEAR NUMBER OF ITEMS
44130      NOPAUSE% = 1                      ' INFORM HELP SCREEN NOT TO
                                               PAUSE
44135      COL% = 1                         ' RESET POSITION COUNTER
44140      HELP$ = IMAGE$ + ".IMG"          ' NAME OF SCREEN FILE
44145      GOSUB 48000                      ' SHOW SCREEN
44150      NOPAUSE% = 0                     ' RESET TO ALLOW PAUSE
44155      GOSUB 44305                      ' SHOW DEFAULT VALUES
44160      GOSUB 44385                      ' EDIT DATA
44165      IF HELP% = 0 THEN RETURN         ' ALL DONE SO EXIT
44170      HELP$ = IMAGE$ + ".HLP"          ' CREATE HELP FILE NAME FOR
                                               THIS SCREEN
44175      GOSUB 48000                      ' SHOW HELP
44180      GOTO 44000                       ' START OVER
44185      '
44190      ' ***************************
44195      '
44200      '
44205      SET FIELD PARAMETERS
```

```
44210     '
44215     IF COL% > 1 THEN PRINT
              LEFT$(A$,COL% - 1);                 ' PRINT TEXT
44220     ITEMS% = ITEMS% + 1                     ' INC FIELD COUNTER
44225     SMASK$(ITEMS%) = ""                     ' CLEAR IT
44230     SROW%(ITEMS%) = ROW% + 1                ' CURRENT ROW NUMBER
44235     SCOL%(ITEMS%) = COL%                    ' CURRENT COLUMN NUMBER
44240     Z = COL% + 1
44245     SMASK$(ITEM%) + MID$(A$,Z,1)            ' GET ONE CHARACTER
44250     X = INSTR(Z,A$," >")                    ' LOOK FOR END OF MASK
44255     IF X = 0 THEN SMAX%(ITEMS%) =
              20 ELSE SMAX%(ITEMS%) =
              VAL(MID$(A$,Z+1,X-Z-1))             ' GET LENGTH
44260     IF LEN(A$) > X + 1 THEN A$ =
              SPACE$(X - Z + 2) +
              MID$(A$,X+1) ELSE A$ = ""           ' PREPARE TO PRINT
44265     RETURN
44270     ' *****************************
44275     '

44305     ' SHOW DEFAULT VALUES
44310     '
44315     PLACE% = 1
44320     FRONT% = 1
44325     FILL$ = "."                             ' SET FOR DISPLAY ROUTINE
44330     FOR Z = 1 TO ITEMS%
44335         ROW% = SROW%(Z)                     ' CURSOR POSITIONING
44340         COL% = SCOL%(Z)
44345         MAXSIZE% = SMAX%(Z)
44350         ENTRY$ = LINES$(Z)
44355         GOSUB 52660                         ' DISPLAY THE DATA
44360     NEXT Z
44365     RETURN
44370     '
44375     ' ***************************
44380     '
44385     ' EDIT THE DATA FIELDS
44390     '
44395     LINES% = 1                              ' START IN DATA FIELD
44400     ENTRY$ = LINES$(LINES%)                 ' FIELD
44405     ROW% = SROW%(LINES%)                    ' ROW
44410     COL% = SCOL%(LINES%)                    ' COL
44415     MASK$ = SMASK$(LINES%)                  ' MASK
44420     MAXSIZE% = SMAX%(LINES%)                ' FIELD LENGTH
```

```
44425       GOSUB 50000                      ' EDIT FIELD
44430       LINES$(LINES%) = ENTRY$          ' SAVE THE EDITED DATA FIELD
44435       IF HELP% > 0 THEN RETURN         ' HELP REQUESTED IN THE FIELD
44440       IF (CTRL% = 3) AND (LINES% > 1)
                THEN LINES% = LINES% - 1:
                GOTO 44400                    ' UP ARROW
44445       IF CTRL% = 3 THEN GOTO 44400     ' UP ARROW BUT ALREADY AT TOP
44450       IF CTRL% = 27 THEN GOTO 44465    ' F1 SO GO TO BOTTOM
44455       IF LINES% < ITEMS% THEN LINES%
                = LINES% + 1: GOTO 44400      ' MOVE DOWN A LINE
44460       '
44465       ' VERIFY ENTRIES
44470       '
44475       LOCATE 24,10                     ' GOTO BOTTOM
44480       COLOR 15,0                       ' HI INTENSITY
44485       PRINT "CHANGE WHICH ITEM?";
44490       MASK$ = "#"                      ' ALLOW UP TO 99 FIELDS
44495       MAXSIZE% = 2
44500       ENTRY$ = "0"                     'DEFAULT
44505       ROW% = 24
44510       COL% = 40
44515       GOSUB 50000                      ' EDIT DATA
44520       COLOR 7,0                        ' LOW INTENSITY
44525       IF CTRL% = 3 THEN LINES% =
                ITEMS% : GOTO 44400          ' UP ARROW
44530       LINES% = VAL(ENTRY$)             ' LINE TO EDIT
44535       IF LINES% = 0 THEN RETURN        ' ALL DONE WITH THIS SCREEN
44540       IF (LINES% < = ITEMS%) AND
                (LINES% > 0) THEN GOTO
                44400                         ' EDIT THE REQUESTED FIELD
44545       GOTO 44465                       ' BAD ENTRY
44550       '
44555       ' ****************************
44560       '
48222       COL% = INSTR(1,A$,"<")           ' LOOK FOR DATA SCREEN MASK
48223       IF COL% > 0 THEN GOSUB 44205     ' CALL DATA ENTRY SYSTEM
48232       COL% = 1                         ' RESET COLUMN COUNTER

51207       IF A.KEY% = 372 THEN CTRL% = 3   ' UP ARROW (SAME AS CHAP 3)
51221       IF A.KEY% = 380 THEN CTRL% = 2   ' DOWN ARROW (SAME AS CHAP 3)

60000       ' STANDARD ERROR PROCESSING ROUTINE
60005       '
60010       X = ERR                          ' GET ERROR NUMBER
```

```
60015      Y = ERL                              ' GET LINE NUMBER
60020      RESUME 60025
60025      KEY OFF                              ' TURN OFF SO WE CAN USE 25TH
                                                    LINE
60030      LOCATE 25,1                          ' DISPLAY ON 25TH LINE
60035      PRINT "ERROR ";X;"ON LINE
               NUMBER";Y
60040      BEEP                                 ' RING THE BELLS
60045      END                                  ' THAT'S ALL FOLKS
60050      '
60055      '
60060      '
```

A MENU SYSTEM

INTRODUCTION

In this chapter we develop a menu display program. A *menu* is a list of actions the computer can perform. The user selects one action, and then either a particular portion of the current program is executed or an entirely new program is loaded and executed. Almost all programs have at least one menu. From a programming standpoint, a menu is similar to a data entry screen. It is a simple (and boring) program to write and time-consuming to adjust and modify.

The menu system presented in this chapter is based on the concepts and techniques developed in the previous chapters. The text editor is used to create a menu screen. Embedded within the text of the menu screen, invisible to the end user, is information about what programs are to be executed when a particular option is selected. The help subroutine is used to display the menu. This subroutine allows highlighting of important information and provides consistency for all of the screens.

In the following sections we define the program and describe its features.

Design

The menu driver should be able either to chain to and run another program or to branch to a subroutine within the current program. The menu program presented allows for these options. In addition, the routines of this chapter build upon the routines developed in Chapters 2 and 4.

Building the Program

The routines of this chapter will be combined with those of Chapters 2 and 4 by using the Merge command in IBM BASIC.

Here is the method to use to build the data entry system.

1. Start with a fresh, formatted diskette.
2. Using PC DOS, transfer a copy of the program from Chapter 2 to the new diskette. Then, using the Merge command, add the program from Chapter 4 to the diskette. Do not forget to delete the test portions of these programs.
3. Using BASIC or the screen editor from Chapter 3, type in the program presented in this chapter and save it with the merged copy of Chapters 2 and 4.

User Features

The menu is the user's road map. Without a menu to remind them about what options are available, most users would be hopelessly lost. The menu text must clearly and unambiguously describe what options are available to the user and what the consequences of a particular selection are. A help file, such as we have provided, is therefore absolutely essential with every menu.

In a menu system it is important that consistency be maintained. Your programs should always use the F1 key to step the user back to the previous menu. By knowing this convention, the users will always be able to retrace their steps and return to the beginning of the program. Another technique is to include an option on every menu that will return the user to the first, or "master," menu.

Our menu selections are always numbered, and the user must press ENTER every time a selection is made. Occasionally you may come across a program that requires ENTER in response to certain questions and not in others. For example, in one place in the program you may have to enter a 1 (CR), while in similar situation a simple 1 is all that is necessary; the computer automatically adds the (CR). Such a program is a prime example of inconsistent programming, and most users find this inconsistency irritating and irrational. Unless a program with such inconsistencies is used on a daily basis, the user is always unnecessarily pressing ENTER and accidently causing an undesired action.

Remember, user-friendly software contains no surprises or hidden pitfalls and is consistent. A good menu should provide the users with the visibility necessary to understand where they are going and why.

Programmer Features

The menu routine can be written by using either one of two methods. Method 1 automatically chains the menu to and runs another program, while method 2 causes a branch to a routine within the current program.

In method 1 the programmer includes the names of the programs to be executed by embedding them within the actual menu text, invisible to the end user. The help screen display routine from Chapter 4 is modified to extract the names and not display them. Method 2 requires either an ON GOSUB or an ON GOTO statement to branch to the appropriate routine within the current program. For either option the programmer simply passes the name of the desired menu screen to the menu routine and it takes over from there.

In the first method, the program names may be placed on any line of the screen file. A name, however, must follow a # symbol, begin on column 1, and contain the option number in columns 2 and 3. For example,

```
#1 ACCREC.BAS
#2 GENLED.BAS
#3 PAYROLL.BAS
```

This listing means that accounts receivable is menu option 1, general ledger is option 2, and so on.

The # symbol was chosen to avoid a conflict with the < and > symbols used for the data entry screen. The choice of symbols is completely arbitrary, and if these symbols conflict with the way you use the data entry or menu screens then change the symbols. To avoid problems, try to be consistent with your choice of symbols so that all the screens of a given type use the same style.

MENU PROGRAM

A flowchart of the menu program is shown in Figure 6.1. This program is very simple. It first uses the help screen display subroutine to display the text and to strip out the options and the names of the programs to chain to or run. It then asks the user to select an option. After verifying that a valid option number has been entered, the menu either runs the requested program or branches somewhere within the current program, depending on what line 46170 of the menu contains.

The program listing is as follows.

```
46000     ' MENU DRIVER
46005     '
46010     '
```

```
46015      '
46020      ' DISPLAYS MENU AND CHAINS TO PROGRAM OF USER'S CHOICE
46025      '
46030      '
46035      ' IMPORTANT VARIABLES USED:
46040      '   LINES$( ) CONTAINS NAME OF PROGRAM TO CHAIN TO
46045      '   IMAGE$ CONTAINS NAME OF MENU FILE
46050      '
46055      ITEMS% = 0                            ' NUMBER OF OPTIONS
46060      NOPAUSE% = 1                          ' INFORM HELP SYSTEM NOT TO
                                                     PAUSE
46065      HELP$ = IMAGE$ + ".MNU"              ' MAKE THE MENU NAME
46070      GOSUB 48000                          ' SHOW THE SCREEN USING HELP
                                                     ROUTINE
46075      NOPAUSE% = 0                          ' RESTORE THE FLAG FOR OTHERS
46080      '
46085      ' ASK FOR OPTION
46090      '
46095      LOCATE 3,15
46100      COLOR 15,0                            ' BRIGHT DISPLAY
46105      PRINT "PLEASE SELECT OPTION";
46110      COLOR 7,0                             ' LOW INTENSITY
46115      ROW% = 3
46120      COL% = 40
46125      MASK$ ="#"                            ' ALLOW HELP REQUEST
46130      MAXSIZE% = 1                          ' ALLOWS ONLY 9 OPTIONS
46135      ENTRY$ = "0"
46140      GOSUB 50000                           ' ACCEPT OPTION
46145      IF HELP% THEN HELP$ = IMAGE$ +
               ".HLP": GOSUB 48000: GOTO
               46000                             ' RESPONDED TO HELP REQUEST
46150      X = VAL(ENTRY$)                       ' OPTION SELECTED
46155      IF X > ITEMS% THEN GOTO 46000         ' BAD ENTRY
46160      IF LINES$(X) = "END" THEN CLS :
               END                               ' RETURN TO BASIC
46165      IF LINES$(X) = "HELP" THEN
               HELP% = 1: HELP$ = IMAGE$ +
               ".HLP" : GOSUB 48000: GOTO
               46000                             ' RESPONDED TO THE HELP
                                                     REQUEST
46170      RUN LINES$(X)                         ' RUN THE REQUESTED PROGRAM
46175      '
46180      ' *********************************
46185      '
```

FIG. 6.1   Menu Program Flowchart

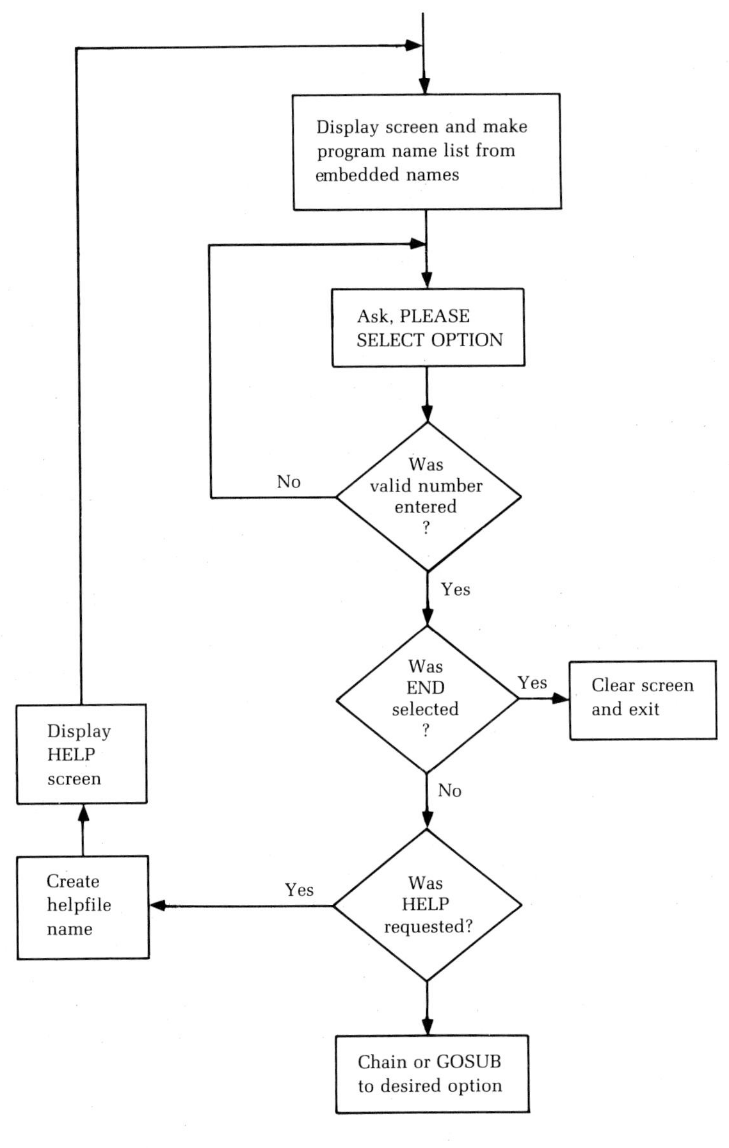

EXPLANATION OF PROGRAM

The menu routine contains a feature that terminates execution and returns to BASIC. This task is accomplished by using the word END in place of the program name. Line 46160 tests to see if the selected option uses END for the program name; if it does, then the program clears the screen and stops the program with an END statement.

Similarly, placing the word HELP in place of a program name will cause line 46165 to display the help screen. This allows you to place the help option on the screen. The user can still press shift F1 for help, but an inexperienced user may not have memorized this command yet.

This procedure is used for both menu types. In the method 2 menu, which normally uses a branch, the END and HELP commands are the only two that need to be defined.

The default option number assigned on line 46135 is 0. Pressing 0 and then ENTER will cause the program to proceed to the next menu. Thus users can exit the menu with a single keystroke, a carriage return (since 0 is defaulted). Also, since this option number always has the same meaning, it is positioned as the last line on the list instead of the first line. When it is at the end of the list, the user is not forced to read it every time a menu appears. This feature is a small touch, but it shows that you have put some thought into the menus and have attempted to make them consistent and easy to use.

The menu routine uses the LINES$() array. This array must be dimensioned to at least the maximum option number before the menu routine is called. If you are also using the data entry screen it is not necessary to dimension the array twice. Be sure to place the dimension statement at the front of the program so that it only executes once.

Other features of the menu program are described in the following subsections.

Chaining or Branching

Line 46170 currently is

```
46170  RUN LINES$(X)              ' RUN THE REQUESTED PROGRAM
```

This line will cause the menu to run another program once a valid option has been selected. If you wish to branch to a point within the current program, this line should be changed as follows.

```
46170 ON X GOSUB 1000,2000,3000,ETC ' BRANCH TO SUBROUTINE
```

where 1000, 2000, 3000, and so on are the subroutine entry points. Do not forget to change these numbers to the correct line numbers in your program.

You will also have to add some lines at the end of your subroutines either to terminate the program on the return or to redisplay the menu. For example,

```
46175  END    ' TERMINATE EXECUTION
```

will terminate the program and

```
46175  GOTO 46000    ' REDISPLAY THE MENU
```

will cause the menu to be redisplayed.

If you are branching to subroutines and not chaining to any other programs, then you do not need to put any program names in your menu screen. It can contain just the text you wish to display and the END and HELP option definitions.

Accepting a Program Name

When the screen display routine encounters a # symbol, it branches to line 46190, where the program name is extracted and inserted into the LINES$() array. ITEMS% contains the value of the largest option found. The program listing for this routine is as follows.

```
46190   ' ACCEPT A PROGRAM NAME
46195   '
46200   Z = VAL(MID$(A$,2,2))                ' GET THE OPTION NUMBER
46205   IF ITEMS% < Z THEN ITEMS% = Z        ' ADJUST COUNTER
46210   LINES$(Z) = MID$(A$,4)               ' MOVE THE FILE NAME
```

```
46215   ROW% = ROW% + 1                          ' INCREMENT COUNTER
46220   RETURN
46225   '
46230   ' *******************************
46235   '
```

Modifications to the Help Screen Display Routine

A line must be added to the existing help screen display routine from Chapter 4 to enable it to process menus. It is:

```
48224   IF MID$(A$,1,1) = "#" THEN
            GOSUB 46190 : GOTO 48165    ' PROCESS MENU FILE NAMES
```

Using the Help Subroutine

The menu system employs the help routine for user on-line help in the same way that the data entry system does. If the user presses shift F1, line 46145 will create the help file name by adding .HLP to IMAGE$ and then it will call the help subroutine. Since the help system is a fundamental part of the menu system, you should use it.

SAMPLE MENU SCREEN

Figure 6.2 illustrates one method of entering a menu. This menu is designed to chain to other programs or terminate execution and return to BASIC. Note that both the title and option 0 will be highlighted since they have been enclosed within ^ symbols.

Menu Test Program

The following routine can be used to help test the menu system. We have not included the standard error processing routine in this program.

FIG. 6.2   Sample menu screen, as typed by the programmer

```
                    ^Accounting Master Menu^

          Please select option
          1. Accounts Receivable Processing
          2. Payroll Preparation
          3. General Ledger Transactions and Reports
          4. Inventory Maintenance
          5. Accounts Payable Processing
          6. ^HELP^
          ^0^. F1 - Exit to BASIC
          #1 ACCREC.BAS
          #2 PAYROLL.BAS
          #3 GENLED.BAS
          #4 INVENT.BAS
          #5 ACCPAY.BAS
          #6 HELP
          #0 END
```

```
100   ' CHAPTER 6 - TEST ROUTINE FOR THE MENU SYSTEM
110   '
120   DIM LINES$(10)      ' PROGRAM NAMES SAVED HERE
130   KEY OFF             ' TURN 25TH LINE OFF
140   IMAGE$ = "CHAP6"    ' NAME OF MENU IMAGE
150   GOTO 46000          ' USE GOTO FOR 'RUN' AND GOSUB FOR
                              'GOSUB' BRANCH
160   END
170   '
180   '
190   '
```

TEST POINT

First, create a menu to chain to a program developed in the earlier
chapters. Run the menu and make sure that the screen is displayed
properly and that the correct program is chained.

Second, change lines 46170 and 46175 presented earlier to branch to some small subroutine that you create. These subroutines can do something clever, such as clear the screen and print "option 1," and so on. After the subroutine executes, the menu should be redisplayed.

USER INSTRUCTIONS

The following subsections contain the user instructions for this menu system. Please add these instructions to your user's manual.

Using a Menu

A *menu* is a list of actions that the computer can perform. After reading the available options, select the one you want by entering its number and then pressing ENTER. For example, if you were looking at the following screen and you wished to run the general ledger program, you would enter 3 (CR).

Requesting Help

If you cannot decide which option to select or you do not understand what is wanted from you, help can be requested by pressing shift F1. The help text contains a detailed explanation of what each option will do. After the help text has been displayed, the menu will be redisplayed.

Exiting, or Which Way Is Out?

To return to the previous menu and eventually back to BASIC, either enter 0 (CR) or simply press the F1 key. [Note: The default option is 0; therefore pressing the ENTER key is the same as entering 0 (CR).]

COMPLETE MENU PROGRAM

The complete listing of the menu processing program is as follows.

```
100        '  CHAPTER 6 - TEST ROUTINE FOR THE MENU SYSTEM
110        '
120        DIM LINES$(10)                    ' PROGRAM NAMES SAVED
                                                 HERE
130        KEY OFF                           ' TURN 25TH LINE OFF
140        IMAGE$ = "CHAP6"                  ' NAME OF MENU IMAGE
150        GOTO 46000                        ' USE GOTO FOR 'RUN'
                                                 AND GOSUB FOR
                                                 'GOSUB' BRANCH

160        END
170        '
180        '
190        '

46000      ' MENU DRIVER
46005      '
46010      '
46015      '
46020      ' DISPLAYS MENU AND CHAINS TO PROGRAM
               OF USER'S CHOICE
46025      '
46030      '
46035      ' IMPORTANT VARIABLES USED:
46040      ' LINES$( ) CONTAINS NAME OF PROGRAM TO
               CHAIN TO
46045      ' IMAGE$ CONTAINS NAME OF MENU FILE
46050      '
46055      ITEMS% = 0                        ' NUMBER OF OPTIONS
46060      NOPAUSE% = 1                      ' INFORM HELP SYSTEM
                                                 NOT TO PAUSE
46065      HELP$ = IMAGE$ + ".MNU"           ' MAKE THE MENU NAME
46070      GOSUB 48000                       ' SHOW THE SCREEN USING
                                                 HELP ROUTINE
46075      NOPAUSE% = 0                      ' RESTORE THE FLAG FOR
                                                 OTHERS
46080      '
46085      ' ASK FOR OPTION
46090      '
```

```
46095     LOCATE 3,15
46100     COLOR 15,0                              ' BRIGHT DISPLAY
46105     PRINT "PLEASE SELECT OPTION";
46110     COLOR 7,0                               ' LOW INTENSITY
46115     ROW% = 3
46120     COL% = 40
46125     MASK$ = "#"                             ' ALLOW HELP REQUEST
46130     MAXSIZE% = 1                            ' ALLOWS ONLY 9 OPTIONS
46135     ENTRY$ = "0"
46140     GOSUB 50000                             ' ACCEPT OPTION
46145     IF HELP% THEN HELP$ = IMAGE$ + ".HLP":
              GOSUB 48000: GOTO 46000             ' RESPONDED TO HELP
                                                    REQUEST
46150     X = VAL(ENTRY$)                         ' OPTION SELECTED
46155     IF X > ITEMS% THEN GOTO 46000           ' BAD ENTRY
46160     IF LINES$(X) = "END" THEN CLS : END     ' RETURN TO BASIC
46165     IF LINES$(X) = "HELP" THEN HELP% = 1:
              HELP$ = IMAGE$ + ".HLP" : GOSUB
              48000: GOTO 46000                   ' RESPONDED TO HELP
                                                    REQUEST
46170     RUN LINES$(X)                           ' RUN THE REQUESTED
                                                    PROGRAM
46175     '
46180     ' ****************************** ***
46185     '
46190     ' ACCEPT A PROGRAM NAME
46190     ' ACCEPT A PROGRAM NAME
46195     '
46200     Z = VAL(MID$(A$,2,2))                   ' GET THE OPTION NUMBER
46205     IF ITEMS% < Z THEN ITEMS% = Z           ' ADJUST COUNTER
46210     LINES$(Z) = MID$(A$,4)                  ' MOVE THE FILE NAME
46215     ROW% = ROW% + 1                         ' INCREMENT COUNTER
46220     RETURN
46225     '
46230     ' *******************************
46235     '

48224     IF MID$ (A$,1,1) = "#" THEN GOSUB
              46190 : GOTO 48165                  ' PROCESS MENU FILE
                                                    NAMES
```

CHAPTER 7

REPORT GENERATION

INTRODUCTION

Generating reports is a time-consuming programming task. Creating a dump of the data is not time-consuming; creating polished and meaningful reports is what takes the time. This chapter deals with the problem of report generation. First, we discuss some philosophical aspects of report creation and making some suggestions. Then we present and explain a program designed to make the task of actually creating a report easier for you, the programmer.

Philosophical Considerations

We have all heard it said many times that "data go into the machine; information comes out." A report containing raw data is usually of little value, unless the only purpose of the report is to record all data, as in a scientific experiment notebook. But a programmer typically is trying to change data into information, and this process can be broken into some definite steps of action. We will describe these steps, giving an example and our recommendations, in the following subsections.

Steps in Report Generation

The first thing to do is to consider what information is to be presented and what data this information is generated from. How much of the data is needed to support the information directly? How much can be left out or output in a separate report (produced only when required).

Second, consider who the report is for. Is it for the vice-president of marketing, the engineering staff, the secretarial pool, or the maintenance team? Even though they are using the same data/information, these users may have individual requirements and formats. Also each group looks at the data from a different perspective.

Third, consider how the report is going to be used. Several different presentations of the same data/information may be required.

An Example

To illustrate what we mean, we'll look at a very common example that most of us come into contact with at one time or another: the quarterly stockholder's report for a corporation. It comes out in one style and one format for everyone. Whether or not you understand it, that's how you get it. It is usually dressed up on slick printing stock with many color photographs. This trick is known as camouflage—no one reads the numbers anyway, right? If the data were really important, we suspect it would not be presented only in standard CPA jargon and format. The information, however, could be presented in several formats within the same report so that the stockholders would have a clear understanding of the company's financial condition and changes without having to learn how to decipher the data.

In any improved reporting format the standard balance sheet and profit/loss statement could be supplied in the report in their formal form, for reference, and in a less formal form where the key points are called out and explained as follows.

1. Our new warehouse in Irvine is now open and has been fully stocked with 1,000,000 Widgets, raising our inventory value by $Z and the overhead by $T.

2. One thousand acres surrounding our Silicon Valley plant have been sold, reducing the value of our physical assets by $X and increasing our cash holdings by $Y.

3. The 10,000,000 model 1963 Widgets stored in Alaska have been donated to the local junior college, giving us a tax credit of $C and an inventory write-off of $D and freeing 60,000 square feet of needed warehouse space.

This type of disclosure tells the stockholders what has transpired. In fact, it may tell them too much. For this reason you must consider the three points listed previously and focus on the target reader as you design the report. A corporation may have to present reports one way because of the huge and varied audience it addresses. You, on the other hand, have a smaller audience for your reports, and so you can be more specific in what and how information is presented.

Recommendations

Since designing a good report requires addressing the three points that focus on user requirements, it follows that you should talk to your potential users and survey their needs. Their responses will vary from "We do not have any idea" or "We do not care" to very specific and well-thought-out requirements. Since these reports are for your users, their requirements should receive your thoughtful attention. For those of you unfortunate enough to get the "no help" answers, try to consider the report from the user's perspective and try to visualize the finished product to create a sample report. Once you provide your users with a sample report, they unfailingly have no problem coming up with criticism (they will call them suggestions).

Trying to make all users happy is an impossible task, and some political skills will be required. For instance, you may want to remind (inform, educate) the users that the computer does not do the organization or report preparation. Together you must design the report, and the user's cooperation is necessary and appreciated.

SIMPLE REPORT GENERATOR

Getting information into the computer is usually easier than getting it out, because you may take a single page of input data and create twenty pages of output information. Designing and programming twenty pages of output is a lot of work. The program presented in this chapter will be helpful for outputting many types of reports but cannot possibly suit everyone.

The report generator is based on a concept similar to that used for the data entry screen. A text file, which describes the page to be printed, is created by either the programmer or the user. This text file contains the regular text, which appears on the page, as well as information describing the variables, their positions on the printed page, special enhanced printing symbols, and special report generator commands. This report file or mask contains complete instructions on how to print the report.

Design

As in the data entry screen subroutine, the variables to be printed by the report generator are contained in an array. The calling program creates this array just as was done for the data entry screen subroutine. In fact, since we expect the data entry and the report generator subroutines to be used together frequently, we have designed the report generator to use the same string array, LINES$(). LINES$() should always be dimensioned at the beginning of the main program for the maximum size required by either subroutine.

This technique, the use of a string array, is a simple one and will generally only be useful on pages containing a small amount of information. You can improve on this technique by adding additional markers to represent special or recurring variables in your report. For example, you might use markers for general ledger account numbers or inventory part numbers.

In addition to printing variables, the report generator can send special commands to the printer. As examples, it can bold print, underline, and print enlarged characters. Other features can be added depending on the capabilities of your printer. The report generator can also number pages, form feed, and automatically print a series of different text files.

Building the Program

The program presented in this chapter does not use any subroutines from the previous chapters. The easiest way to enter the program is to use the screen editor from Chapter 3.

Programmer Features

With this program you will be able to create and modify a report layout without having to modify the BASIC program used to create the report. The text editor from Chapter 3 can be used to create and edit the report. There are three types of commands: variable insert, printer control, and dot commands. To insert a variable into the report, the number of the array element to be printed is placed between a pair of symbols. The printer control commands work much like the way the help subroutine highlights. Matching symbols are placed on either side of the text of interest. These symbols will turn underlining, enlarged lettering, or bold printing on and off. A dot command gives commands to the report generator. This is done by beginning a line in the report text file with a period or dot followed by the command name. The various options available are described in Figure 7.1.

FIG. 7.1   Report generator controls

SYMBOL	DESCRIPTION
{ }	Insert variable and concatenate
[ ]	Insert variable do not concatenate
^	Bold print text
~	Print enlarged text
—	Underline text
.FF	Form feed the paper
.PAGE	Page numbering
.RPT	Print new report
.ASC	Print these ASCII characters

There are two possible ways of inserting information into an existing line of text: Expand the line to fit new data or truncate the data to fit existing space. The { } symbols are used to concatenate the data, regardless of its length, into the text line. The [ ] symbols are used to insert the data into the text line without altering the position of the text in the line. If the data to be inserted into the line is too long or too short to fill the space between the [ ] symbols, the line is adjusted so that the data fits exactly in the space described.

A simple code is used to tell the report generator which method is desired. If a space is included between the symbols, then a short line will be filled with spaces and not expanded. For example, suppose we wish to insert "Marty and Alan" into these lines:

    {1} divide their lives into daily subroutines.
    [1   ] divide their lives into daily subroutines.
    [1   ] 100   200   3000   100

These lines become

    Marty and Alan divide their lives into daily subroutines.
    Marty divide their lives into daily subroutines.
    Marty and Alan 100   200   3000   100

The first example uses the { } symbols, and therefore the line is expanded to accept the entire insert.

The second example has the [ ] symbols, the array reference number (one digit or space), and two spaces, totaling five spaces for the mask. Therefore the report generator only accepts the first five characters of the insert.

The third example has a mask size in excess of the size of the insert. Thus the report generator prints the entire insert along with the spaces to preserve the overall length.

As these examples show, if you want the entire insert and are not sure how long it is going to be, either use the { } or the [ ] symbols with lots of extra spaces.

PROGRAM FEATURES

The flowchart for the report generator is shown in Figure 7.2. After the report file is opened, the file is read one line at a time. Each line is processed looking for an insert or printer-control symbol or a dot command.

An option has been included that allows the report to be sent to either the diskette or the printer. If PRT% equals 0, the report is sent to the printer; otherwise, the report will be sent to a diskette.

Why would you want to send the report to the diskette? Convenience is the main reason. A report can be created and stored on the diskette much faster than the average printer can print. Therefore, the operator can use the computer again sooner, and the report can be printed later, perhaps at a more convenient time. If a large number of reports are being created and user input is required in between each report, a lot of time can be wasted waiting on the printer.

Explanation of Variables

The report subroutine requires one array, LINES$() (line 120). LINES$() contains the data to be printed. It must be dimensioned to at least the maximum number of array elements used.

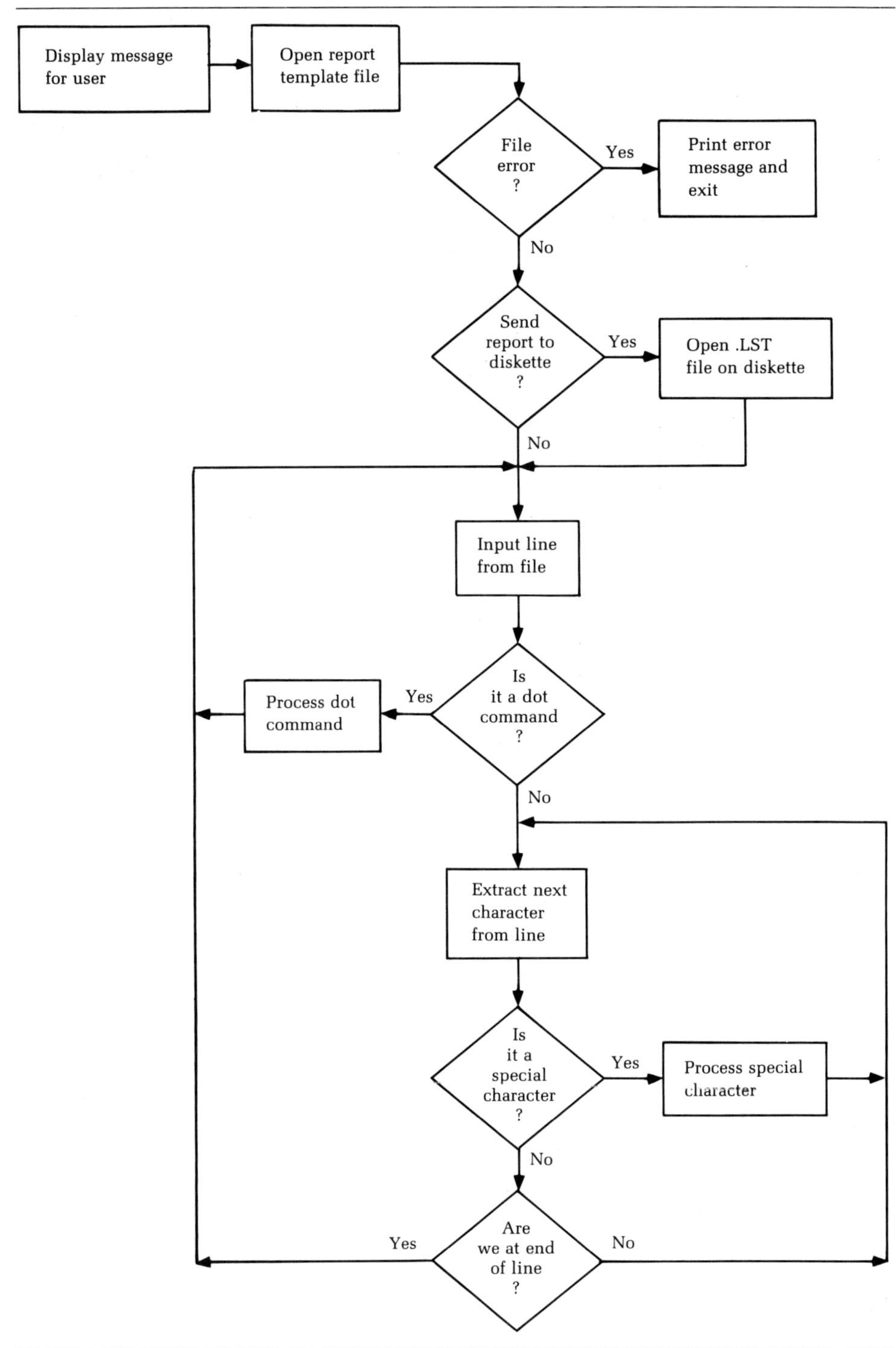

Display message for user
Open report template file
File error ?
Yes
Print error message and exit
No
Send report to diskette ?
Yes
Open .LST file on diskette
No
Input line from file
Is it a dot command ?
Yes
Process dot command
No
Extract next character from line
Is it a special character ?
Yes
Process special character
No
Are we at end of line ?
Yes
No

The report mask is saved on diskette with the extension .RPT (for "report"), and the finished report is saved using the same prefix and the extension .LST (for "list").

The file name is passed to the report generator subroutine in the variable IMAGE$.

The report generator main program follows.

```
55000    ' DATA PRINT SUBROUTINE
55005    '
55010    ' THIS FILLS IN A DATA PAGE AND SENDS IT
             TO THE PRINTER OR DISK
55015    '
55020    ' IMPORTANT VARIABLES:
55025    '      IMAGE$              NAME OF REPORT TO PRINT
55030    '      LINES$()            ARRAY CONTAINS DATA TO PRINT
55035    '      PRT%                0 = SEND TO PRINTER 1 = SEND TO DISK
55040    '
55045    CLS                                        ' INFORM THE USER OF
                                                      PRINTING
55050    LOCATE 10,10
55055    PRINT "PLEASE WAIT"
55060    LOCATE 12,10
55065    A$ = IMAGE$ + ".RPT"                       ' IMAGE SAVED WITH .RPT
                                                      EXTENSION
55070    PRINT "PROCESSING ";A$;
55075    ON ERROR GOTO 55705                        ' IN CASE FILE MISSING
55080    OPEN A$ FOR INPUT AS #1
55085    ON ERROR GOTO 60000                        ' NORMAL ERROR
                                                      PROCESSING
55090    IF PRT% = 0 THEN GOTO 55100 ELSE A$ =
             IMAGE$ + ".LST"
55095    OPEN A$ FOR OUTPUT AS #2                    ' OUTPUT TO PRINTER OR
                                                      DISK
55100    A$ = ""                                    ' CLEAR FOR USE BELOW
55105    '
55110    ' PAGE PROCESS LOOP
55115    '
55120    LINE INPUT#1, ENTRY$                       ' GET A LINE FROM THE
                                                      DATA PAGE
55125    IF LEFT$(ENTRY$,1) = "." THEN GOSUB
             55490 : GOTO 55270                      ' TEST FOR DOT COMMAND
55130    '
55135    ' PRINTS AND LOOKS FOR SPECIAL
             COMMANDS
```

```
55140    '
55145    ' SYMBOL                DESCRIPTION
55150    '    ^                  BOLD PRINT TOGGLE
55155    '    ~                  ENLARGED PRINT TOGGLE
55160    '    _                  UNDERLINE PRINT TOGGLE
55165    '    {                  INSERT AND CONCATENATE
55170    '    [                  INSERT AND DO NOT CONCATENATE
55175    '
55180    ' LOOK FOR SPECIAL COMMANDS ONE
             CHARACTER AT A TIME
55185    '
55190    FOR X = 1 TO LEN(ENTRY$)
55195        C$ = MID$(ENTRY$,X,1)                    ' EXTRACT ONE
                                                          CHARACTER
55200         IF C$ = "^" THEN GOSUB 55885 : GOTO
             55245                                     ' TEST FOR BOLD
55205         IF C$ = "~" THEN GOSUB 55950 : GOTO
             55245                                     ' TEST FOR LARGE PRINT
55210         IF C$ = "_" THEN GOSUB 56015 : GOTO
             55245                                     ' TEST FOR UNDERLINE
55215         IF C$ = "{" THEN GOSUB 55295 : GOTO
             55245                                      ' TEST FOR INSERT
55220         IF C$ = "[" THEN GOSUB 55370 : GOTO
             55245                                     ' TEST FOR INSERT
55225    '
55230    ' SPACE LEFT HERE FOR YOU TO ADD MORE
             COMMANDS IF YOU SO DESIRE
55235    '
55240    IF PRT% = 0 THEN LPRINTC$; ELSE
             PRINT #2,C$;                              ' PRINT IT
55245    NEXT X
55250    '
55255    '
55260    '
55265    IF PRT% = 0 THEN LPRINT "" ELSE
             PRINT #2,""                               ' ADD THE CARRIAGE
                                                          RETURN
55270    IF EOF(1) THEN GOTO 55450                    ' ALL DONE SO EXIT
55275    PRINT ".";                                   'SHOW THE USER SOME
                                                          PROGRESS
55280    GOTO 55120                                   ' GET NEXT LINE
55285    '
55290    '

55450    ' CLOSE EVERYTHING AND RETURN
```

```
55455    '
55460    CLOSE                               ' CLOSE THE OPEN FILES
55465    '
55470    CLS                                 ' CLEAR THE SCREEN
55475    RETURN
55480    ' ********************************
55485    '
```

Report Generator Test Program

The report generator can be tested with the following routines. This test program not only allows you to test this program as you enter it, but it can be used as you design your own programs to test the new report pages you create.

```
100      ' CHAPTER 7 - TEST ROUTINE FOR REPORT
             GENERATOR
105      '
110      CLS
115      PRINT "CHAPTER 7 REPORT GENERATOR TEST
             PROGRAM"
120      DIM LINES$(10)
125      '
130      PRINT
135      INPUT "ENTER 0 TO SEND TO PRINTER 1 TO
             WRITE TO .LST FILE: ";PRT%
140      '
145      INPUT "ENTER NAME OF REPORT (SAMPLE IS
             CHAP7): ";IMAGE$            ' ACCEPT REPORT NAME
150      GOSUB 57000                     ' FILL THE LINES$()
                                             PRINT DATA ARRAY
155      GOSUB 55000                     ' PRINT A PAGE
160      PRINT
165      PRINT "PRINTING COMPLETED."
170      BEEP                            ' RING THE BELL
175      END
180      '
185      '
190      '

57000    ' SAMPLE DATA FOR TEST (CHAP7.RPT)
57010    '
```

```
57020    LINES$(1) = "JOHN DOE"
57030    LINES$(2) = "1234 FIRST STREET"
57040    X = 1000                          ' A VALUE
57050    LINES$(3) = MID$(STR$(X),2)        ' REMOVE LEADING
                                                SPACE
57060    LINES$(4) = MID$(STR$(X * 3),2)    ' DITTO
57070    RETURN
57080    ' ************************
57090    '
57100    '
```

The first routine, lines 100–190, is the calling or main program. The second routine, lines 57000–57100, sets up the LINES$() array for printing in much the same manner as the data entry screens. In this program the values of the array are assigned directly. In your programs you will usually use variables.

A sample report form is:

```
NAME        {1}
STREET      {2}
ZIP CODE    {3}
AMOUNT      {4}
{1} lives at {2} and owes us $ {4}
```

This produces the following output:

```
NAME        John Doe
STREET      1234 First Street
ZIP CODE    1000
AMOUNT      3000
John Doe lives at 1234 First Street and owes us $ 3000
```

Before the report generator can be tested, however, an insert routine must be entered.

Insert and Concatenate

The curvey brackets, { }, are used to insert and concatenate variables into the text line. The text lines are processed one character at a time by the loop on lines 55190 through 55245. When line 55215 discovers a left bracket, {, it branches to the insert subroutine at line 55295.

The insert subroutine first searches for a right bracket, and then it extracts the array element number from between the brackets. After it verifies that a valid number has been entered, it prints the field and increments the line character counter to the character past the right bracket. Since this adjusts the line length based on the variable length, we say that the variable has been concatenated into the line.

The insert and concatenate subroutine follows.

```
55295    ' INSERT A FIELD INTO THE LINE AND
             CONCATENATE {}
55300    '
55305    END.INSERT% = INSTR(X,ENTRY$,"}")      ' LOOK FOR OTHER END
55310    IF END.INSERT% = 0 THEN RETURN          ' ALL DONE
55315    '
55320    ' NOW WE SHOULD HAVE VALID ELEMENT
             NUMBER
55325    '
55330    Y = VAL(MID$(ENTRY$,X+1,2))             ' ALLOW UP TO 99
55335    IF Y <= 0 THEN RETURN                   ' ERROR SO EXIT
55340    PRINT #2,LINES$(Y);                     ' PRINT THE FIELD
55345    X = END.INSERT%                         ' SKIP INSERT AREA
55350    RETURN                                  ' TRY AGAIN
55355    '
55360    '
55365    '
```

TEST POINT

Using the text editor, create a test report. To save time include examples of all possible options.

Run the program and verify that inserting works correctly.

Insert and Do Not Concatenate

The square brackets, [ ], are used to insert but not to concatenate variables into the text line. The text lines are processed one character at a time by the loop on lines 55190 through 55245. When line 55220 discovers a left bracket, [, it branches to the insert subroutine at line 55370.

The insert subroutine first searches for a right bracket, and then it extracts the array element number from between the brackets. After it verifies that a valid number has been entered, it prints the field and increments the line character counter to the character past the right bracket. Since this does not make any adjustments to the line length, we say that the variable has been inserted into the line.

The insert subroutine follows.

```
55370    ' INSERT A FIELD AND DO NOT
             CONCATENATE [ ]
55375    '
55380    END.INSERT% = INSTR(X,ENTRY$,"]")          ' LOOK FOR THE OTHER
                                                       END
55385    IF END.INSERT% = 0 THEN RETURN             ' ALL DONE
55390    '
55395    ' NOW WE SHOULD HAVE VALID ELEMENT
             NUMBER
55400    Y = VAL(MID$(ENTRY$,X+1,2))                ' ALLOW UP TO 99
55405    IF Y <= 0 THEN RETURN                      ' ERROR SO EXIT
55410    IF LEN(LINES$(Y)) > (END.INSERT%+1-
             X) THEN LINES$(Y) =
             LEFT$(LINES$(Y), END.INSERT%+1-
             X)
55415    IF PRT% = 0 THEN LPRINT LINES$(Y);
             PRINT #2,LINES$(Y);                     ' PRINT THE FIELD
55420    IF LEN(LINES$(Y)) < (END.INSERT% + 1 -
             X) THEN X = (END.INSERT% + 1 - X -
             LEN(LINES$(Y))); ELSE X = 0            ' FILL WITH SPACES
55422    IF PRT%=0 THEN LPRINT SPACE$(X); ELSE
             PRINT#2, SPACE$(X);
55425    X = END.INSERT%                            ' SKIP INSERT AREA
55430    RETURN                                     ' TRY AGAIN
55435    ' *****************************
55440    '
55445    '
```

TEST POINT

Use the test report to verify that this function works.

PRINTER CONTROLS

Most of the printers currently available have numerous built-in capabilities beyond simply printing text. Many can bold print, compress or enlarge the text, justify each line, and print graphics characters. This report generator has provisions for using a few of these capabilities. Since there are so many printers available on the market, we cannot hope to address all the possible features. What we have done is create a framework that you can adapt for your own brand of printer and style of reports.

Most printers have options that can be turned on and off through the use of control sequences. These control sequences usually begin with a nonprinting character; typically the ESCape character (ASCII value 27) is used, but your printer may be different. There is no real standard. The printer monitors every character it receives, and when it finds the leading control character, it begins to interpret the control sequence and adjusts its printing accordingly.

The example printer used here is the Epson FX-100. The options chosen are available on most of the popular dot matrix printers. Refer to your printer's user manual for the control sequences specific to your printer.

Bold Printing

Since the same character, ^, is used in the report format to turn the options on and off, we must maintain a variable or flag to inform us what the current state of the option is. BOLD% is the bold flag. When BOLD% equals 1, the printer is in the bold print mode. It is in the normal print mode when BOLD% equals 0.

The subroutine tests BOLD%. If it equals 1, it turns bold print off; otherwise, it turns it on.

The Epson FX-100 bold print command is ESC E. Bolding is turned off with an ESC F. Your printer may use different commands.

The bold print routine is:

```
55885    ' BOLD PRINT COMMAND ROUTINE
55890    '
55895    ' COMMANDS ARE FOR EPSON FX-100 PRINTER
55900    '
55905    '
55910    '
55915    IF BOLD% <> 0 THEN BOLD% = 0 : L$=
             CHR$(27)+"F" : GOTO 55930          ' CANCEL MODE
55920    BOLD% = 1                              ' SET FLAG SO WE KNOW
                                                    MODE SET
55925    L$ = CHR$(27)+"E"                      ' TURN EMPHASIZED MODE
                                                    ON
55930    IF PRT%=0 THEN LPRINT L$; ELSE
             PRINT #2, L$;
55935    RETURN
55940    '
55945    '
```

TEST POINT

Run a sample printing of the test case, and demonstrate that bold printing works after inserting the ^ character in the text file CHAP7.RPT.

Enlarged Printing

Another common feature that can be used very effectively in reports is enlarged printing. With enlarged printing the characters are typically printed at twice their normal size.

As with bold printing, a flag is maintained. You might have guessed that we used ENLARGED% for the flag name.

The Epson FX-100 turns enlarged printing on with ESC W CHR$(1) and off with ESC W CHR$(0).

You should note that in the PRINT statement (line 55990), a semicolon is used between the characters. The semicolon will not insert spaces the way the comma does. It is important that extra characters, like spaces, not be inserted in between the control characters.

The subroutine for enlarged printing is:

```
55950  ' ENLARGED PRINT MODE
55955  '
55960  ' COMMANDS ARE FOR EPSON FX-100
55965  '
55970  '
55975  '
55980  IF ENLARGED% <> 0 THEN ENLARGED% = 0 :
           L$ = CHR$(27)+"W"+CHR$(0) : GOTO
           55995                                    ' TURN MODE OFF
55985  ENLARGED% = 1                               ' SET FLAG SO WE KNOW
                                                        MODE IS ON
55990  L$ = CHR$(27)+"W"+CHR$(1)                    ' TURNS ENLARGED PRINT
                                                        ON
55995  IF PRT%=0 THEN LPRINT L$; ELSE
           PRINT#2,L$;
56000  RETURN
56005  '
56010  '
```

TEST POINT

Print the test report, and verify that enlarged printing functions properly by embedding the ∼ character in CHAP7.RPT.

Underlining

Underlining is an effective way to highlight text. The Epson FX-100
begins underlining with ESC — CHR$(1) and stops with ESC —
CHR$(0).
    The underline subroutine is:

```
56015  ' UNDERLINE PRINT MODE
56020  '
56025  ' COMMANDS ARE FOR EPSON FX-100
56030  '
56035  '
56040  '
56045  IF UNDERLINE% THEN UNDERLINE% = 0 : L$
           = CHR$(27)+"-"+CHR$(0): GOTO 56060     ' TURN MODE OFF
56050  UNDERLINE% = 1                             ' SET FLAG SO WE KNOW
                                                      MODE IS ON
56055  L$ = CHR$(27)+"-"+CHR$(1)                  ' BEGINS UNDERLINING
```

```
56060    IF PRT%=0 THEN LPRINT L$; ELSE PRINT#2,L$;
56065    RETURN
56070    '
56075    '
```

TEST POINT

Print the test report again and verify that underline works by embedding the — symbol in CHAP7.RPT.

DOT COMMANDS

Dot commands are used to send additional commands to the report generator. This technique of issuing commands by including them in the actual text file to be printed is used by many popular word processors. Only four commands are developed here. Our intention is not to include every possible feature but to give you a basis for creating your own programs. Please experiment and add your own commands.

The dot commands begin with a period, or dot, in the first character of any line. Line 55125 tests the first character of each line for a dot. If it finds one, it branches to the dot command processor, line 55490, where the dot command processor first converts the remainder of the line to uppercase (an error correction or prevention feature) and then tries to identify the command name. When a valid command name is found, it branches to the appropriate routine for processing. An invalid command name causes the line to be ignored.

The dot command process is:

```
55490    ' DOT COMMAND PROCESSOR
55495    ' SPECIAL PRINTER COMMANDS THAT START IN COLUMN 1 WITH A.
55500    ' COMMANDS ARE:
55505    '        .FF          PRINTER FORM FEED
55510    '        .PAGE        PAGE NUMBERING CONTROL
55515    '        .RPT         NEW REPORT NAME
55520    '        .ASC         PRINTER CONTROL CHARACTER ROUTINE
55525    '
55530    '
```

```
55535     ENTRY$ = MID$(ENTRY$,2)              ' REMOVE . MARK
55540     FOR X = 1 TO LEN(ENTRY$)             ' MAKE SURE LINE IS ALL
                                                   UPPERCASE
55545         Y = ASC(MID$(ENTRY$,X,1))        ' GET ASCII VALUE
55550         IF Y >= 97 AND Y <= 122 THEN
                  MID$(ENTRY$,X,1) =
                  CHR$(Y-32)                    ' FORCE UPPERCASE
55555     NEXT X
55560     IF LEFT$(ENTRY$,2) = "FF" THEN GOSUB
              55605 : RETURN                    ' FORM FEED
55565     IF LEFT$(ENTRY$,3) = "RPT" THEN GOSUB
              55660 : RETURN                    ' OPEN NEW REPORT
55570     IF LEFT$(ENTRY$,4) = "PAGE" THEN
              GOSUB 55745 : RETURN              ' PAGE NUMBERING
                                                   ROUTINE
55575     IF LEFT$(ENTRY$,3) = "ASC" THEN GOSUB
              55795 : RETURN                    ' SPECIAL PRINTER
                                                   CONTROLS
55580     GOSUB 55830                          ' BAD COMMAND SO PRINT
                                                   AND SKIP THIS LINE
55585     RETURN                               ' EXIT
55590     '
55595     '
55600     '
```

The Test Points for all dot commands follow the detailed explanation below.

Form Feed

Without a form feed command we would be limited to short or single-page reports. The form feed command allows multiple page reports and lets us not be overly concerned about keeping track of the number of lines used on each page.

The form feed command is FF. When line 55560 finds an FF it branches to line 55605. The form feed routine prints the universal form feed character CHR$(12) and prints a page number if page numbering is turned on.

The form feed subroutine is:

```
55605     'FORM FEED AND LABEL PAGES
55610     '
55615     IF PRT%=0 THEN LPRINT CHR$(12); ELSE
              PRINT#2,CHR$(12);                    ' FORM FEED COMMAND
55620     IF PAGE% = 0 THEN RETURN                 ' NO PAGE NUMBERING
55625     IF PRT%=0 THEN LPRINT TAB(70);
              "PAGE";STR$(PAGE%) ELSE
              PRINT#2,TAB(70);"PAGE";
              STR$(PAGE%)                           ' PRINT PAGE NUMBER
55630     PRINT STR$(PAGE%);                        ' SHOW USER PROGRESS
55635     PAGE% = PAGE% + 1                         ' INCREMENT PAGE
55640     RETURN                                        COUNTER
55645     '
55650     '
55655     '
```

TEST POINT

Execute the report generator test report and verify that form feed works.

Page Numbering

Page numbering is a necessary feature for reports of more than one page. Line 55570 searches for the command PAGE. When it finds a match, it branches to 55745, where the value of variable PAGE% is set.

Page numbering is normally off. The PAGE command not only turns numbering on but it also sets the starting page number. The command is:

    .PAGE ##

or

    .PAGE

where the first option turns page numbering on beginning with the number ## and the second option turns numbering off.

The page numbering routine is:

```
55745    ' PAGE NUMBERING CONTROL
55750    '
55755    ' .PAGE          TURNS NUMBERING OFF
55760    ' .PAGE ##       NUMBERS NEXT PAGE STARTING WITH ##
55765    '
55770    IF LEN(ENTRY$) = 4 THEN PAGE% = 0 ELSE PAGE% =
             VAL(MID$(ENTRY$,6))
55775    RETURN
55780    '
55785    '
55790    '
```

The actual printing of the page number occurs on line 55630, in the form feed subroutine.

TEST POINT

Repeat the report generator test one more time with all the dot commands included. By now you are probably getting very tired of doing this testing, but it will not surprise you to discover that most errors are in the untested portions of a program. An ounce of prevention is ... (you know the rest).

Automatic Report Generation

Everyone has a different way of creating reports. We prefer to create single-page reports (mainly because they fit on one page) and group them together into a final massive document. The RPT command does the grouping and allows a page to specify the next page to be printed.
The format for this command is:

```
.RPT fn
```

where fn is the name of another report page. The program listing is:

```
55660    ' OPEN ANOTHER REPORT PAGE
55665    '
```

```
55670    CLOSE#1                              ' CLOSE CURRENT FILE
55675    ON ERROR GOTO 55705                  ' SET NEW ERROR TRAPPING
                                                  ROUTINE
55680    A$ = MID$(ENTRY$,5) + ".RPT"         ' EXTRACT FILE NAME AND
                                                  ADD EXTENSION
55685    OPEN A$ FOR INPUT AS #1              ' OPEN NEW FILE
55690    ON ERROR GOTO 60000
55695    PRINT : PRINT TAB(10); "PROCESSING ";A$;
55700    RETURN                               ' EVERYTHING OK SO
                                                  CONTINUE
55705    RESUME 55710                         ' FILE NOT FOUND SO
                                                  ERROR CREATED
55710    PRINT
55715    PRINT A$;" NOT FOUND.";CHR$(7)       ' PRINT ERROR MESSAGE
                                                  AND RING BELL
55720    CLOSE
55725    END
55730    '
55735    '
55740    '
```

TEST POINT

Add this command to the end of the current test report, and print out
a second report page after creating the next page of data.

Special Printer Commands

Printers have so many options that it is unlikely that you would want
to create a special subroutine for every option. Occasionally, however-
er, you will want to use an unusual option. You can do this with the
ASC command. It will send a printer-control sequence, and so a special subroutine will not be necessary.

The command format is:

```
.ASC ## ## ##...##
```

where ## is the decimal value of the ASCII character to be printed.

As examples, ESC (escape) = 27, M = 77. The Epson FX-100 Elite character command (ESC M) becomes

    .ASC 27 77

This subroutine works by first looking for the space between the numbers, then extracting the value of the number, and finally using CHR$() to print the ASCII character. The ASCII value is used because this is the easiest way to describe nonprinting control characters.

    The program listing follows.

```
55795    ' PRINTER CONTROL COMMANDS
55800    '
55805    ' .ASC ## ## ## ## ##
55810    '
55815    ' USES CHR%() TO PRINT CHARACTER FOR EACH VALUE
55820    ' EG. ESCAPE IS ASCII 27 THEREFORE TO PRINT AN
             ESCAPE WE WOULD USE
55825    ' .ASC 27
55830    '
55835    ENTRY$ = MID$(ENTRY$,5)                ' STRIP OFF ASC
55840    IF LEN(ENTRY$) =
             0 THEN RETURN                      ' ALL DONE
55845    X = INSTR(1,ENTRY$," ")                ' LOOK FOR SEPARATOR
55850    IF X = 0 THEN Y =
             VAL(ENTRY$) : ENTRY$ = ""          ' AT END OF LINE
55855    IF X <> 0 THEN Y =
             VAL(LEFT$(ENTRY$,X-1)) :
             ENTRY$ = MID$(ENTRY$,X+1)          ' IN THE MIDDLE OF THE
                                                    LINE
55860    IF PRT%=0 THEN LPRINT CHR$(Y);
             ELSE PRINT#2,CHR$(Y);              ' SEND THE CHARACTER TO
                                                    THE PRINTER
55865    GOTO 55840                             ' GET NEXT CHARACTER
55870    '
55875    '
55880    '
```

TEST POINT

First the good news: This is the final test for this chapter. Now the bad news: Yes, you have to test it.

STANDARD ERROR PROCESSING

This program uses our standard error processing routine. It is repeated here for convenience.

```
60000      ' STANDARD ERROR PROCESSING ROUTINE
60005      '
60010      X = ERR                      ' GET ERROR NUMBER
60015      Y = ERL                      ' GET LINE NUMBER
60020      RESUME 60025
60025      KEY OFF                      ' TURN OFF SO WE CAN USE 25TH LINE
60030      LOCATE 25,1                  ' DISPLAY ON 25TH LINE
60035      PRINT "ERROR ";X;" ON LINE NUMBER ";Y
60040      BEEP                         ' RING THE BELLS
60045      END                          ' THAT'S ALL FOLKS
60050      '
60055      '
60060      '
```

HOW TO USE THIS PROGRAM

One further suggestion on how to use this program. As you develop programs that use this report generator, include in the LINES$() array any variables that could possibly be printed, even those you do not plan to use immediately. Also clearly document the arrangement in LINES$() of all variables. Once this is done it will be very easy for you or your users to create new reports without having to modify the program.

To make the printing of these new or custom reports simple, you can include a custom report option in your menus. This option should ask for the report name and then branch to a subroutine that will print the report.

Enhancements

There is an endless list of enhancements possible for this program. Simple arithmetic abilities, printer graphics, right-hand justification of text, plus many word processor features can be added. If you approve of this style of report creation, you should consider adding some of your own enhancements.

USER INSTRUCTIONS

(Note: Since the user of the report generator is not likely to have read this book, and the narrative used earlier in this chapter can serve effectively as instructions, that text is repeated here as part of the User Instructions.)

The report generator allows you to take existing data and to arrange the data in any way you desire to create a printed report. In addition to printing the data, the report generator also allows you to use special printer features such as bold printing, enlarged printing, and underlining. The basic options for the report generator are listed in Figure 7.3.

FIG. 7.3   Report generator controls

SYMBOL	DESCRIPTION
{ }	Insert variable and concatenate
[ ]	Insert variable do not concatenate
^	Bold print text
~	Print enlarged text
—	Underline text
.FF	Form feed the paper
.PAGE	Page numbering
.RPT	Print new report
.ASC	Print these ASCII characters

There are two possible ways of inserting information into an existing line of text: Expand the line to fit new data or truncate the data to fit existing space. The { } symbols are used to concatenate the data, regardless of its length, into the text line. The [ ] symbols are used to insert the data into the text line without altering the position of the text in the line. If the data to be inserted into the line is too long or too short to fill the space between the [ ] symbols, the line is adjusted so that the data fits exactly in the space described.

A simple code is used to tell the report generator which method is desired. If a space is included between the symbols, then a short line will be filled with spaces and not expanded. For example, suppose we wish to insert "Marty and Alan" into these lines:

{1} divide their lives into daily subroutines.

[1   ] divide their lives into daily subroutines.

[1   ] 100   200   3000   100

These lines become

Marty and Alan divide their lives into daily subroutines.

Marty divide their lives into daily subroutines.

Marty and Alan 100   200   3000   100

The first example uses the { } symbols, and therefore the line is expanded to accept the entire insert.

The second example has the [ ] symbols, the array reference number (one digit or space), and two spaces, totaling five spaces for the mask. Therefore, the report generator only accepts the first five characters of the insert.

The third example has a mask size in excess of the size of the insert. Thus the report generator prints the entire insert along with the spaces to preserve the overall length.

As these examples show, if you want the entire insert and are not sure how long it is going to be, either use the { } or the [ ] symbols with lots of extra spaces.

There are three special symbols used for printer control. These allow you to bold, enlarge, and underline text. To print any text (in the report text file) in one of these special printer modes, simply surround the text with a pair of these symbols.

There are four commands, called dot commands, used to control the report generator program. These commands are entered in the report text file along with the regular text to be printed. They must, however, always begin in the first column of a line. The four commands are:

.FF	Start a new page or form feed.
.PAGE #	Page numbering
.RPT fn	Print the report with the file name fn. This must be the last line in a report file.
.ASC # #	Embedding .ASC # #...# (where # is an ASCII value) in the text file forces the printer to execute the feature defined by the ASCII sequence given. The command allows you to use any feature of your printer.

COMPLETE REPORT GENERATOR PROGRAM

Here is the complete program listing for the report generator program.

```
100     ' CHAPTER 7 - TEST ROUTINE FOR REPORT GENERATOR
105     '
110     CLS
115     PRINT "CHAPTER 7 REPORT GENERATOR TEST PROGRAM"
120     DIM LINE$(10)
125     '
130     PRINT
135     INPUT "ENTER 0 TO SEND TO PRINTER 1 TO WRITE TO .LST FILE: ";PRT%
140     '                                                       '
145     INPUT "ENTER NAME OF REPORT (SAMPLE IS
            CHAP7): ";IMAGE$                    ' ACCEPT REPORT NAME
150     GOSUB 57000                             ' FILL THE LINE$()
                                                  PRINT DATA ARRAY
155     GOSUB 55000                             ' PRINT A PAGE
160     PRINT
```

```
165      PRINT "PRINTING COMPLETED."
170      BEEP                                        ' RING THE BELL
175      END
180      '
185      '
190      '


55000    ' DATA PRINT SUBROUTINE
55005    '
55010    ' THIS FILLS IN A DATA PAGE AND SENDS IT TO THE PRINTER OR DISK
55015    '
55020    ' IMPORTANT VARIABLES:
55025    '      IMAGE$              NAME OF REPORT TO PRINT
55030    '      LINES$()            ARRAY CONTAINS DATA TO PRINT
55035    '      PRT%                0 = SEND TO PRINTER 1 = SEND TO DISK
55040    '
55045    CLS                                         ' INFORM THE USER OF
                                                       PRINTING
55050    LOCATE 10,10
55055    PRINT "PLEASE WAIT "
55060    LOCATE 12,10
55065    A$ = IMAGE$ + ".RPT"                        ' IMAGE SAVED WITH .RPT
                                                       EXTENSION
55070    PRINT "PROCESSING ";A$;
55075    ON ERROR GOTO 55705                         ' IN CASE FILE MISSING
55080    OPEN A$ FOR INPUT AS #1
55085    ON ERROR GOTO 60000                         ' NORMAL ERROR
                                                       PROCESSING
55090    IF PRT% = 0 THEN GOTO 55100 ELSE A$ = IMAGE$ + ".LST"
55095    OPEN A$ FOR OUTPUT AS #2                     ' OUTPUT TO PRINTER OR
                                                       DISK
55100    A$ = ""                                      ' CLEAR FOR USE BELOW
55105    '
55110    ' PAGE PROCESS LOOP
55115    '
55120    LINE INPUT#1, ENTRY$                         ' GET A LINE FROM THE
                                                        DATA PAGE
55125    IF LEFT$(ENTRY$,1) = "." THEN GOSUB
             55490 : GOTO 55270                       ' TEST FOR DOT COMMAND
55130    '
55135    ' PRINTS AND LOOKS FOR SPECIAL COMMANDS
55140    '
55145    ' SYMBOL                  DESCRIPTION
55150    '    ^                     BOLD PRINT TOGGLE
55155    '    ~                     ENLARGED PRINT TOGGLE
```

```
55160     '                                  UNDERLINE PRINT TOGGLE
55165     '     {                            INSERT AND CONCATENATE
55170     '     [                            INSERT AND DO NOT CONCATENATE
55175     '
55180     ' LOOK FOR SPECIAL COMMANDS ONE CHARACTER AT A TIME
55185     '
55190     FOR X = 1 TO LEN(ENTRY$)
55195         C$ = MID$(ENTRY$,X,1)                    ' EXTRACT ONE
                                                         CHARACTER
55200         IF C$ = "^" THEN GOSUB 55885 :
                  GOTO 55245                            ' TEST FOR BOLD
55205         IF C$ = "~" THEN GOSUB 55950 :
                  GOTO 55245                            ' TEST FOR LARGE PRINT
55210         IF C$ = "_" THEN GOSUB 56015 :
                  GOTO 55245                            ' TEST FOR UNDERLINE
55215         IF C$ = "{" THEN GOSUB 55295 :
                  GOTO 55245                            ' TEST FOR INSERT
55220         IF C$ = "[" THEN GOSUB 55370 :
                  GOTO 55245                            ' TEST FOR INSERT
55225     '
55230     ' SPACE LEFT HERE FOR YOU TO ADD MORE COMMANDS IF YOU SO DESIRE
55235     '
55240     IF PRT%=0 THEN LPRINT C$; ELSE
              PRINT#2,C$;                               ' PRINT IT
55245     NEXT X
55250     '
55255     '
55260     '
55265     IF PRT%=0 THEN LPRINT "" ELSE
              PRINT#2,""                                ' ADD THE CARRIAGE
                                                         RETURN
55270     IF EOF(1) THEN GOTO 55450                     ' ALL DONE SO EXIT
55275     PRINT ".";                                    ' SHOW THE USER SOME
                                                         PROGRESS
55280     GOTO 55120                                    ' GET NEXT LINE
55285     '
55290     '
55295     ' INSERT A FIELD INTO THE LINE AND CONCATENATE {}
55300     '
55305     END.INSERT% = INSTR(X,ENTRY$,"}")             ' LOOK FOR OTHER END
55310     IF END.INSERT% = 0 THEN RETURN                ' ALL DONE
55315     '
55320     ' NOW WE SHOULD HAVE VALID ELEMENT NUMBER
55325     '
55330     Y = VAL(MID$(ENTRY$,X+1,2))                   ' ALLOW UP TO 99
55335     IF Y <= 0 THEN RETURN                         ' ERROR SO EXIT
```

```
55340   IF PRT%=0 THEN LPRINT LINES$(Y); ELSE
            PRINT#2,LINES$(Y);                          ' PRINT THE FIELD
55345   X = END.INSERT%                                 ' SKIP INSERT AREA
55350   RETURN                                          ' TRY AGAIN
55355   '
55360   '
55365   '
55370   ' INSERT A FIELD AND DO NOT CONCATENATE [ ]
55375   '
55380   END.INSERT% =
            INSTR(X,ENTRY$,"]")                         ' LOOK FOR OTHER END
55385   IF END.INSERT% = 0 THEN RETURN                  ' ALL DONE
55390   '
55395   ' NOW WE SHOULD HAVE VALID ELEMENT NUMBER
55400   Y = VAL(MID$(ENTRY$,X+1,2))                     ' ALLOW UP TO 99
55405   IF Y <= 0 THEN RETURN                           ' ERROR SO EXIT
55410   IF LEN(LINES$(Y)) < (END.INSERT%+1-X)
            THEN LINES$(Y) =
            LEFT$(LINES$(Y),END.INSERT%+1-X)
55415   IF PRT%=0 THEN LPRINT LINES$(Y); ELSE
            PRINT#2,LINES$(Y);                          ' PRINT THE FIELD
55420   IF LEN(LINES$(Y)) < (END.INSERT% + 1 -
            X) THEN X =(END.INSERT% + 1 - X -
            LEN(LINES$(Y))) ELSE X = 0                  ' FILL WITH SPACES
55422   IF PRT%=0 THEN  LPRINT SPACE$(X); ELSE
            PRINT#2,SPACE$(X);
55425   X = END.INSERT%                                 ' SKIP INSERT AREA
55430   RETURN                                          ' TRY AGAIN
55435   ' ******************************
55440   '
55445   '
55450   ' CLOSE EVERYTHING AND RETURN
55455   '
55460   CLOSE                                           ' CLOSE THE OPEN FILES
55465   '
55470   CLS                                             ' CLEAR THE SCREEN
55475   RETURN
55480   ' **********************************
55485   '
55490   ' DOT COMMAND PROCESSOR
55495   ' SPECIAL PRINTER COMMANDS THAT START IN COLUMN 1 WITH A.
55500   ' COMMANDS ARE:
55505   '       .FF             PRINTER FORM FEED
55510   '       .PAGE           PAGE NUMBERING CONTROL
55515   '       .RPT            NEW REPORT NAME
55520   '       .ASC            PRINTER CONTROL CHARACTER ROUTINE
```

```
55525   '
55530   '
55535   ENTRY$ = MID$(ENTRY$,2)                    ' REMOVE . MARK
55540   FOR X = 1 TO LEN(ENTRY$)                   ' MAKE SURE LINE IS ALL
                                                     UPPERCASE
55545       Y = ASC(MID$(ENTRY$,X,1))             ' GET ASCII VALUE
55550       IF Y >=97 AND Y <= 122 THEN
                MID$(ENTRY$,X,1) =
                CHR$(Y-32)                         ' FORCE UPPERCASE
55555   NEXT X
55560   IF LEFT$(ENTRY$,2) = "FF" THEN GOSUB
            55605 : RETURN                         ' FORM FEED
55565   IF LEFT$(ENTRY$,3) = "RPT" THEN GOSUB
            55660 : RETURN                         ' OPEN NEW REPORT
55570   IF LEFT$(ENTRY$,4) = "PAGE" THEN GOSUB
            55745 : RETURN                         ' PAGE NUMBERING
                                                     ROUTINE
55575   IF LEFT$(ENTRY$,3) = "ASC" THEN GOSUB
            55795 : RETURN                         ' SPECIAL PRINTER
                                                     CONTROLS
55580   GOSUB 55830                               ' BAD COMMAND SO PRINT
                                                     AND SKIP THIS LINE
55585   RETURN                                     ' EXIT
55590   '
55595   '
55600   '

55605   ' FORM FEED AND LABEL PAGES
55610   '
55615   IF PRT%=0 THEN LPRINT CHR$(12); ELSE
            PRINT#2,CHR$(12);                      ' FORM FEED COMMAND
55620   IF PAGE% = 0 THEN RETURN                   ' NO PAGE NUMBERING
55625   IF PRT%=0 THEN LPRINT TAB(70);"PAGE";
            STR$(PAGE%) ELSE PRINT#
            PRINT#2,TAB(70);"PAGE"; STR$(PAGE%)    ' PRINT PAGE NUMBER
55630   PRINT STR$(PAGE%);                         ' SHOW USER PROGRESS
55635   PAGE% = PAGE% + 1                          ' INCREMENT PAGE COUNTER

55640   RETURN
55645   '
55650   '
55655   '
55660   ' OPEN ANOTHER REPORT PAGE
55665   '
55670   CLOSE#1                                    ' CLOSE CURRENT FILE
55675   ON ERROR GOTO 55705                        ' SET NEW ERROR
                                                     TRAPPING ROUTINE
```

```
55680    A$ = MID$(ENTRY$,5) + ".RPT"           ' EXTRACT FILE NAME AND
                                                     ADD EXTENSION
55685    OPEN A$ FOR INPUT AS #1                 ' OPEN NEW FILE
55690    ON ERROR GOTO 60000
55695    PRINT : PRINT TAB(10);"PROCESSING "; A$;
55700    RETURN                                  ' EVERYTHING OK SO
                                                     CONTINUE
55705    RESUME 55710                            ' FILE NOT FOUND SO
                                                     ERROR CREATED
55710    PRINT
55715    PRINT A$;" NOT FOUND.";CHR$(7)          ' PRINT ERROR MESSAGE
                                                     AND RING BELL
55720    CLOSE
55725    END
55730    '
55735    '
55740    '
55745    ' PAGE NUMBERING CONTROL
55750    '
55755    '.PAGE                                  TURNS NUMBERING OFF
55760    '.PAGE ##                               NUMBERS NEXT PAGE
                                                 STARTING WITH ##
55765    '
55770    IF LEN(ENTRY$) = 4 THEN PAGE% = 0 ELSE
             PAGE% = VAL(MID$(ENTRY$,6))
55775    RETURN
55780    '
55785    '
55790    '
55795    ' PRINTER CONTROL COMMANDS
55800    '
55805    ' .ASC ## ## ## ## ##
55810    '
55815    ' USES CHR$() TO PRINT CHARACTER FOR
             EACH VALUE
55820    ' EG. ESCAPE IS ASCII 27 THEREFORE TO
             PRINT AN ESCAPE WE WOULD USE
55825    ' .ASC 27
55830    '
55835    ENTRY$ = MID$(ENTRY$,5)                 ' STRIP OFF ASC
55840    IF LEN(ENTRY$) = 0 THEN RETURN          ' ALL DONE
55845    X = INSTR(1,ENTRY$," ")                 ' LOOK FOR SEPARATOR
55850    IF X = 0 THEN Y = VAL(ENTRY$) : ENTRY$ = ""
                                                 ' AT END OF LINE
```

```
55855   IF X <> 0 THEN Y = VAL(LEFT$(ENTRY$,X-          ' IN THE MIDDLE OF THE
           1)) : ENTRY$ = MID$(ENTRY$,X+1)                 LINE

55860   IF PRT%=0 THEN LPRINT CHR$(Y); ELSE           ' SEND THE CHARACTER TO
           PRINT#2,CHR$(Y);                              THE PRINTER
55865   GOTO 55840                                    ' GET NEXT CHARACTER
55870   '
55875   '
55880   '
55885   ' BOLD PRINT COMMAND ROUTINE
55890   '
55895   ' COMMANDS ARE FOR EPSON FX-100
           PRINTER
55900   '
55905   '
55910   '
55915   IF BOLD% <> 0 THEN BOLD% = 0 : L$ =
           CHR$(27)+"F" : GOTO 55930                   ' CANCEL MODE
55920   BOLD% = 1                                     ' SET FLAG SO WE KNOW
                                                          MODE SET
55925   L$ = CHR$(27)+"E"                             ' TURN EMPHASIZED MODE
                                                          ON
55930   IF PRT%=0 THEN LPRINT L$; ELSE PRINT#2,L$;
55935   RETURN
55940   '
55945   '
55950   ' ENLARGED PRINT MODE
55955   '
55960   ' COMMANDS ARE FOR EPSON FX-100
55965   '
55970   '
55975   '
55980   IF ENLARGED% <> 0 THEN ENLARGED% = 0 :
           L$ = CHR$(27)+"W"+CHR$(10) : GOTO
           55995                                       ' TURN MODE OFF
55985   ENLARGED% = 1                                 ' SET FLAG SO WE KNOW
                                                          MODE IS ON
55990   L$ = CHR$(27)+"W"+CHR$(1)                     ' TURNS ENLARGED PRINT
                                                          ON
55995   IF PRT%=0 THEN LPRINT L$; ELSE
           PRINT#2,L$;
56000   RETURN
56005   '
56010   '
```

```
56015     ' UNDERLINE PRINT MODE
56020     '
56025     ' COMMANDS ARE FOR EPSON FX-100
56030     '
56035     '
56040     '
56045     IF UNDERLINE% THEN UNDERLINE% = 0 :
              L$ = CHR$(27)+"-"+CHR$(0) : GOTO
              56060                                ' TURN MODE OFF
56050     UNDERLINE% = 1                           ' SET FLAG SO WE KNOW
                                                       MODE IS ON
56055     L$ = CHR$(27)+"-"+CHR$(1)                ' BEGINS UNDERLINING
56060     IF PRT%=0 THEN LPRINT L$; ELSE
              PRINT#2,L$;
56065     RETURN
56070     '
56075     '


57000     ' SAMPLE DATA FOR TEST (CHAP7.RPT)
57010     '
57020     LINES$(1) = "JOHN DOE"
57030     LINES$(2) = "1234 FIRST STREET"
57040     X = 1000                                 ' A VALUE
57050     LINES$(3) = MID$(STR$(X),2)              ' REMOVE LEADING SPACE
57060     LINES$(4) = MID$(STR$(X * 3),2)          ' DITTO
57070     RETURN
57080     ' ************************
57090     '
57100     '


60000     ' STANDARD ERROR PROCESSING ROUTINE
60005     '
60010     X = ERR                                  ' GET ERROR NUMBER
60015     Y = ERL                                  ' GET LINE NUMBER
60020     RESUME 60025
60025     KEY OFF                                  ' TURN OFF SO WE CAN USE
                                                       25TH LINE
60030     LOCATE 25,1                              ' DISPLAY ON 25TH LINE
60035     PRINT "ERROR ";X;" ON LINE NUMBER ";Y
60040     BEEP                                     ' RING THE BELLS
60045     END                                      ' THAT'S ALL FOLKS
60050     '
60055     '
60060     '
```

PERSONAL CALENDAR: A SAMPLE PROGRAM

INTRODUCTION

Thus far, several flexible subroutines have been developed. This chapter will illustrate how easy it is to use these subroutines to create larger programs. The sample program developed in this chapter will maintain a personal appointment calendar. This is a moderately-sized program that is easily and quickly constructed using the building blocks developed in the previous chapters. We will use the same methods to create this program that we used in the previous chapters.

In addition to using the routines developed in the previous chapters, the personal calendar program introduces a few new routines and concepts. A subroutine is used to calculate the number of days a given date is from the beginning of the year. Another subroutine uses a random-access file to store the appointment information.

In the following subsections we first design the input screens and the reports. Then we create the various program modules necessary to connect everything together.

Building the Program

The calendar program builds on the routines that have been developed in previous chapters. The routines of this chapter are merged with those of Chapters 2, 4, 5, 6, and 7 to produce a working personal calendar program.

Design

The personal calendar program displays, accepts, and prints hourly appointment information. The features of this program can best be seen by looking at the various input screens and reports.

The menu, shown in Figure 8.1, lists the available options: review, print, help, and exit. When options 1 and 2 are selected, the program will ask for the date to be reviewed or printed, as shown in Figure 8.2. When option 3 is selected, the range of dates of interest is entered, as illustrated in Figure 8.3.

FIG. 8.1   Appointment Calendar Menu

```
             ^Appointment Calendar Menu^

        1. Review Day's Appointments

        2. Print One Day's Appointments

        3. Print Group of Days

        4. ^HELP^

        ^0 Exit to BASIC^

        #0 END
        #4 HELP
```

FIG. 8.2   Single-date entry screen

```
                        ^Appointment Date^

     1. Month of Appointment              <# 2>
     2. Day of Month                      <# 2>
```

The appointment data entry screen is shown in Figure 8.4. It is designed to accept hourly appointments between 8:00 A.M. and 5:00 P.M. The report generator template, shown in Figure 8.5, is very similar to the data entry screen.

Since any date may be edited, random-access files are used to store the data on the disk.

BASIC CALENDAR PROGRAM

The calendar program, flowcharted in Figure 8.6, uses the following subroutines.

- Menu,
- Accept single date,
- Load data from disk,

FIG. 8.3   Data entry screen for group of dates

```
                    ^Appointment Calendar^

     1. Beginning Month                    <# 2>
     2. Day of Beginning Month             <# 2>
     3. Last Month                         <# 2>
     4. Day of Last Month                  <# 2>
```

FIG. 8.4   Data entry screen for appointments

```
              ^Appointment Calendar^

               1.  8 AM   <a 30>
               2.  9 AM   <a 30>
               3.  10 AM  <a 30>
               4.  11 AM  <a 30>
               5.  12 PM  <a 30>
               6.  1 PM   <a 30>
               7.  2 PM   <a 30>
               8.  3 PM   <a 30>
               9.  4 PM   <a 30>
              10.  5 PM   <a 30>
```

FIG. 8.5   Appointment report generator template

```
              ^Appointment Calendar^

                8 AM     {1}
                9 AM     {2}
               10 AM     {3}
               11 AM     {4}
               12 PM     {5}
                1 PM     {6}
                2 PM     {7}
                3 PM     {8}
                4 PM     {9}
                5 PM     {10}
```

FIG. 8.6   Menu flowchart

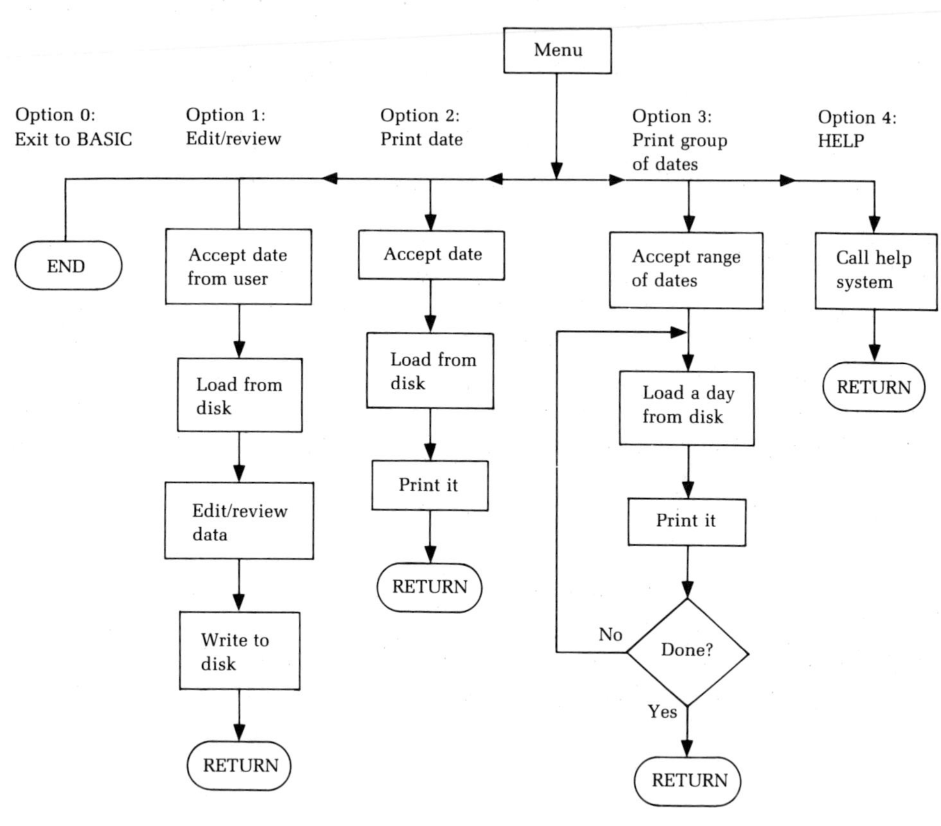

- Edit/review appointment data,
- Write data to disk,
- Print data,
- User help text.

Most of these routines are based on subroutines developed in the previous chapters.

In the following subsections the personal calendar program will be created one menu option at a time, beginning with the menu itself.

Before you begin editing the program, however, you should merge the subroutines from Chapters 2, 4, 5, 6, and 7. Remember to set the test portions of each program.

Menu

The menu uses the menu system from Chapter 6 to display the options, accept an option, and branch to the requested routine. This program could be considered the master or main program because it calls the other routines.

The menu routine is as follows.

```
100      ' CHAPTER 8 - PERSONAL CALENDAR PROGRAM
110      '
120      ' THIS MAINTAINS AN ANNUAL PERSONAL CALENDAR. IT IS AN EXAMPLE
130      ' OF HOW A LARGE PROGRAM CAN BE BUILT FROM THE SUBROUTINES
140      ' DEVELOPED THROUGHOUT THE BOOK.
150      '
160      '
170      ON ERROR GOTO 60000            ' STANDARD ERROR PROCESSING
180      LAST% = 10                     ' NUMBER OF FIELDS ON A DATA
                                           ENTRY SCREEN
190      DIM LINES$(LAST%)              ' THESE ARE FOR DATA ENTRY
                                           ROUTINE
200      DIM SROW%(LAST%)               ' AND REPORT GENERATOR
210      DIM SCOL%(LAST%)
220      DIM SMASK$(LAST%)
230      DIM SMAX%(LAST%)
240      PRT% = 1                       ' SEND PRINTOUTS TO DISK
250      A.PRINTER$ = "COM1:1200,N,8,1,
            CS10000,DS,LF"              ' SET UP FOR COMM PORT PRINTER
260      KEY OFF                        ' TURN THE FUNCTION KEYS OFF
270      FOR X = 1 TO 10                ' CLEAR THE KEYS
280      KEY X, " "
290      NEXT X
300      CALENDAR.FILE$ = "PERCAL.DAT"  ' NAME OF PERSONAL CALENDAR
                                           FILE
310      '
320      ' THE CALENDAR FILE IS A RANDOM ACCESS FILE WITH RECORD SIZE OF 300
            BYTES
330      '
340      OPEN CALENDAR.FILE$ AS #3 LEN=
            300                         ' OPEN FOR RANDOM ACCESS
```

```
350      IMAGE$ = "CHAP8"                      ' NAME OF MENU SCREEN
360      '
370      ' CALL THE MENU SUBROUTINE AND BRANCH TO REQUESTED FUNCTION
380      '
390      GOSUB 46000                           ' CHAPTER 6 MENU ROUTINE
400      GOTO 350                              ' RESET NAME AND DO MENU AGAIN
410      '
420      '
430      '
```

In addition to using the above program, you must change some lines in the original menu subroutine. Lines 46170 and 46175 must be changed to

```
46170 ON X GOSUB 1000,2000,3000 ' BRANCH TO DESIRED ROUTINE
46175 RETURN                     ' RETURN TO MAIN PROGRAM
```

So instead of chaining to another program, we now branch to a subroutine, where the subroutines perform as follows.

1000 edit/reviews a day's appointments,

2000 prints a single day's appointments,

3000 prints a group of dates.

The help text is saved on the diskette as CHAP8.HLP and is shown below.

TEST POINT

When you execute the program it should display the menu of Figure 8.1. Only the exit option, 0, should be working. Verify that it does clear the screen, and stop the program.

Option 1: Edit/Review a Day's Appointments

Option 1 combines two features: editing and reviewing the data. In some programs you may want to separate these features. For example, you may have several people using a program, and you may not want all of them to be able to edit the data. If you are not concerned about keeping people from editing, then we feel it is more convenient to keep both features combined. Since this program is a personal calendar program, anyone who has access to the calendar can change it.

The program for option 1, shown below, is quite simple.

```
1000      ' OPTION 1 - EDIT/REVIEW ONE DATE
1005      '
1010      GOSUB 7000                        ' ACCEPT THE DATE
1015      GOSUB 8000                        ' LOAD DATA FROM DISK
1020      IMAGE$ = "CHAP8C"                 ' DATE EDIT SCREEN NAME
1025      GOSUB 44000                       ' EDIT THE DATA - CHAPTER 5
1030      GOSUB 9000                        ' SAVE DATA TO DISK
1035      RETURN                            ' ALL DONE WITH THIS DATE
1040      '
1045      '
1050      '
```

Subroutines 7000, 8000, and 9000 are described in succeeding sections. Subroutine 44000 is the data entry system from Chapter 5.

In addition, a data entry screen, shown in Figure 8.4, and the four help screens called calendar help screens must be entered.

Accepting a Date

Two functions are performed by subroutine 7000: It accepts a month and day from the user, and then it calculates the number of days this date is from the beginning of the year.

The number of days between any two dates can be found by calculating a value for both dates, using the following formulas, and then subtracting these values (subroutine 7500). The formula for dates in January and February is:

$$\text{value} = 365(\text{year}) + \text{day} + 31(\text{month} - 1) +$$
$$\text{INT}[(\text{year} - 1)/4)] \; \text{INT}(.75 \; \{\text{INT}[(\text{year} - 1)/100] + 1\})$$

For dates between March and December the formula is:

$$\text{value} = 365(\text{year}) + \text{day} + 31(\text{month} - 1) + \text{INT}[(\text{year} - 1)/4]$$
$$- \text{INT}(.75 \; \{\text{INT}[(\text{year} - 1)/100] + 1 \}) - \text{INT}[.4(\text{month}) + 2.3]$$

The terms in the above equations have the following meanings.

- Year is the calendar year (e.g., 1984).
- Month is the number of the month (e.g., March is 3).
- Day is the number of the day's date.
- INT is the BASIC integer command.

INT INT (N) command returns the integer (whole-number) part of the argument N.

EXAMPLE

```
100 X = 100.25
110 PRINT "INTEGER" ; INT (X)
```

When this is executed the computer will print

```
INTEGER 100
```

The program listing for this subroutine is as follows.

```
7000      ' ACCEPT A DATE FROM THE USER
7005      '
7010      IMAGE$ = "CHAP8A"                    ' NAME OF DATA ENTRY
                                                   SCREEN
7015      LINES$(1) = ""                       ' CLEAR OLD DATE
7020      LINES$(2) = ""
7025      GOSUB 44000                          ' EDIT THE DATA -
                                                   CHAPTER 5
7030      MM = VAL(LINES$(1))                  ' RESTORE DATE DATA
7035      DD = VAL(LINES$(2))
7040      GOSUB 7500                           ' TRANSLATE TO DISK
                                                   RECORD NUMBER
7045      RETURN
7050      '
7055      '
7060      '
7500      ' CALCULATE DAY NUMBER
7505      '
7510      YY = 1985                            ' CURRENT YEAR
```

```
7515    IF (MM = 0) OR (DD = 0) THEN DAY = 1 :
            RETURN                                  ' ERROR SO FORCE JAN 1
7520    IF (MM > 12) OR (DD > 31) THEN DAY = 1 :
            RETURN                                  ' DITTO HERE
7525    JAN1 = 365 * YY + INT((YY - 1)/4) -
            INT(.75 * INT((YY - 1)/100) + 1)        ' VALUE OF JAN 1, YY
7530    IF MM > 3 THEN GOTO 7550                    ' LAST HALF DIFFERENT
7535    DAY = 365 * YY + DD + 31 * (MM-1) +
            INT((YY - 1)/4) - INT(.75 *
            (INT((YY - 1)/100) + 1)) - JAN1
7540    RETURN
7545    '
7550    ' NOW FOR MARCH THROUGH DECEMBER
7555    '
7560    DAY = 365 * YY + DD + 31 * (MM - 1) +
            INT(YY/4) - INT(.75 * (INT(YY/100)
            + 1)) - INT(.4 * MM + 2.3) - JAN1
7565    RETURN
7570    '
7575    '
7580    '
```

The data entry routine of Chapter 5 (line 7025, GOSUB 44000) calls routine 8000 (shown below) to fill the LINE$() array with the original, or default, values and routine 9000 (below) to move LINE$() values into the regular variable names.

Subroutine 8000 is as follows.

```
8000    ' LOAD A DAY'S DATA FROM THE DISK
8005    '
8010    FIELD 3,30 AS L1$,30 AS L2$,30 AS L3$,30 AS L4$,30 AS L5$,30 AS
            L6$,30 AS L7$,30 AS L8$,30 AS L9$,30 AS L10$
8015    GET #3,DAY                                  ' READ THE RECORD FOR
                                                      DISK
8020    LINES$(1) = L1$                             ' EQUATE TO ARRAY
                                                      ELEMENTS
8025    LINES$(2) = L2$
8030    LINES$(3) = L3$
8035    LINES$(4) = L4$
8040    LINES$(5) = L5$
8045    LINES$(6) = L6$
8050    LINES$(7) = L7$
8055    LINES$(8) = L8$
```

```
8060      LINES$(9) = L9$
8065      LINES$(10) = L10$
8070      ' STRIP TRAILING SPACES
8075      FOR X = 1 TO 10                              ' DO FOR EVERY FIELD
8080              IF LEN(LINES$(X)) = 0 THEN
          GOTO 8090                                    ' DONE?
8085              IF RIGHT$(LINES$(X),1) = " "
          THEN LINES$(X) =
          LEFT$(LINES$(X),LEN(LINES$(X)) -
          1) : GOTO 8080                               ' REMOVE SPACE AND TRY
                                                         AGAIN

8090      NEXT X
8095      RETURN
8100      '
8105      '
8110      '
```

TEST POINT

Execute the program and verify that option 1 allows you to enter a month and a day. While in the data entry screen program, test the help feature and the various editing commands available.

Random-Access Files

To edit any date's data, we must use random-access diskette files. A random-access file, as the name suggests, is a data file that can be read from or written to in any order—that is, randomly. Up to this point all the diskette files used were sequential or text files. A sequential file is read in exactly the same order in which it is written.

Random-access files require a little more programming and bookkeeping than sequential files require because the computer stores random files slightly differently than it stores sequential files. The following analogy will help explain the difference. A sequential file can be compared with a stack of papers. Such a stack is very compact, but it is difficult to insert or remove papers from the stack unless they happen to be next to each other in the stack. In contrast, a random-access file can be thought of as a stack of identical shoe boxes numbered sequentially, 1, 2, 3, ... Each box contains pieces of paper. Some of the boxes are full, some partially full, and some empty. When the contents of a box are to be read or changed, you tell your assistant to go get box number XX. The shoe boxes take up more room than the stack of papers, but with the boxes you can generally get to a particular set of papers faster.

In the computer, sequential files are written to the disk with the text packed tightly together (the stacks of paper). Random files are written in pieces called *records* (the shoe boxes); all the records in a file use exactly the same amount of space. When a random file is opened for processing, the computer is told how large the records are. The computer must also be told which record is to be accessed. The length of the data stored in a record must be less than or equal to the record size. Since, in general, the data is smaller than the record size, some space is wasted. Because the computer can easily calculate exactly where the beginning of each record is, however, it can quickly read or write the data.

In the personal calendar program we wish to store 10 lines of data with a maximum length of 30 characters each, for a record size of 300 characters. The records are consecutively numbered, beginning with 1. In our program January 1 is record 1, January 2 is record 2, and so on.

As a matter of practice, random-access files should be initialized before they are used. A file is initialized by writing blank or null lines into every record. The following program initializes a one-month calendar.

```
100        ' CHAPTER 8 CALENDAR INITIALIZATION ROUTINE
110        '
120        ' CREATES AND CLEARS THE CALENDAR FILE
130        '
140        CLS
150        PRINT "CREATING THE PERSONAL CALENDAR FILE"
160        OPEN "PERCAL.DAT" AS #1 LEN =
               300                         ' OPEN THE FILE
170        FIELD #1,150 AS A$,150 AS B$    ' DEFINE THE RANDOM ACCESS
                                               FIELD
180        LSET A$ = " "                   ' CREATE A BLANK OR NULL STRING
190        LSET B$ = " "
200        DAYS = 31                       ' EXAMPLE ONE MONTH ONLY, 366 =
                                               ONE YEAR
```

```
210        FOR X = 1 TO DAYS          ' WRITE NULL$ FOR DAYS TIMES
220            PUT #1,X               ' SAVE FIELD 1 AT RECORD X
230        NEXT X
240        CLOSE#1
250        END
260        '
270        '
280        '
```

Adjust the number of days in the routine above to the size of calendar you want. Note that a full, one-year calendar will fill most of the blank diskette, and so do not try to put a calendar on a diskette already containing other files.

FIELD There are several BASIC statements associated with random-access files. The FIELD statement is combined with the LSET and RSET statements to move data into and out of the random buffer.

The OPEN statement contains a term that sets the size of the record or random buffer. The FIELD statement assigns data to specific places within this buffer. This is done by giving each variable a length and a position relative to the other variables in the record. In the following example,

```
FIELD 1,20 AS N$, 10 AS ID$, 40 AS ADD$
```

means, for file 1, the first 20 characters contain N$, the next 10 contain ID$, and the final 40 contain ADD$. The variables have to be assigned a position so that we know where they are.

Unfortunately there is one more complication, LSET and RSET.

LSET AND RSET The variables used in the actual FIELD statement cannot be used as regular variables. In fact, the only place you should use them is in LSET, RSET and when another value is being equated to them. This is an oddity of IBM BASIC and is not something inherent with all BASICs. In IBM BASIC the physical location or address of a string is frequently changed. In other words, BASIC freely moves data around as it sees fit. This is normally not a problem, but the physical address of the random buffer is fixed and does not move. Therefore, to make sure the random-buffer string variable does not get moved, the special FIELD and RSET and LSET statements were invented.

The FIELD statement makes sure that the physical address of a string is assigned to its location in the random buffer. The LSET and RSET move data into the strings in a way that does not change the string's physical address. Therefore the data ends up in the random buffer and not somewhere else. The LSET moves the data into the buffer area and left-justifies it. RSET also moves the data, but it right-justifies it.

GET   The GET statement reads the specified diskette record into the random buffer area. The GET statement is

```
GET 1,number
```

where 1 is the OPEN file number and "number" is the record number to be read.

PUT   PUT writes the random buffer to the diskette file at the record specified.

```
PUT 1,number
```

where 1 is the OPEN file number and "number" is the record number to be written.

Calendar Help Screens

The following illustrations show the four help screens that will be displayed. Please enter them using the editor as four separate files with the names specified.

```
1.  File 'CHAP8.HLP'
```

```
^APPOINTMENT MENU HELP^
```

```
THIS PROGRAM MAINTAINS A PERSONAL APPOINTMENT CALENDAR. YOU
CAN EDIT, REVIEW, OR PRINT ANY DAY'S APPOINTMENTS.
```

^OPTION 1^ ALLOWS YOU TO EDIT OR REVIEW ANY SINGLE DAY'S
SCHEDULE.

^OPTION 2^ PRINTS A SINGLE DAY'S APPOINTMENTS.

^OPTION 3^ PRINTS SEVERAL DAYS APPOINTMENTS.

^OPTION 4^ DISPLAYS THIS HELP PAGE.

^OPTION 0^ STOPS THE PROGRAM AND RETURNS TO BASIC.

^SELECT OPTION, ENTER ITS NUMBER, AND STRIKE RETURN^

2. File 'CHAP8A.HLP'

^APPOINTMENT DATE HELP^

PLEASE ENTER THE MONTH AND DAY YOU
WISH TO EDIT OR REVIEW. IF YOU ENTER
AN IMPROPER DATE, THE COMPUTER WILL
ASSUME THAT YOU WISH TO EDIT JANUARY 1.

3. File 'CHAP8B.HLP'

^PRINTING GROUP OF DATES^

THIS SECTION PRINTS A GROUP OF DAYS'
APPOINTMENTS. ENTER THE MONTH AND DAY
YOU WISH TO BEGIN PRINTING AND THE
LAST MONTH AND DAY YOU WISH TO PRINT.

4. File 'CHAP8C.HLP'

^PERSONAL CALENDAR^

THIS IS A PERSONAL CALENDAR PROGRAM.
YOU MAY ENTER TEXT ON ANY LINE. TO
EXIT, STEP THROUGH THE LINES, USING
THE RETURN KEY, UNTIL YOU REACH THE
LINE THAT ASKS WHAT YOU WANT TO CHANGE
AND ENTER 0 (CR).

Calendar Data Entry Subroutine

The data entry system needs the name of the entry screen and two subroutines to move the data between the regular variable names and LINES$(). Since we are not manipulating the data other than with the data entry system, we are taking a shortcut here and not assigning regular variable names. The data-save routine follows.

```
9000    ' WRITE A DAY'S DATA TO THE DISK
9005    '
9010    FIELD 3,30 AS L1$,30 AS L2$,30 AS L3$,30 AS L4$,30 AS L5$,
            30 AS L6$,30 AS L7$,30 AS L8$,30 AS L9$,30 AS L10$
9015    LSET L1$ = LINES$(1)     ' EQUATE TO ARRAY ELEMENTS
9020    LSET L2$ = LINES$(2)
9025    LSET L3$ = LINES$(3)
9030    LSET L4$ = LINES$(4)
9035    LSET L5$ = LINES$(5)
9040    LSET L6$ = LINES$(6)
9045    LSET L7$ = LINES$(7)
9050    LSET L8$ = LINES$(8)
9055    LSET L9$ = LINES$(9)
9060    LSET L10$ = LINES$(10)
9065    PUT #3,DAY                ' WRITE IT TO THE DISK
9070    RETURN
9075    '
9080    '
9085    '
```

TEST POINT

In the menu select option 1. In the data screen enter a date in January, and verify that appointment information can be entered and edited. After the appointments have been edited, the program returns to the menu. Repeat this test now to verify that the data has been properly written to the diskette and read from the diskette. Finally, repeat the test again and press shift F1 and verify that the help routine is working.

Option 2: Print a Day's Appointments

Option 2 uses some of the previous routines plus the report generator of Chapter 7. The report generator needs a report template name and a routine to move the data between the regular variable names and the LINES$() array. As in the data entry screen, since we are not manipulating the data we can leave it in the LINES$() array. We take another shortcut here and use the data entry routine 8000. For this reason, the report generator program is quite small.

```
2000   ' OPTION 2 - PRINT A SINGLE DAY
2005   '
2010   GOSUB 7000          ' ACCEPT THE DATE
2015   GOSUB 8000          ' LOAD DATA FROM DISK
2020   IMAGE$ = "CHAP8"    ' NAME OF REPORT PAGE
2025   GOSUB 55000         ' REPORT GENERATOR
2030   RETURN
2035   '
2040   '
2045   '
```

TEST POINT

Run the program and select option 2. If everything goes according to plan, the report should appear on your printer, and the program should return to the menu.

Option 3: Print a Group of Dates

Option 3 is only a little more complicated than option 2. The option 3 subroutine accepts two dates instead of one; it then uses a loop to print all the days' schedules between the two dates.

Here is option 3.

```
3000   ' OPTION 3 - PRINT A GROUP OF DATES
3005   '
3010   FOR X = 1 TO 4                  ' CLEAR ARRAY
3015   LINES$(X) = ""
3020   NEXT X
3025   IMAGE$ = "CHAP8B"              ' NAME OF DATA ENTRY SCREEN
3030   GOSUB 44000                    ' DATA ENTRY PAGE
3035   MM = VAL(LINES$(1))            ' SETUP FOR DATE CONVERSION
3040   DD = VAL(LINES$(2))
3045   GOSUB 7500                     ' CONVERT DATE TO RECORD NUMBER
3050   D1 = DAY                       ' SAVE THIS
3055   MM = VAL(LINES$(3))            ' REPEAT FOR SECOND DATE
3060   DD = VAL(LINES$(4))
```

```
3065   GOSUB 7500                      ' CONVERT DATE
3070   D2 = DAY
3075   IF D1 > D2 THEN SWAP D1,D2      ' MAKE D1 SMALLEST
3080   IMAGE$ = "CHAP8"                ' REPORT NAME
3085   FOR DAY = D1 TO D2              ' LOOP AND PRINT EACH DAY
3090       GOSUB 8000                  ' READ THE DAY'S DATA
3095       GOSUB 55000                 ' PRINT THE REPORT
3100   NEXT DAY
3105   RETURN                          ' ALL DONE
3110   '
3115   '
3120   '
```

TEST POINT

Execute and select option 3. Enter two dates about three days apart, and verify that three reports are printed. Repeat and test the help system. You may wish to enter several days' appointments to make sure that the correct data have been printed.

Option 4: Help

Option 4 uses the help subsystem and requires nothing to be added.

TEST POINT

Select option 4 from the menu, and the menu help text should appear.

Summary

You now have a working personal calendar program built from reusable subroutines. The number of new program lines required to create this program is small compared with its overall size. We hope this example has shown you the value of a library of subroutines.

USER INSTRUCTIONS

The calendar program maintains a daily personal calendar. You can edit, review, or print any day's or group of days' schedules. Help is available with every screen.

This menu is the first screen seen.

```
            APPOINTMENT CALENDAR MENU

  1. REVIEW DAY'S APPOINTMENTS
  2. PRINT ONE DAY'S APPOINTMENTS
  3. PRINT GROUP OF DAYS
  4. HELP
  0. EXIT TO BASIC
```

Option 1: Edit/Review a Day's Appointments

Option 1 allows you to edit or review any day's appointments . After
the option is selected, you will be asked to enter a month and a day.
The appointments for this day will be displayed and can be edited if
desired.

Option 2: Print a Day's Appointments

Option 2 asks for the month and the day to be printed. Make sure that
the printer is turned on and ready.

Option 3: Print a Group of Dates

In option 3 you will be asked to enter the beginning month and day
and the last month and day to be printed. These appointments will be
printed one day to a page. Make sure that the printer is turned on and
ready.

Option 4: Help

When you select option 4, a brief description of the various HELP options is presented.

COMPLETE PERSONAL CALENDAR PROGRAM

```
100    ' CHAPTER 8 - PERSONAL CALENDAR PROGRAM
110    '
120    ' This maintains an annual personal calendar. It is an example
130    ' of how a large program can be built from the subroutines
140    ' developed throughout the book.
150    '
160    '
170    ON ERROR GOTO 60000                    ' STANDARD ERROR
                                                  PROCESSING
180    LAST% = 10                             ' NUMBER OF FIELDS ON A
                                                  DATA ENTRY SCREEN
190    DIM LINES$(LAST%)                      ' THESE ARE FOR DATA
                                                  ENTRY ROUTINE
200    DIM SROW%(LAST%)                       ' AND REPORT GENERATOR
210    DIM SCOL%(LAST%)
220    DIM SMASK$(LAST%)
230    DIM SMAX%(LAST%)
240    PRT% = 1                               ' SEND PRINTOUTS TO
                                                  DISK
250    A.PRINTER$ =
           "COM1:1200,N,8,1,CS10000,          ' SET UP FOR COMM
           DS,LF"                                PORT PRINTER
260    KEY OFF                                ' TURN THE FUNCTION
                                                  KEYS OFF
270    FOR X = 1 TO 10                        ' CLEAR THE KEYS
280          KEY X, ""
290    NEXT X
300    CALENDAR.FILE$ = "PERCAL.DAT"          ' NAME OF PERSONAL
                                                  CALENDAR FILE
310    '
320    ' THE CALENDAR FILE IS A RANDOM ACCESS FILE WITH RECORD SIZE OF
           300 BYTES
330    '
340    OPEN CALENDAR.FILE$ AS #3 LEN=300      ' OPEN FOR RANDOM
                                                  ACCESS
350    IMAGE$ = "CHAP8"                       ' NAME OF MENU SCREEN
360    '
370    ' CALL THE MENU SUBROUTINE AND BRANCH TO REQUESTED FUNCTION
380    '
390    GOSUB 46000                            ' CHAPTER 6 MENU
                                                  ROUTINE
400    GOTO 350                               ' RESET NAME AND DO
                                                  MENU AGAIN
```

```
410    '
420    '
430    '

1000    ' OPTION 1 - EDIT/REVIEW ONE DATE
1005    '
1010    GOSUB 7000                          ' ACCEPT THE DATE
1015    GOSUB 8000                          ' LOAD DATA FROM DISK
1020    IMAGE$ = "CHAP8C"                   ' DATE EDIT SCREEN NAME
1025    GOSUB 44000                         ' EDIT THE DATA -
                                              CHAPTER 5
1030    GOSUB 9000                          ' SAVE DATA TO DISK
1035    RETURN                              ' ALL DONE WITH THIS
                                              DATE
1040    '
1045    '
1050    '

2000    ' OPTION 2 - PRINT A SINGLE DAY
2005    '
2010    GOSUB 7000                          ' ACCEPT THE DATE
2015    GOSUB 8000                          ' LOAD DATA FROM DISK
2020    IMAGE$ = "CHAP8"                    ' NAME OF REPORT PAGE
2025    GOSUB 55000                         ' REPORT GENERATOR
2030    RETURN
2035    '
2040    '
2045    '

3000    ' OPTION 3 - PRINT A GROUP OF DATES
3005    '
3010    FOR X = 1 TO 4                      ' CLEAR ARRAY
3015        LINES$(X) = ""
3020    NEXT X
3025    IMAGE$ = "CHAP8B"                   ' NAME OF DATA ENTRY
                                              SCREEN
3030    GOSUB 44000                         ' DATA ENTRY PAGE
3035    MM = VAL(LINES$(1))                 ' SETUP FOR DATE
                                              CONVERSION
3040    DD = VAL(LINES$(2))
3045    GOSUB 7500                          ' CONVERT DATE TO
                                              RECORD NUMBER
3050    D1 = DAY                            ' SAVE THIS
3055    MM = VAL(LINES$(3))                 ' REPEAT FOR SECOND
                                              DATE
```

```
3060    DD = VAL(LINES$(4))
3065    GOSUB 7500                              ' CONVERT DATE
3070    D2 = DAY
3075    IF D1 > D2 THEN SWAP D1,D2              ' MAKE D1 SMALLEST
3080    IMAGE$ = "CHAP8"                        ' REPORT NAME
3085    FOR DAY = D1 TO D2                      ' LOOP AND PRINT EACH
                                                   DAY
3090        GOSUB 8000                          ' READ THE DAY'S DATA
3095        GOSUB 55000                         ' PRINT THE REPORT
3100    NEXT DAY
3105    RETURN                                  ' ALL DONE
3110    '
3115    '
3120    '

7000    ' ACCEPT A DATE FROM THE USER
7005    '
7010    IMAGE$ = "CHAP8A"                       ' NAME OF DATA ENTRY
                                                   SCREEN
7015    LINES$(1) = ""                          ' CLEAR OLD DATE
7020    LINES$(2) = ""
7025    GOSUB 44000                             ' EDIT THE DATA -
                                                   CHAPTER 5
7030    MM = VAL(LINES$(1))                     ' RESTORE DATE DATA
7035    DD = VAL(LINES$(2))
7040    GOSUB 7500                              ' TRANSLATE TO DISK
                                                   RECORD NUMBER
7045    RETURN
7050    '
7055    '
7060    '

7500    ' CALCULATE DAY NUMBER
7505    '
7510    YY = 1985                               ' CURRENT YEAR
7515    IF (MM = 0) OR (DD = 0) THEN DAY = 1 :
            RETURN                              ' ERROR SO FORCE JAN 1
7520    IF (MM > 12) OR (DD > 31) THEN DAY =1 :
            RETURN                              ' DITTO HERE
7525    JAN1 = 365 * YY + INT((YY - 1)/4) -
            INT(.75 * INT((YY - 1)/100) + 1)    ' VALUE OF JAN 1, YY
7530    IF MM > 3 THEN GOTO 7550                ' LAST HALF DIFFERENT
7535    DAY = 365 * YY + DD + 31 * (MM-1) + INT((YY - 1)/4) - INT(.75 *
            (INT((YY - 1)/100) + 1)) - JAN1
```

```
7540    RETURN
7545    '
7550    ' NOW FOR MARCH THROUGH DECEMBER
7555    '
7560    DAY = 365 * YY + DD + 31 * (MM - 1) + INT(YY/4) - INT(.75 *
           (INT(YY/100) + 1)) - INT(.4 * MM + 2.3) - JAN1
7565    RETURN
7570    '
7575    '
7580    '

8000    ' LOAD A DAY'S DATA FROM THE DISK
8005    '
8010    FIELD 3,30 AS L1$,30 AS L2$,30 AS L3$,30 AS L4$,30 AS L5$,30 AS
           L6$,30 AS L7$,30 AS L8$,30 AS L9$,30 AS L10$
8015    GET #3,DAY                              ' READ THE RECORD FOR
                                                     DISK
8020    LINES$(1) = L1$                         ' EQUATE TO ARRAY
                                                     ELEMENTS
8025    LINES$(2) = L2$
8030    LINES$(3) = L3$
8035    LINES$(4) = L4$
8040    LINES$(5) = L5$
8045    LINES$(6) = L6$
8050    LINES$(7) = L7$
8055    LINES$(8) = L8$
8060    LINES$(9) = L9$
8065    LINES$(10) = L10$
8070    ' STRIP TRAILING SPACES
8075    FOR X = 1 TO 10                         ' DO FOR EVERY FIELD
8080          IF LEN(LINES$(X)) = 0 THEN GOTO
                 8090                           ' DONE
8085          IF RIGHT$(LINES$(X),1) = " " THEN LINES$(X) =
                 LEFT$(LINES$(X),LEN(LINES$(X)) - 1) :
                 GOTO 8080
                                                ' REMOVE SPACE AND TRY
                                                     AGAIN
8090    NEXT X
8095    RETURN
8100    '
8105    '
8110    '

9000    ' WRITE A DAY'S DATA TO THE DISK
9005    '
```

```
9010   FIELD 3,30 AS L1$,30 AS L2$,30 AS L3$,30 AS L4$,30 AS L5$,30 AS
         L6$,30 AS L7$,30 AS L8$,30 AS L9$,30 AS L10$
9015   LSET L1$ = LINES$(1)                        ' EQUATE TO ARRAY
                                                     ELEMENTS
9020   LSET L2$ = LINES$(2)
9025   LSET L3$ = LINES$(3)
9030   LSET L4$ = LINES$(4)
9035   LSET L5$ = LINES$(5)
9040   LSET L6$ = LINES$(6)
9045   LSET L7$ = LINES$(7)
9050   LSET L8$ = LINES$(8)
9055   LSET L9$ = LINES$(9)
9060   LSET L10$ = LINES$(10)
9065   PUT #3,DAY                                  ' WRITE IT TO THE DISK
9070   RETURN
9075   '
9080   '
9085   '

46170  ON X GOSUB 1000,2000,3000                  ' BRANCH TO DESIRED
                                                     ROUTINE
46175  RETURN                                      ' RETURN TO MAIN
                                                     PROGRAM
```

INDEX

Alphanumeric character accept, 42
ASC, 39
ASCII character codes, 38
Auto line numbering, 122
Automatic report generation, 233

Backspace key, 45
BEEP, 60

Chaining, 205
Clear, 130
CLOSE command, 117
CLS, 21
COLOR, 37

COL%, 25
Compiler, 11
Concantenating two lines, 99
Control keys
  END, 44
  HOME, 85
Control-left arrow, 44
Control-right arrow, 44
Controls, editing, 44–45
Copy text block, 102

Data entry program, 179
Data entry screen, creation of, 176
Date formula, 254

Delete
  block of text, 103
  character, 51
  line, 97
  word, 58
DEL key, 45
DIM, 80
Directory, 124
Displaying
  a character, 47
  a cursor, 36
  messages, 96
  original values, 185
Display subroutine, 26
Dot commands, 230
  .ASC, 234
  .FF, 231
  .PAGE, 232
  .RPT, 233

Edit command, 114
Editing controls, 44
Edit subroutine, 35
END key, 44
End-of-file, 121
ENTER key, 45
ENTRY$, 25
EOF, 121
Erase to end of line, 54
ERL, 60
ERR, 60
Error processing routine, 59
ESC key, 45
Exiting data entry screen, 191

Flowchart
  for data entry screen, 180
  for field-editing routine, 188
  for help subroutine, 159
  for menu program, 204

for personal calendar, 251
  for report generator, 220
  for text editor, 109
flowchart, display subroutine, 27
flowchart search and replace, 127
FIELD command, 259
FILES command, 124
FILL$, 26
FIRST%, 80
FOR-NEXT, 31
FRE ( ), 110
Form feed, 231
F1 key, 85
F2 key, 45
F3 key, 85
F4 key, 85
F5 key, 85
F6 key, 85
F7 key, 85
F8 key, 85
F9 key, 85

GET command, 260
Global, 129
GOSUB, 2

HELP%, 25
Hints, 12
HOME key, 85

IF-THEN, 21
INKEY$, 36
INPUT, 15
Insert and concatenate, 224
Insert and do not concatenate, 225
Inserting blank line, 95
Inserting characters, 53
INS key, 45
INT command, 255
Integer, 25

Jump to end of line, 51
Jump to front of line, 57
Jump to home page, 92
Jump to last page, 93
Jump to next word, 49
Jump to previous word, 50

KEY, 21
Keyboard overlay, 86

LCOL%, 80
Left arrow, 44
LEFT$, 29
LEN, 29
Line editor, 16
Line editor overview, 23
LOAD command, 131
LOCATE, 21
LROW%, 80

Mask, 19
MASK$, 25
MAXSIZE%, 25
Menu, 199
MERGE command, 131
MID$, 30
MLINES%, 80
Move a block of text, 105
Moving cursor right and left, 48
Moving down a line, 88
Moving up a line, 89

NOPAUSE%, 163
Numerical accept routine, 42

ON ERROR, 21
OPEN command, 116

Page numbering, 232
Pause subroutine, 164

PLACE%, 37
PRESERVE$, 54
PRINT, 21
Printer commands, special, 234
Printer control sequences, 227
Printing enlarged letters, 228
Printing underlines, 229
Processing control keys, 45
Processing input keys, 40
Processing a key, 37
Program testing hints, 33
PUT command, 260

Quit, 130

Random-access files, 257
Records, 258
REM 7
Remark statement, 7
Report generator controls, 218
Report generator text program, 223
Restoring original field, 55
RESUME, 60
RETURN, 2
Right arrow, 44
ROW%, 25

Save block of text to diskette, 100
Screen display routine, 82
Screen editing commands, 84
Screen editor command words, 108
Screen editor test routine, 83
Screen intensity, 165
Scroll down a page, 91
Scroll up a page, 91
Search and replace, 125
Setting block markers, 100
Shift
    F1 key, 45
    F2 key, 45

Shift (*Continued*)
    F3 key, 85
    F4 key, 85
    F5 key, 85
    F6 key, 85
    F7 key, 85
    F8 key, 85
    TAB, 45
Splitting a line, 98
Subroutine, 2
SYNTAX ERROR, 132

TAB key, 44
Tab stop routine, 56

TEMP.TXT, 101
Text editor flowchart, 78
Text loading subroutine, 120
Text-saving and printing subroutine, 116

Uppercase convert subroutine, 43

Variable exchange, 178

Word wrap, 105

Yes/no accept routine, 42

Other books in the Microcomputer Books Series are available from your local computer store or bookstore.

For more information, write:
Addison-Wesley Publishing Co., Inc.
Microcomputer Books & Consumer Software
Reading, MA 01867
(617) 944–3700

05663   *BASIC Business Subroutines for the Apple II and IIe*
Alan G. Porter and Martin G. Rezmer

06516   *Using BASIC on the IBM PC*
Angela and Michael Trombetta

11162   *A Bit of IBM BASIC*
Thomas A. Dwyer and Margot Critchfield

13433   *Back to BASIC*
John G. Kemeny and Thomas E. Kurtz

03115   *A Bit of BASIC*
Thomas A. Dwyer and Margot Critchfield

01589   *BASIC and the Personal Computer*
Thomas A. Dwyer and Margot Critchfield

10341   *Pascal: A Problem Solving Approach*
Elliot B. Koffman

08296   *Pascal for FORTRAN Programmers*
Robert Weiss and Charles Seiter

06577   *Pascal for BASIC Programmers*
Charles Seiter and Robert Weiss

05464   *Pascal for the IBM Personal Computer*
Ted G. Lewis

12080   *Looking at LISP*
Tony Hasemer

05208   *The Netweaver's Sourcebook: A Guide to Micro Networking and Communications*
Dean Gengle

10483   *Database for the IBM PC*
Sandra L. Emerson and Marcy Darnovsky

11358   *Database: A Primer*
C. J. Date

11065   *A Buyer's Guide to Microcomputer Business Software: Accounting and Spreadsheets*
Amanda C. Hixson

13047   *1-2-3 Go!*
Julie Bingham

10241   *Executive SuperCalc³*
Roger E. Clark

14276   *The Integrated Software Book*
Jules H. Gilder

10924   *Starting with UNIX*
P. J. Brown

08848   *The Business Guide to the UNIX System*
Jean L. Yates and Sandra L. Emerson

08847   *The Business Guide to the XENIX System*
Jean L. Yates, Sandra L. Emerson, and Candice Basham

05793   *Thinking Small: The Buyer's Guide to Portable Computers*
Charles Rubin and Michael McCarthy

04191   *The Under-$800 Computer Buyer's Guide: Evaluating the New Generation of Small Computers*
Anthony T. Easton and Tony Seton

05158   *Microcomputer Graphics for the IBM PC*
Roy E. Myers

06599   *Basic Money: Managing Personal Finances on Your Microcomputer*
Charles Seiter

06598   *Advanced Money: Planning Investments on Your Computer*
Charles Seiter and Steven Nichols

09666   *The Urgently Needed Parent's Guide to Computers*
Brian Williams and Richard Tingey

06896   *The IBM Personal Computer from the Inside Out*
Murray Sargent III and Richard Shoemaker

09660   *The Practical Guide to the Apple IIc*
Peter C. Weiglin and Joyce Conklin

07961   *The KoalaPad Book*
David D. Thornburg

05155   *Computers for Kids Over 60*
Greg Kearsley and Mary Furlong

00105   *Marketing Your Software*
William Nisen, Allan Schmidt, and Ira Alterman

12021   *The Addison-Wesley Book of IBM Software 1985*
Dennis L. Foster and Editors of D. L. Foster Book Co.